Macmillan Professional Masters

Conveyancing

Macmillan Professional Masters

Titles in the series

Conveyancing

Priscilla Sarton
LL.M
Senior Lecturer
in Law at the College of Law

Law series editor: Marise Cremona
Principal Lecturer in Law
at the City of London Polytechnic

MACMILLAN

First published 1991 by
THE MACMILLAN PRESS LTD
Houndmills, Basingstoke, Hampshire RG21 2XS
and London
Companies and representatives
throughout the world

ISBN 0–333–49028–2

A catalogue record for this book is available
from the British Library.

Printed in Hong Kong

10   9   8   7   6   5   4   3   2
00   99 98 97 96 95 94 93 92

Contents

Preface

It has been surprisingly difficult when writing this book to decide on the correct words to use. A professional conveyancer can be either female or male, and to add to the complexity of the matter, either a solicitor or a licensed conveyancer.

There has been no wish to imply that every legal adviser is a male solicitor, but the pressing need for brevity has meant that 'he' has had to be used for both sexes and 'solicitor' for both professions. It is hoped that readers will not take offence. Another difficulty has been the replacement of the traditional words 'vendor' and 'purchaser' by the modern 'seller' and 'buyer' in the new form of contract for sale. 'Seller' is used throughout this book, but the word 'purchaser' is not so easily displaced, as in the context of the Land Registration Act 1925, the Land Charges Act 1972 and other property legislation, 'purchaser' has a technical meaning that 'buyer' does not. The choice was either to use 'purchaser' in some chapters and 'buyer' in others, or stick consistently to 'purchaser'. The second course has been chosen.

The Law Society has helpfully given permission for the use of questions from its past examination papers. The answers are the author's, and are in no way connected with the Society. Thanks are due to the Law Society and Oyez for their permission to reproduce the protocol documentation, including the form of contract for sale, and to the Law Society for its permission to quote from its 'Introduction to the Protocol'.

The book is dedicated to Mark Sarton, for without him it would never have been written, yet he has suffered so much through its writing.

PRISCILLA SARTON

Table of Cases

Table of Statutes

Table of Statutory Instruments

1 Stages in a Conveyancing Transaction from the Seller's Point of View

1.1 Introduction

This chapter introduces you to the stages of a conveyancing transaction from the point of view of the seller's solicitor. It does not attempt to set out everything that needs to be done, but does detail the major steps and serves to put the other chapters into context.

At one time, this would have been an easy chapter to write, for a transaction trod a stately measure, the order of the steps never varying. Searches were always made by the purchaser, and title deduced and investigated after the contract for sale was made. In recent years things have changed. Sellers now sometimes do things traditionally done by purchasers. Things are now done pre-contract that used to be done post-contract. We live in exciting times.

In March 1990 the Law Society introduced the National Protocol for the sale of domestic freehold and leasehold property. The protocol sets out procedures which the Society recommends all solicitors to use. The purpose is to speed the transaction through, and particularly to reduce the time lag between the parties coming to an agreement and the formation of the actual contract. Use of the protocol also involves the use of standardised documentation, namely a form of agreement for sale, property information forms (with optional client questionnaires) and a 'fixtures, fittings and contents' form.

The protocol relates only to domestic transactions and even then it is not compulsory for a solicitor to use it, but its use is described by the Law Society as 'preferred practice'. It does anyway reflect procedures that were already becoming fairly widespread. Every solicitor acting in a domestic transaction should notify the solicitor on the other side whether or not the protocol will be used. Once the protocol has been adopted for that transaction it must be followed, except that a solicitor may depart from it provided that he gives notice to the other side of his decision to do so. The protocol only governs procedures between the two solicitors. It does not affect matters between the solicitor and his client, or third parties such as mortgagees. It is anticipated that the protocol will also be used between solicitors and licensed conveyancers.

It is stressed again that a solicitor who uses the protocol might find himself doing little different from what he would have done anyway. The only departures from his previous practice might be the use of the standardised forms, and the amount of documentation (what the protocol calls 'the package') supplied to the purchaser's solicitor before the contract. Nor is the protocol designed to be an exhaustive list of steps to be taken, and the Law Society in its introduction to the protocol states that 'at all stages the solicitor's professional skills, knowledge and judgement will need to be applied in just the same way as it has been in the past'.

This chapter describes a protocol transaction, but also attempts to explain how the transaction would proceed if it were not governed by the protocol. Exclusive attention to the protocol is discouraged by the fact that it is not exhaustive as to what steps must be taken, and that the Law Society states that the protocol is 'evolutionary', that 'some changes might be necessary', and that the Society is receptive to 'constructive criticism'.

1.2   Your client

Imagine that Robert Oates is planning to sell his present home. The house is freehold and is mortgaged to the Potteries Bank plc. He is also planning to instruct you to act for him. In what it calls the first step, the protocol suggests that Robert should call on you as soon as he decides to put his home on the market, so that you can immediately start to put together the pre-contract 'package'. It can then be sent without delay to the prospective purchaser as soon as he is found.

You probably have only a slender hope of Robert coming to you at this stage. The first person Robert will approach is the estate agent, and he will not approach you until the prospective purchaser is actually found. When this happens Robert will instruct you to act for him.

1.3   Gathering Information

(a)   General

Your first task is to gather information. You need this in order to draft the contract. You also need it to complete the property information form which you will be sending to the purchaser's solicitor. This form is in the Appendix to this book. Read it, and you will know the sort of information you need to collect.

This gathering of information is what the protocol calls 'preparing the package: assembling the information' (the 'package' being the documents that you will send as soon as possible to the purchaser's solicitor). It is nothing new; a seller's solicitor has always needed this information. The sources of information include your client, possibly the estate agent, and the documents of title. So imagine you have Robert sitting in your office.

(b) Interview with Client – Gathering Information about His Title

(i) You must ask your client where his title deeds or land certificate are as you need to investigate his title in order to draft the contract. The deeds might be in the possession of your client, but if the house is mortgaged, the lender will have them. Robert's deeds are with the Potteries Bank, his mortgagee. The Bank may, when it learns of the proposed sale, be prepared to instruct you to act for it in the redemption of the mortgage. It will then send you the original deeds or, in the case of registered title, the charge certificate. The Bank will expect an undertaking from you to the effect that you hold the deeds on its behalf, and if the sale falls through, will return the deeds in the same condition as they were when you received them.

If the Bank will not be instructing you, then it may be reluctant to let you have the originals. If the title is unregistered, the Bank will send you an abstract or epitome of the deeds.

If the title is registered, you only need to be given the title number of the property. You can then obtain an office copy of the entries on the register and of the filed plan from the District Land Registry. (Note that it is always possible for you to discover if a title is registered, and the title number, by making a search in the public index map at the District Land Registry. See Chapter 5; 2 (d).

(ii) Ask Robert if his neighbours have any sort of rights over his property, such as a right-of-way? The point is that such easements do not always appear on the deeds or on the register of title. They may have arisen from long use. If the house is one of a terrace there is often a right-of-way for each owner over the backyards of the houses, for access to a side entrance. Similarly, does your client exercise rights over a neighbour's property? Does he obtain his gas, electricity, water, etc., directly from the public road, or across a neighbour's property?

If the last-mentioned, you have to find out if the pipes, etc., are there merely by the permission of the neighbour, or if Robert has easements over the neighbour's land (see question 5 on the property information form).

(iii) Does Robert live in the house with his wife? If so, is she a co-owner? Has she agreed to the sale? (If the answer to these questions is 'yes' you need instructions from her (see Chapter 11).

(iv) Could anyone else have a claim to own part of the house? For example, did anyone contribute to the original purchase price with the intention of owning a share? If the answer is 'yes', it will affect the provisions put in the contract, (see Chapter 11) and the answer to question 8 on the property information form.

(*c*) *Interview with Client: Completing the Property Information Form*

The property information form has to be completed by you on the basis of information supplied by your client. You can go through the form with him now. Alternatively, you can give Robert a property information questionnaire to take away with him to complete at home. The completed questionnaire will give you the facts you need to complete the property information form. (The questionnaire is an optional part of the protocol documentation). The sort of topics covered by the property information form is discussed in Chapter 6.

(*d*) *Interview with Client: Completing the Fixtures, Fittings and Contents Form*

This form (which is part of the protocol documentation) lists most of the items likely to be found in an average house and about which there could possibly be an argument as to whether or not they are included in the sale. The items range from aerials to door-knockers. You may hand this form to Robert at the interview, but you will doubtless ask him to complete it at home. He will have to indicate which of the items are to be sold with the house.

(*e*) *Interview with Client: His Financial Position*

What is your client's financial position? The mortgage to the Bank must be redeemed. The Bank should be asked for a redemption figure, on the basis that completion will take place in, say, six weeks time.

Ask Robert if there is a second mortgage. He may have borrowed money some time ago, signed a paper and not realised its significance.

If Robert's title is unregistered, a second mortgage may be revealed by a search against his name at the Land Charges Registry, where it would be registered as a CI or CIII land charge. If his title is registered, a search at HM District Land Registry may reveal a registered charge or an entry protecting an informal mortgage.

Robert, by virtue of an express or implied condition in the contract, will be promising that all mortgages will be redeemed. You need to check that the purchase price will be sufficient to discharge all the mortgages. If it is not, then he will have to find other funds with which to redeem them, or abandon the idea of selling the house. Usually, if your client is selling his house, he will be buying a new one. An example of the calculation of a client's financial position in such circumstances is given in Chapter 17.

(*f*) *Your Charges*

Robert may ask you for an estimate of your charges for acting for him in the sale. You must calculate the disbursements that you will have to make, and your fees. You might wish to make it clear that you are giving an estimate only, and that you are not bound to the figure quoted. Nevertheless, any estimate must be realistic, based on a knowledge of the details of the transaction, and include all disbursements, e.g. stamp duty and VAT. No client will be favourably impressed if the quoted figure is greatly exceeded. If you offer a fixed charge, the prospective client should be told the length of time this will remain valid.

The Law Society recommends that any indication of charges should be either given, or confirmed, in writing, and has drawn up a form (the domestic conveyancing charges form) to be completed and given to the client. The use of this form is optional.

1.4 Preparing the Package

If the seller's solicitor is following the protocol he must now assemble a package of documents to be sent to the purchaser's solicitor. For a freehold property this involves:

1. Making what are called the pre-contract searches and enquiries. Traditionally these are made by the purchaser's solicitor, but it may save time if they are made instead by the seller's solicitor as soon as he is instructed by his client to act in the transaction, and the results forwarded to the other side. These searches are discussed in greater detail in Chapter 6.
2. In the case of an unregistered title, making a land-charges search against the name of the seller and any previous estate owners whose names are not already covered by a satisfactory search certificate. (see Chapters 4 and 9). Apart from the protocol, it is always sensible for a seller's solicitor to make this search before drafting the contract, as without it he cannot be sure that he has full knowledge of his client's title (see the workshop section of Chapter 5).
3. In the case of an unregistered title, preparing an epitome of title, and where possible, marking copies of all deeds that will not be given to the purchaser on completion as having been examined against the originals. (see Chapter 8).
4. If the title is registered, obtaining office copy entries of the register, and of copy documents filed at the registry.

    (Items 3 and 4 mean that the purchaser is at this stage being given evidence of the seller's ownership of the property – see later).

The package to be sent to the purchaser on the sale of a freehold consists of:

(a) the draft contract,
(b) the office copy entries or the epitome of title,
(c) the results of the pre-contract searches,

(d) a completed property information form,
(e) the completed fixtures, fittings and contents form.

(For the sale of a leasehold see Chapter 15).

1.5 Drafting the Contract

When you have seen your client and obtained either the deeds or an up-to-date office copy of the entries on the register of title, you should be able to draft the contract. The essential thing is that you do not allow your client to enter into a contract which he has no hope of fulfilling. Remember that it is essential that you thoroughly investigate your client's title. Your investigation must be every bit as thorough as if you were buying, rather than selling, on his behalf. The contract will contain express or implied promises as to the title, and if you find that your client cannot live up to these promises, because there is something wrong with his title, the promises must be altered.

The contract is prepared in duplicate, usually on a standard printed form (see Chapter 5). Both copies are sent to the purchaser's solicitor for approval. The purchaser's solicitor may make amendments. If so, a copy of the amended contract will be returned to you for your consideration.

When the contract is finally approved on behalf of both parties, one part will be signed by the seller and one part by the purchaser. The signature must usually be that of the client, not the solicitor. It is not generally part of the solicitor's authority actually to sign the contract. So if you find that the contract *has* been signed by the purchaser's solicitor, you need evidence that his client has given him express authority to do this.

The reason why the contracts are in duplicate is that the parties intend to *exchange* the two parts. The seller will then have the part signed by the purchaser, and the purchaser will have the part signed by the seller. As exchange is contemplated by the parties, the contract will not come into existence until exchange takes place.

1.6 Exchanging Contracts

Once the purchaser's solicitor is satisfied that the results of all the pre-contract searches and enquiries are satisfactory and that his client can safely enter into the contract, exchange will take place. Once contracts are exchanged, the parties are bound: the seller to transfer ownership, and the purchaser to pay the purchase price.

(a) Personal Exchange

This is where the seller's solicitor meets the purchaser's solicitor and the two parts of the contract are exchanged. This method of exchange is rare because a solicitor cannot usually spare the time involved in travelling to a colleague's office.

(b) Exchange through the Post

The purchaser's solicitor posts his client's part of the contract to the seller's solicitor, together with a cheque for the deposit. When he receives these, the seller's solicitor posts the part of the contract signed by the seller back to the purchaser.

Despite the long use of this method of exchange, there is still controversy as to the exact moment that the exchange takes place. One view is that exchange has occurred (and that the contract therefore exists) as soon as the second part of the contract is put in the post. The other view is that exchange has not taken place until the second part of the contract is actually received by the addressee. If the contract incorporates the standard conditions (see Chapter 5) the contract will provide that exchange is to be treated as taking place on the *posting* of the second part, not on its receipt. (See standard condition 2:1.1). If Robert is not buying a new house, this method of exchange would be satisfactory. If he is buying a new house, the exchange of contracts on his sale needs to be synchronised with the exchange of contracts on his purchase, and this is not easily done if contracts are exchanged by post.

(c) Exchange by Telephone

In this case, exchange takes place by an agreement over the telephone that the contracts are to be *treated* as exchanged.

Suppose that this method of exchange is contemplated on Robert's sale. The purchaser's solicitor might send his part of the contract, together with a cheque for the deposit, to you. The accompanying letter is likely to say that these are not sent by way of exchange, but that you are to hold them to the order of the purchaser. This means that you cannot foist an exchange on the purchaser by posting the part of the contract signed by Robert. Exchange cannot take place until the purchaser is ready. When the purchaser is ready, his solicitor will telephone you, and say that he is ready to exchange contracts. It will then be agreed on the telephone that contracts are now exchanged. You, as Robert's solicitor, will agree that you now hold his part of the contract to the order of the purchaser, and that you will post it that day.

It is possible that exchange could be agreed over the telephone before either seller or purchaser has parted with his part of the contract. In such a case, the purchaser's solicitor will give an undertaking to post his client's part of the contract and deposit cheque that day, and you will undertake to post Robert's part of the contract.

You can see that although the exchange takes place when agreement is reached on the telephone, this is always followed (or possibly preceded) by the exchange of the documents themselves.

The drawback to this method of exchange is that it has taken place through a conversation, which might later be denied. For this reason, the Law Society recommends that written notes be taken by both parties as to what was said. It also recommends that the solicitors should agree that the telephone exchange be governed by either Law Society formula A (to be used where the purchaser has already sent a signed contract to the seller's solicitor) or formula B (to be used when each party still holds his own part of the contract).

Both formulae provide for the insertion in the contract of an agreed completion date, for confirmation that the contracts are in the form agreed, and for the giving of the undertakings outlined above.

Exchange can be similarly effected through telex, with the added advantage that the 'conversation' is automatically recorded in writing.

(An attempt to explain Law Society formula C is made in Chapter 17).

Warning **Whatever method of exchange is used, exchange will not be treated as having taken place unless the contents of the two parts of the contract are identical. This is why it is essential that any alteration to the draft contract is written into *both* parts before they are exchanged. It is salutory to read the case of *Harrison* v. *Battye* [1974].**

1.7 The Deposit

On exchange of contracts, the purchaser will normally have to pay a deposit of 10 per cent of the purchase price (see Chapter 5). This is part-payment of the purchase price, but it is also something more. It is a pledge of the purchaser's intention to fulfil the contract. If the purchaser unjustifiably refuses to complete, the deposit is forfeited to the seller.

If the contract provides for payment of a deposit, and the purchaser fails to do this (either because no payment is ever made, or because his cheque is dishonoured) the purchaser is considered to have broken the contract in such a fundamental way as to enable the seller to treat the contract as discharged (see standard condition 2:2.4). The seller is released from the contract, and can also sue for the unpaid deposit (see *Damon Cia Naviera SA* v. *Hapag-Lloyd International SA* [1985].

1.8 Insurance

If nothing is said to the contrary in the contract, the risk of capital loss passes to the purchaser as soon as contracts are exchanged. So if, for example, the house burns down, the purchaser bears the loss and remains liable for the full purchase price. Two things might mitigate his loss:

1. after exchange the seller owes the purchaser a duty to take reasonable care of the property until completion of the sale. So if the fire could be

traced back to the negligence of the seller, he would be liable to compensate the purchaser;
2. if the seller had maintained his own insurance on the house (which is likely, although he is under no duty to the purchaser to do so), then the insurance money due under the policy is held by the seller on trust for the purchaser. (This is the effect of s.147 of the Law of Property Act 1925).

If the contract incorporates the standard conditions of sale (see Chapter 5) standard condition 5.1 alters these rules entirely. In Condition 5.1.1 the seller promises the purchaser to transfer the property in the same physical state as it was at the date of the contract (with the exception of fair wear and tear, i.e. ordinary dilapidation). This means that the risk of physical damage remains with the seller. It is therefore essential for the seller to continue to insure the property until the sale is completed, for his own protection. (Condition 5.3 makes it clear that the seller does not owe a duty to the purchaser to insure the property, and s.147 of the Law of the Property Act 1925 is excluded.)

If, for example, the house burns down before completion, or is in any way physically damaged, the seller must compensate the purchaser, which will amount to the purchaser paying a reduced purchase price.

Condition 5.1.2 creates rights to rescind the contract, i.e. set it aside as if it had never existed. It applies when, before completion, the change in the physical state of the property makes the property unusable for its purpose at the date of the contract. In these circumstances the purchaser can rescind the contract, i.e. he does not merely pay a reduced price; he need not buy the property at all, unless he wishes.

In the same circumstances, a right of rescission is also given to the seller, but in his case only if the damage is of a sort that he could not reasonably have insured against, or if it is damage that it is not legally possible for him to make good. For instance, this could be because he could not get planning permission. Why should a seller wish to rescind if the property is severely damaged? Presumably because faced with a greatly reduced purchase price, he prefers not to sell at all, perhaps because it will leave him without enough money to buy a new house. (Remember that the seller has the right of rescission if he *could not* insure; not because he *did not* insure.)

Condition 5.1 applies only to an alteration in the physical state of the property, but this is not the only thing that can decrease its value. The fact that the property is listed as being of exceptional historical or architectural merit can remove any development value from the land for instance. The risk of this sort of capital loss continues to pass to the purchaser on exchange of contracts.

Despite Condition 5.1 some purchasers will still prefer to insure the property themselves as from the date of the contract, preferring to have a claim against an insurance company rather than against the seller. If a purchaser does this the property will be doubly insured, i.e. by both seller and purchaser. The effect of double insurance is that each insurance company will pay only part of the claim, so the seller may find that his insurance company will pay only, say, half the loss, leaving the other half to be paid by the purchaser's insurer. The seller should consider putting into the contract a condition saying that if the seller's payment from the insurance company is reduced for this reason, then the compensation to be paid by him to the purchaser will be reduced by the same amount. The purchaser will recoup himself from the proceeds of his own policy.

1.9   Proving Title

If the seller is following the protocol, the package of documents sent to the purchaser before contract will have included details of the seller's title. If the transaction is following a more traditional route, the purchaser may not be sent details of the seller's title until the contract is in existence. This is explained more fully in Chapter 5. However, in case you are asking yourself how it is at all possible that investigation of title could be left until after contract, it is because the contract will contain a promise (usually implied rather than expressed) by the seller that he has a good title. If the purchaser does not investigate title until after exchange of contracts, he agrees to buy in reliance on this promise. If after contract his investigation of title reveals that there are defects in the title that he was not told about at the time of contract, he can say that the defect is a breach of contract, and possibly that the contract is discharged by the breach. The purchaser is then released from his obligation to buy.

Of course, there is considerable inconvenience for a purchaser in this position, who is probably committed to a contract to sell his existing house, and so you may be asking yourself 'why does the purchaser not always investigate title *before* the contract'? He *can* do so if he is given the necessary evidence of title at that stage. Whether he *has* to, depends on the terms of the contract. If the purchaser is entitled to raise requisitions on the title (i.e. object that the title is not as promised in the contract) after exchange of contracts he can leave investigation of title until then if he wishes to do so. This is the position envisaged by the standard conditions of sale (see Chapter 5). If a special condition in the contract precludes the purchaser from raising requisitions after exchange, the purchaser *must* investigate title before contract, as it will generally be too late to object to the title after the contract is made.

The promises as to title given by the seller are explained in Chapter 5, and the evidence of title that has to be supplied is explained in Chapters 7 and 8.

1.10   Dealing with the Purchaser's Requisitions on Title

If the purchaser is dissatisfied either with the soundness of the title or with the evidence of the title that is given, he will 'raise a requisition on title'. In other words, he will complain to you about what is wrong and ask you to put it right. When faced with the purchaser's complaint, the seller may be able to put the matter right. He may, for example, be able to supply a missing document, or prove that a third-party interest is no longer enforceable against the land.

If the seller cannot put the matter right, his position depends on whether the purchaser is investigating title before or after contract. If the former, the purchaser will not enter into the contract. If the purchaser is investigating title after contract, then generally the seller must face the fact that he is in breach of his contract. He cannot live up to his promise as to title. He awaits the purchaser's decision. The purchaser may be able to treat the contract as discharged by the breach, and cease to be under any obligation to buy. He may also be able to sue for damages. The damages may be heavy. The seller perhaps wishes he had never entered into the contract in the first place. A seller in such a position should read Chapter 18, section 3(b).

It is unfortunately true that the fact that your client is in breach of contract *may* be your fault. Why did you not notice that his title was defective when you investigated it prior to drafting the contract? You could then, by a special condition in the contract, have disclosed the defect and prevented the purchaser from raising the requisition (turn to Chapter 5).

1.11 Checking the Draft Conveyance or Transfer

Assuming that you are able to deal with any requisition, you now read the draft conveyance or transfer. This is drawn up by the purchaser's solicitor, but has to be approved by the seller's solicitor, who must check that it is not drawn so as to give the purchaser more than the seller contracted to give.

Once the draft has been approved by you, the purchaser's solicitor will 'engross' it, i.e. prepare a fair copy of it. This will be sent to you so that you can arrange to have it executed by your client.

1.12 Completion Statement

When you send to the purchaser's solicitor your replies to his requisitions on title, and the approved draft conveyance, you will also send him a completion statement, setting out the sum that the purchaser must pay on completion. This may consist merely of the purchase price, less the deposit already paid. There may sometimes be other items, for example:

(a) *apportionments of outgoings.* At one time it was usual to apportion the water and sewage charges, gas and electricity bills, so that if the seller had paid for a period extending beyond the completion date, he was credited with an apportioned part of the payment. This is not now usually done. The seller usually tells the relevant authorities of his date of departure and ensures that the meters are read as close as possible to the date of completion. He is then sent bills from the bodies concerned. The purchaser is responsible for the charges arising from the date of completion. The community charge is a personal matter. It does not relate to the property and cannot be apportioned.

An apportionment is still usual in an assignment of a lease. The rent might have to be apportioned, and so might payments made to the landlord in respect of insurance or maintenance.

(b) *interest*. If completion takes place later than the date agreed in the contract, either seller or purchaser might be liable to pay interest on the unpaid balance of the purchase price. The amount involved will be deducted from, or added to, the purchase price (see Chapter 18).

1.13   Completion

Completion at its simplest is a swop. The purchaser pays the balance of the purchase price in return (in the case of an unregistered title) for the deeds and the conveyance to him. The purchaser will then own the legal estate and the beneficial interest. If the seller's title is registered, the purchaser will receive the land certificate and the transfer. He will then own the beneficial interest, but will not own the legal estate until he is registered as the new proprietor (see Chapter 3). In our case, Robert's title is mortgaged. The purchaser will want evidence that the mortgage has been paid off. In unregistered title, he will demand that a receipt be endorsed on the mortgage deed, and executed by the mortgagee. In registered title, he will be given the charge certificate (or charge certificates, if there is more than one registered charge) and a form 53 for each charge. This is discussed further in Chapters 7 and 9.

1.14   After Completion

(a) You should now account to Robert for the proceeds of sale. You will usually have secured your client's authority to deduct from them your fees and disbursements, and any fees due to the estate agent. The balance, with a statement showing clearly how the balance is arrived at, is remitted according to your client's instructions.

(b) Any undertakings that have been given to the purchaser's solicitor must be complied with, e.g. in connection with the redemption of your client's mortgage.

2 Stages in a Conveyancing Transaction: The Purchaser's Point of View

2.1 Introduction

This chapter takes you through a transaction again, but this time from a purchaser's point of view. Imagine that you are acting for Susan Holt in her purchase of a house. She has applied for a mortgage loan from a building society, and you find that the society is prepared to instruct you to act for it in the creation of the mortgage. You have, therefore, two clients (see Chapter 2, section 2.18 on conflict of interest).

2.2 Gathering Information

(a) Susan must give you details of the bargain that has been struck so that you can judge if the draft contract prepared by the seller represents that bargain. Were fittings included in the sale, and at what price? What sort of completion date has been arranged between the parties?

(b) Was there anything about the property that struck her? Did anyone appear to have any sort of access over the property? Who appeared to be living on the property apart from the seller?

2.3 You need to know your Client's Financial Position

(a) Total purchase price

The first point is that you must make sure that she realises the *total* cost of the purchase. This may well take her by surprise. She needs an estimate of your fees and details of your foreseeable disbursements. These will include stamp duty (currently at 1 per cent of the entire purchase price, if this exceeds £30 000) and land registry fees. Again, you may decide to use the Law Society's domestic conveyancing charges form (see Chapter 1, section 3(f).

(b) Mortgage offer

The second point is that as she is buying with the aid of a mortgage loan, you must be sure that the lender has made a *formal* offer of a loan before you commit your client to the contract to buy.

When you read the formal offer, check the amount of the loan. Is this the amount your client expects? Is there any retention clause (see Chapter 17). Is there any condition that must be satisfied before the loan is made? (An example might be that the Society wants a specialist survey done on some part of the house, e.g. for risk of subsidence. The money will only be available when the survey is done, and if the Society considers the result to be satisfactory.) If the mortgage is an endowment mortgage, the offer will be conditional on the life policy being on foot before completion. The proposal form for the assurance should be completed now and forwarded either to the lender or the assurance company, and confirmation that the proposal has been accepted by the company is needed *before contract*.

(c) Deposit

A contract usually provides for a deposit of 10 per cent of the purchase price to be paid on exchange of contracts. Your client must realise that this may be forfeited to the seller if it is your client's fault that completion does not take place. So any failure by her to complete will involve her in severe financial loss, even if the seller is in fact able to sell the house to someone else at the same, or even an increased, price. Of course, if the failure to complete is the seller's fault, Susan will be entitled to the return of the deposit.

If Susan does not have enough money to pay a 10 per cent deposit on exchange of contracts, there are various solutions:

(i) If she is selling her existing house to buy the new one, she will be receiving a deposit from her purchaser, and this may be used to finance the deposit which she has to pay to her seller (see Chapter 5 for details on the drafting of the contract for sale). However, if she is trading up – e.g. selling an £80 000 house and buying a new one for £120 000, she will still have to find £4000.

(ii) She may be able to persuade the seller to accept a smaller deposit, e.g. on the above example £8000 rather than £12 000. The seller may be unhappy with this, as he knows that if she fails to complete she will be forfeiting to him a significantly smaller sum.

However, he may be comforted by standard condition 6.6.5. This gives a seller who accepts less than the 10 per cent deposit a right to sue for the balance if he is forced to serve a completion notice because of the purchaser's delay in completion. So if things go wrong, the seller may be able to recover the missing £4000, always provided, of course, that Susan is not insolvent.

(iii) She may have to borrow the deposit, the loan either to be repaid when the mortgage loan is forthcoming at completion, or to be added to the mortgage debt. The customer's bank is a traditional source for such a loan, but building societies now have the power to lend on unsecured loans, as well as secured ones, so the building society may provide the deposit at exchange of contracts, instead of withholding the entire advance until completion. The mortgage, when made, will then charge the land with repayment of the total loan, including the amount lent to fund the deposit;

(iv) She may be able to use a deposit insurance scheme. The idea is that an insurance company, in return for a one-off premium (to be paid by the purchaser), promises the seller that if the contract is not performed owing to the purchaser's default, the company will pay the seller the 10 per cent deposit. It usually costs less to pay the premium than to pay the interest on a loan for the deposit. It is often not possible to use such a scheme in a chain transaction (see Chapter 17).

2.4 The Pre-contract Searches and Enquiries

As you will see in Chapter 5 the seller has a limited duty to tell the purchaser about defects in his title to the property and about third-party rights over it, such as restrictive covenants or easements. The duty stops there. So there is a great deal of information which might well affect the purchaser's decision as to whether or not to buy the property and which might be known to the seller, but which he does not have to tell the purchaser. The purchaser must therefore find out for herself, and must do so *before* the contract. To take a simple example, the seller may know that the Motorway M1001 is to be built on the far side of the garden fence. The purchaser, however, does not learn this interesting fact until after she has agreed to buy the house. It is too late. The seller was under no duty to inform the purchaser about the proposed motorway. He has not broken a term of the contract, so the purchaser must either complete or lose her deposit and face a claim for damages. This is why it is so important for the purchaser to make enquiries about the property *before* contract.

Pre-contract searches and enquiries are dealt with in Chapter 6.

You will realise, having read Chapter 1, that if the seller's solicitor is following the National Protocol, these searches will be provided for the purchaser as part of the pre-contract package. It still remains the responsibility of the purchaser's solicitor to check the results of the searches, and to consider if any further searches need to be made.

2.5 Consideration of the Draft Contract

Once the draft contract has been received in duplicate from the seller, you must consider if it represents the bargain that your client expects. If there is any doubt, Susan must again be consulted. She should also be asked on what date she wishes to complete as the completion date will be put in the contract on exchange.

2.6   The Deposit

The deposit payable on exchange must now be obtained from the client.
(The need to provide this deposit has already been discussed with her.) If
your client is to give you a cheque, you should receive it sufficiently early
for the cheque to be cleared before you draw on it to pay the seller.
According to standard condition 2.2.1. (see Chapter 5) the deposit should
be paid to the seller by banker's draft or by a cheque drawn on a solicitor's
bank account. This, if complied with, should remove any possibility that
the cheque will bounce. Condition 2.2.4 provides that if any cheque for the
deposit is dishonoured, the seller can treat the contract as discharged.

2.7   Exchange of Contracts

Once you are satisfied:

(a) that the purchaser will have the necessary funds on completion to buy
     the property and to pay all attendant expenses;
(b) that the replies to all the pre-contract searches and enquiries are
     satisfactory;
(c) that the draft contract is satisfactory;
(d) if it is to be investigated before contract, that the title is satisfactory;

you may exchange contracts on behalf of your client. On exchange, a date
for completion, previously settled between the parties, will be put in the
contract.

2.8   Insurance

We have seen that if the contract incorporates the standard conditions, the
risk of physical damage to the property no longer passes to the purchaser
on exchange of contract. It is therefore not essential for a purchaser to
insure against that risk until completion. However, as Susan is buying with
the aid of a mortgage loan, you must check the *lender's* requirements as to
insurance. The lender may require the borrower to take out comprehensive
insurance as from the time the money is made available, which may be
earlier than actual completion.

2.9   Investigation of Title

Once the contract is made, the purchaser will investigate title (see Chapters
7 and 9) and may raise requisitions on title. (Remember, though, what was

said in Chapter 1, section 10. If the contract, by a special condition, prevents the purchaser from raising requisitions after contract, the purchaser *must* investigate title before exchange of contracts.)

The contract will, through the general conditions, provide a timetable for the stages of the transaction. Standard condition 4 says that requisitions must be raised within six working days of receipt of the seller's evidence of title, or if this was provided with the contract, within six days of the contract. The purchaser must be careful to observe this particular time limit as the condition provides that the purchaser's right to raise requisitions is lost after the six days have passed. In other words, if the purchaser does not object to the title *within* the time limits, she may be unable to object at all, and will have to accept the title with its defects. This condition will not prevent requisitions being raised out of time in some circumstances. A requisition can be raised out of time if it is as to a defect that is only revealed when the original title deeds themselves are seen, which may not be until completion. An example would be a memorandum of severance endorsed on a conveyance to joint tenants (see Chapter 11) if the abstract of title did not disclose the existence of this memorandum. Another exception is where the pre-completion search reveals a defect which was not disclosed by the abstract of title. Again, a requisition can be raised out of time.

The purchaser's solicitor must also remember that there is a time limit in standard condition 4 for the purchaser to raise observations on the seller's replies to the requisitions, and that this limit must be strictly observed.

2.10 Report on Title to the Building Society

You are investigating title not only on behalf of Susan Holt, but also on behalf of her mortgagee. Once you are satisfied that the title, and the evidence of the title, are satisfactory, you will report to that effect to the Building Society.

You might, however, have found a defect in title, and one that you consider to be sufficiently serious to affect the value of the property. Susan, because she likes the house so much, might be willing to press ahead. You owe a duty to the Building Society. You must report on the defect to the Society, with the possible result that the offer of the mortgage will be withdrawn. (This should not leave Susan Holt stranded, as if the defect is sufficiently serious to lead to the withdrawal of the mortgage offer, it will probably be a ground for Susan treating the contract to buy as discharged by the seller's breach.)

If Susan Holt will not consent to your informing the Society, you will have to tell the Society you can no longer act for it. The Society will instruct another solicitor, who will investigate title and discover the defect. So Susan might as well accept the inevitable.

2.11   Drafting the Conveyance or Transfer

It is your task to draft the purchase deed, and two copies of your draft will be sent, with your requisitions on title, to the seller's solicitor. Drafting is discussed in Chapters 13 and 14.

The seller's solicitor will return one copy of the draft, either approved or amended. Once any amendments have been negotiated and agreed, you will have the deed engrossed. You must then consider whether or not it is necessary for your client to execute it. It is often unnecessary for the purchaser to execute the deed, but she should do so if the deed contains covenants given to the seller. The deed should also be executed by co-purchasers, if it contains a declaration as to how they own the beneficial interest, i.e. whether as joint tenants or in shares. Execution of the deed makes this declaration binding upon them.

The deed is then sent to the seller's solicitor for execution by his client. The deed will then be retained by the seller's solicitor until completion.

2.12   Drafting the Mortgage

Your client will have a choice of mortgage. There are two main types, the repayment mortgage, and the endowment mortgage.

Under the repayment mortgage, the borrower promises monthly payments of capital and interest over a period of years. The maximum is usually 40 years. The capital debt is therefore slowly reduced. If the borrower expects to be survived by a spouse or by dependants for whom a home must be provided, he would be well advised to take out a mortgage protection policy. If the borrower dies before the mortgage loan is repaid, the policy will provide the money to pay off the balance due.

For an endowment mortgage, the borrower must take out an assurance policy on his life. The premiums are calculated so that at the end of the agreed number of years, the policy will yield at least sufficient money to repay the capital loan. When the mortgage over the land is created, the policy is assigned by the borrower to the lender. Over the term of the mortgage, the borrower pays the interest on the loan and the premiums on the policy. At the end of the mortgage term, the policy matures, and provides the money needed for redemption of the mortgage. The premiums can be calculated so that the policy yields more than the sum needed to redeem the mortgage. This means that the borrower will also have a capital sum for his own use. The endowment policy is then called a 'with profits' policy. If the policy will yield only the amount needed to repay the loan, it is called a 'minimum cost' policy. As the policy also matures if the borrower dies before the loan is repaid, there is no need for a mortgage protection policy.

Which mortgage is best for your client depends on his circumstances, and it is difficult to generalise. A 'with profits' endowment mortgage is sometimes preferred as it offers an effective means of saving. However any sort of life assurance must be looked upon as a long-term investment, as a borrower who attempts to surrender a policy in the early years (i.e. who asks the assurance company to end the contract early) will receive back from the company less than he has paid into it in premiums). This is no disadvantage if the mortgagor wishes to sell his house to buy another, as the same policy will be used as security for repayment of the new loan, and will not be surrendered. It is a disadvantage if the mortgagor, perhaps because of financial difficulties or marriage, wishes to sell his house and not buy another. The policy must be kept alive for several years if the assured wants anything like a real return for the premiums paid.

There is often no advantage at all in taking out a minimum-cost endowment policy. It has no savings element and the overall cost can be higher than a straight repayment mortgage. You must realise that your client is coming to you from the estate agent who has probably arranged the mortgage finance and possibly a life policy. Many estate agents are now owned by insurance companies, building societies or banks, and so may not, or perhaps cannot (because of the Financial Services Act 1986) give a choice of lender or assurance policy to the customer. Consider the suitability of the financial package that has been arranged, and whether a straight repayment mortgage might not be more suitable for your client than an endowment mortgage (see the statement of the Council of the Law Society on the 1986 Act in connection with life policies and tied agents, published in the *Guardian Gazette*, 23 March 1988.)

A mortgagor who pays interest on a loan for the purchase of his principal residence is entitled to income-tax relief. This relief can only be claimed on the first £30 000 of the loan. If two or more people are responsible for the repayment of the loan, the relief is shared between them. Relief is usually given under what is known as the MIRAS scheme (mortgage interest relief at source). This provides that the borrower pays interest to the lender after deduction of the tax relief. The lender claims the balance from the Inland Revenue. So, for example, if the monthly interest is £100, and income tax is 25p in the £1, the borrower pays the lender £75. The system only copes with basic-rate tax, so if the borrower pays higher-rate tax, the extra relief has to be claimed separately.

As, in this case, you are also the solicitor for the Building Society, it will be your task to draft the mortgage documents. The Society will send you its standard form of mortgage, and you will only have to fill in the blanks with details of the property, the borrower, amount of loan, etc. In the case of an endowment mortgage you may have to prepare the deed of assignment of the assurance policy. (The policy will, of course, be reassigned when the loan is repaid.) It will also be necessary after completion to give notice to the assurance company that the policy has been assigned. This is important for two reasons. It ensures that when the policy monies are payable they will be paid to the Building Society rather than to Susan. It also preserves the priority of the mortgage, and prevents a later mortgagee of the policy gaining priority over the Society's mortgage. Two copies of the notice are prepared. After completion, both copies are sent to the assurance company which is asked to receipt one copy of the notice and return it. This is then carefully preserved for fear the company might one day deny having been given notice. (Increasingly, lenders do not ask the borrower actually to assign the policy, but only *to promise* to assign it if required to do so. Nor is any notice of the assignment given to the assurance company. This is because it is likely that the house will be sold before the policy matures, and the loan repaid from the sale proceeds rather than the policy proceeds.)

Susan will have to execute the mortgage and the assignment of the policy as well as, possibly, the conveyance or transfer (see earlier). Your instructions from the Building Society may tell you to ensure that the mortgage documents are signed in the presence of a solicitor, or legal executive, or licenced conveyancer. This will mean that she will have to come into your office. So ensure that she has had your completion statement (see Chapter 2, section 13) and can bring the balance of the purchase price with her when she comes, and be sure that the appointment leaves time for any personal cheque of hers to be cleared before completion.

2.13   Obtaining the Balance of the Purchase Money

(a) From the Building Society. When you reported to the Society that the title was in order, you would also have asked them to send you the advance in time for completion.
(b) From your client. You need to send a statement to Susan, setting out the sum needed from her to complete the purchase. It will consist of the purchase price (less the deposit paid on contract) plus any apportionment of outgoings, plus your fees for acting in the purchase and in the mortgage, plus all the disbursements, minus the net mortgage loan.

2.14   The Pre-completion Search

Shortly before completion, you must make the pre-completion search. This really represents the final step in the investigation of the seller's title.

Completion must not take place until the results of the search are known, and must then take place before the priority period given by the official search certificate expires.

If you are buying a registered title, the search is made at the appropriate District Land Registry. If you are buying an unregistered title, the search is made at the Central Land Charges Registry at Plymouth (see Chapters 7 and 9 for a further explanation of these searches).

2.15 Completion

On completion you will pay the balance of the purchase price to the seller's solicitor. This will usually be paid by banker's draft or it may be telegraphed directly to the bank account of the seller's solicitor.

You will expect to pick up:

(a) if the title is unregistered, the deeds and the conveyance to Susan executed by the seller. If the seller had a mortgage, the purchaser is entitled to see that this is discharged. The mortgage deed itself will be handed over, properly receipted by the lender, or instead the solicitor acting for the mortgagee (who will probably be the same solicitor as is acting for the seller) will give you 'the usual undertakings' (these are explained in Chapter 7);

(b) in registered conveyancing, the land certificate and the transfer executed by the seller. If the seller had a mortgage, you will pick up the charge certificate, the transfer, Land Registry Form 53, or the usual undertakings in respect of it (see Chapter 7).

If the parties' solicitors are actually going to attend completion, it will usually take place at the offices of the seller's solicitor. (On this point, see standard condition 6.2.) (If this involves a long journey for the purchaser's solicitor, he can instruct another solicitor to act as his agent.) These civilised meetings are becoming things of the past, and completion increasingly takes place through the post. The purchaser's solicitor telegraphs the purchase price to the seller's solicitor, and in return the seller's solicitor posts the deeds to the purchaser's solicitor. Certain tasks have to be undertaken by the seller's solicitor as agent for the purchaser's solicitor, e.g. the examination and marking of the deeds, and endorsement of memoranda. An important point for the purchaser's solicitor to have confirmed is that the seller's solicitor has authority from the seller's mortgagee to receive the money to be used to redeem the mortgage. Otherwise, if the seller's solicitor disappears with the money, the seller's mortgagee can refuse to discharge the mortgage (see *Edward Wong Finance Co. Ltd* v. *Johnson Stokes and Master [1984]*).

The Law Society has published a code for postal completions, designed to define the solicitors' responsibilities and to reduce risk. If the solicitors are following the protocol, they must agree to adhere to the code, but otherwise do not have to do so.

2.16 After Completion

(a) You must report to your client that completion has taken place and that she can now move in. Keys are usually left with the estate agents, rather than with the solicitors.

(b) You can now transfer the sums paid to you by Susan Holt in respect of your fees and disbursements from your clients' account to your office account.

(c) If your client has bought the property subject to a lease, the tenant should be given written notice of the identity of his new landlord. If you fail to give this notice to a residential tenant, any rent or service charge due from him will be treated as not being due, and so no action for non-payment can be taken (section 48 of the Landlord & Tenant Act 1987).

(d) Perfecting the title. As purchaser's solicitor, ask yourself two questions:

   (i) does the conveyance or transfer need stamping with *ad valorem* stamp duty, and/or the 'particulars delivered' stamp?
   (ii) is the purchaser affected by the Land Registration Act 1925?

If you have bought an unregistered title, you need to consider whether or not you must apply for first registration of your client's title (see Chapter 3). You have two months in which to apply. You will be applying for registration of Susan as proprietor, and also for registration of the Society's mortgage.

If you have bought a registered title, you must apply for registration of the transfer to your client. Only when registered will your client obtain the legal estate. The application for registration should be made before the priority period given by the pre-completion search expires (see Chapter 7). You will also be applying for registration of the Society's mortgage as a registered charge.

2.17   A Note on the Stamping of Documents by the Purchaser after Completion

(*a*)   *Rates of Duty*

 (i) *Ad valorem* and fixed-rate stamp duty   A conveyance or transfer on sale of a freehold or existing leasehold estate is liable to *ad valorem* stamp duty at the rate of 1 per cent of the consideration. The conveyance or transfer will be exempt from stamp duty if it contains a certificate to the effect that the consideration does not exceed £30 000. (For full wording of this certificate, see the conveyance in Chapter 13.)

 (ii) Stamp duty does not have to be paid on mortgages or vacating receipts executed after 1971.

(iii) A conveyance or transfer by way of gift executed after 30 April 1987 is exempt from stamp duty, provided it contains a certificate that it is an instrument within one of the categories of exempt documents under Stamp Duty (Exempt Instruments) Regulations 1987 (SI 1987/516).

(iv) An assent executed as a deed, an appointment of a new trustee, a conveyance or transfer in consideration of marriage, or as part of rearrangement of property on a divorce are now exempt from the 50p deed stamp, provided they are certified as in paragraph (iii) above.
(v) A power of attorney is not liable for stamp duty (s.85 of the Finance Act 1985).
(vi) An assent not executed as a deed is not liable for stamp duty.

(*b*)   *Time Limit for Stamping*

The conveyance or other document should be presented for stamping within thirty days of its execution. The date of execution is taken as the date which the conveyance bears (i.e. usually the date of completion). There are financial penalties (which can be severe) if a document is presented for stamping after the thirty-day period, and the Land Registry will not register any conveyance or transfer that is not properly stamped.

(*c*)   *'Particulars Delivered' Stamp*

The Finance Act 1931 provides that certain documents must be produced to the Inland Revenue, together with a form giving particulars of the documents and any consideration received. The form is kept by the Inland Revenue (it provides useful information for the assessment of the value of the land) and the document is stamped with a stamp (generally cal'ed the PD stamp) as proof of its production. Without this PD stamp the document is not properly stamped and the person who failed in his responsibility to produce it (i.e. the original purchaser) can be fined.
   The documents that need a PD stamp are:

 (i) a conveyance on sale of the freehold;
 (ii) a grant of a lease for seven years or more;
(iii) the transfer on sale of a lease of seven years or more.

If a conveyance or transfer is being sent to the Land Registry for registration, and it is not liable for *ad valorem* stamp duty but does need a PD stamp (i.e. the sale was for £30 000 or less) the document need not be produced at the Inland Revenue before the application for registration is made. Instead, the form giving particulars is sent with the application for registration to the Land Registry, which forwards the form to the Inland Revenue.

2.18   Acting for Both Parties

We have treated acting for the seller and acting for the purchaser as alternatives. Is it possible for a solicitor to act for both?

The usual answer is 'no' because of the inherent conflict of interest. Similarly, the same solicitor (or two or more solicitors acting in partnership or association) cannot act for both landlord and tenant. However, rule 6 of the Law Society Practice Rules 1990 does permit a solicitor to act for both parties in a very limited number of cases. Even in one of these cases, a solicitor cannot act for both parties if there is a conflict of interest between them. A licenced conveyancer cannot act for both parties if there is a conflict of interest between them.

A conflict of interest may become apparent to you when you are drafting the contract for sale. As soon as you find yourself putting in a special condition that is to the disadvantage of the purchaser, e.g. cutting down his power of investigating title or preventing him from objecting to a defect in title, you should realise that you cannot also advise the purchaser on the wisdom of accepting the condition.

There is no rule of professional conduct to prevent a solicitor acting for co-sellers, or for co-purchasers unless there is a conflict of interest between them. Usually there will not be a conflict, but see Chapter 17 for an example of how this might arise.

There is not usually a conflict in acting for the seller and the seller's mortgagee as they both have the same objective in mind, i.e. successful redemption of the mortgage. Nor is there usually a conflict of interest in acting for the purchaser, and the purchaser's mortgagee, if the mortgagee is not a private person. However, there are two points that might arise:

(i) any defect in title that might affect the value of the property or the security of the mortgage must be made known to the mortgagee even though this might result in the mortgage offer being withdrawn;
(ii) any renegotiation in the terms of sale must be made known to the mortgagee, particularly any reduction in the purchase price. If the purchase price is reduced, a lender who is lending a substantial part of the price may also wish to reduce the amount of the loan.

If the mortgagee is a private person, you should not act for him and for the purchaser. This is because of the need to negotiate the terms of the mortgage.

3 Registered Title

Note: *Unless it is otherwise indicated, a reference in this Chapter to 'the Act' is a reference to the Land Registration Act 1925.*

3.1 Introduction

Conveyancing is bedevilled by the fact that the title to a legal estate may be either unregistered, or registered under the Land Registration Act 1925.

Whether or not the title is registered has no great effect on conveyancing procedure. The stages in the transaction remain the same. It does greatly affect investigation of title. It is also true to say that on some matters, such as the question of third-party interests in land, there is a different land law for registered title than there is for unregistered title.

If a title is unregistered, ownership of the legal estate is proved by the production of past conveyances, which show a transfer of the legal estate from one owner to another, and ultimately to the seller. The conveyances cannot guarantee ownership. To take a simple – although unlikely – example, a deed may be forged. A deed may also be voidable, for example, because it is a purchase of trust property by a trustee. However, the production of deeds, coupled with the fact that the seller is in possession of the house, i.e. either living there or receiving rent, usually offer assurance of ownership.

Just as the conveyances cannot guarantee ownership, neither can they guarantee that there are no third-party rights other than those mentioned in them. Some third-party rights may have been created by deeds predating those which the purchaser sees. Other third-party rights may have arisen independently of conveyances of the legal estate. A contract for sale, an option, an equitable interest arising from a resulting trust, would all be examples, as would an easement or restrictive covenant granted not in a conveyance of the land, but in a separate deed.

The Land Charges Act 1972, by providing for registration of some third-party interests affecting an unregistered title, does assist a purchaser who wishes to check on the existence of third-party rights. However, not all interests need to be registered under that Act. Nor can all interests that are registered necessarily be discovered by a purchaser. (Chapter 4 elaborates both these points.)

The purpose of the Land Registration Act 1925 is to simplify the investigation of title to a legal estate. If the title to, say, the freehold estate in Blackacre is registered, there is what amounts to a guarantee that the person named in the register as proprietor of the estate really does own it. This guarantee comes from what is known as the 'statutory vesting' (see later). As regards third-party interests, a transferee for value of the registered title will take the estate subject only to interests that are protected by an entry on the register, or that are 'overriding' interests. The reading of the title deeds in unregistered conveyancing is, therefore, replaced by the reading of the register.

Unfortunately, from the point of view of a purchaser, even in registered conveyancing, reading the register is not enough. A transferee will take the title subject to overriding interests, and an overriding interest is, by definition, an interest that is not entered on the register, but which will bind anyone who acquires the title (s.3 of the Act). You will see that it is the existence of overriding interests that introduce risk into registered conveyancing.

3.2   How does a Title Come to be Registered?

Since 1925, bit by bit, counties or parts of counties have been designated as areas of compulsory registration of title by Order in Council. (To tie this down to a concrete example, Rochester upon Medway, in Kent, became an area of compulsory registration on 1 March 1957). Indeed, as from 1 December 1990, the whole of England and Wales will be an area of compulsory registration.

The mere fact that land with an unregistered title lies in such an area does not mean that the title has to be registered. Only certain transactions necessitate an application for first registration of the title to the legal estate. These transactions are:

  (i) a conveyance on sale of the freehold estate;
 (ii) an assignment on sale of a leasehold estate, provided the lease has over twenty-one years to run at the date of assignment;
(iii) the grant of a lease having over twenty-one years to run at the date of the grant (s.123 of the Act as amended by s.2(1) of the Land Registration Act 1986).

Some examples may make this clearer.

Example 1

Samuel owns Blackacre, a house in Rochester. The title to it is unregistered. This is because it has not been sold since 1957. Patience, the purchaser, is now buying the freehold. Samuel will prove his ownership of the legal estate by producing past conveyances of it, ending with a conveyance to him. The legal estate will vest in Patience at completion of the sale. Patience, having stamped the conveyance to her (see Chapter 2, sections 16 and 17) must now consider the effect of s.123. She has *bought* Blackacre, and it is in an area of compulsory registration. She must now apply for first registration of the freehold title. She will apply to the District Land Registry that deals with Kent, i.e. the one at Tunbridge Wells.

The Act does not *compel* her to apply for first registration, but there is a sanction if she does not bother. Section 123 provides that if she does not apply within two months of the date of the conveyance, then the conveyance at the end of the two months will become void for the purpose of passing the legal estate. She will retain the equitable interest, and so have every right to live on the property. She will feel the pinch, however, when she decides to sell. Her title will be defective, as she will not own the legal estate. She can acquire the legal estate by applying for late registration of her title. Late applications are accepted by the Registrar, and the effect of registration will be to revest the legal estate in her.

Example 2

Terry owns the lease of a house in Kent. The lease has fifty years to run. The title to it is unregistered. Terry dies, and the lease vests in his personal representative, who vests it in Ben, the beneficiary named in Terry's will.

Neither the personal representative nor Ben has to apply for first registration. Neither bought the lease. The title to it will, quite properly, remain unregistered.

If the personal representative had instead sold the lease to Peter, Peter would have had to apply for first registration of the title to the lease.

Notice that it is only the title to the estate that has been sold that has to be registered. The freehold will remain unregistered, until this is itself sold.

'Sale' is not generally defined by the Act. It seems to have the usual meaning of a disposition for money. A conveyance or assignment by way of exchange for other land is specifically defined as a 'sale' if equality money is paid (s.123(3) of the Act).

It is doubtful if a conveyance for consideration other than money, e.g. in return solely for shares, or solely for other land, is a conveyance on sale.

Example 3

Len owns the freehold of a house in Kent, the title to which is unregistered. He grants a lease of thirty years to Teresa. Within two months of the grant of the lease Teresa must apply for registration of the title to it, otherwise, at the end of the two months, the lease will become equitable. The title to the freehold will not be registered until the freehold is sold.

(Suppose that Len granted a lease of twenty-one years and one month. The title should be registered by virtue of s.123. However, s.8 of the Act provides that it is impossible to register a lease that has twenty-one years or less to run. So Len would seem to be in difficulties if he delays his application for registration. He is compelled to register the unregistrable. This is why s.8(1A) provides that a lease that has less than twenty-one years to run when the application for first registration is made will be registered, if it had over twenty-one years to run when granted or assigned.)

Example 4

Although all areas are areas of compulsory registration, it is still important when buying an *unregistered* title to know when the area became subject to compulsory registration. To return to Rochester and Example 1, if Patience finds that Samuel had bought Blackacre after Rochester became an area of compulsory registration she knows that his title is bad. It should not have remained unregistered. His failure to apply for first registration within two months of his purchase means that he has lost the legal estate. It can only be restored by registration of the title.

3.3 Voluntary Registration

It is always possible for an estate owner to volunteer for registration of his title, if his land is in an area of compulsory registration. Voluntary registration would clearly be convenient for an owner, such as a developer, who intends to sell his land off in parts. It will be easier to prove title to several purchasers, if the title is registered.

3.4 What Titles Can be Registered?

It is possible to register the title to

(a) the freehold estate
(b) a legal leasehold estate. It is not however, possible to register the title to a lease granted for twenty-one years or less. Nor is it possible to apply for first registration of a lease that has less than twenty-one years to run at the time the application is made (but see s.8 (1A) of the Act previously mentioned).

These titles can be independently registered. It is also possible to register the title to an easement and to a mortgage or charge by deed. Such a registration will not be independent, but will be a registration against the title of the land affected. Registration of easements is discussed in Chapter 12. A mortgage or charge by deed can be registered as a registered charge in the charges register of the land affected.

3.5 The Effect of First Registration of a Title

The registration of a purchaser as proprietor of a legal estate automatically vests the legal estate in him (ss. 5 and 9 of the Act). This statutory vesting ensures that if you are dealing with the registered proprietor, you must be dealing with the owner of the estate.

Usually, the purchaser who has applied for first registration will already have acquired the legal estate on completion, so the statutory vesting merely confirms the pre-existing position. However, if, for example, the conveyance to the purchaser had been a forgery, no legal estate would have vested in him at completion, but would vest in him as soon as he is registered as proprietor. This example shows that registration can 'cure' a title.

3.6 Classes of Title

A proprietor can be registered with different classes of title. The class of title warns a purchaser about the extent of risk in dealing with that proprietor.

(a) Absolute Title to a Freehold Estate

Look at Example 1 in section 3.2. Patience has acquired the legal freehold estate on completion and must now apply for first registration of her title to it. She will do this by sending to the District Land Registry:

 (i) all the conveyancing documents, i.e. the pre-contract searches and enquiries (but not the local land charge search and additional enquiries), the contract, the requisitions on title, the land charge search certificates and the title deeds, together with a list in triplicate of all these documents;
 (ii) the Land Registry application form;
(iii) the fee.

The title will be investigated by the Registry staff. If there is nothing greatly wrong with the title, the Registrar will register Patience as proprietor of the freehold estate, with absolute title. (The date of registration is backdated to the date of application for first registration, Rule 42 of the Land Registration Rules 1925).

Section 5 of the Act says that a proprietor registered with an absolute title takes the legal estate, together with all rights appurtenant to it, subject only to:

 (i) *Incumbrances Protected by an Entry on the Register* Suppose for instance, that on investigation of Patience's title, the Registrar realises that the title is subject to restrictive covenants, created by a past conveyance, and properly registered as a DII land charge. When he draws up the register of Patience's title, a notice of these covenants will be entered on the charges register. Patience now owns the legal estate subject to these covenants.

    Notice that when Patience's title was unregistered, she was bound by the covenants because they had been protected by registration as a land charge. Once her title is registered, she is bound by the covenants because they are entered on the charges register of the registered title. The registration as a land charge is now completely irrelevant. This is why it is so important for incumbrances existing at the date of first registration to be entered on the register (that is, unless they can take effect as overriding interests, e.g. legal easements). If the restrictive covenants were not entered on the charges register they would cease to bind Patience, as they would not be protected by an entry on the register, nor would they be overriding interests. The person with the benefit of the covenants would have been seriously prejudiced by the registration of the title. His remedy would be to apply for rectification of the title, to ensure that the covenants are entered in the charges register. (but see *Freer* v. *Unwins Ltd* [1976]).

Adverse interests entered on the register carry no risk to a purchaser of the registered title from Patience, as the interests are discovered by reading the register.

(ii) *Overriding Interests*   This is the area of risk. An overriding interest is one that is not on the register, but which will bind a purchaser. These are discussed in 3.15. Some may be discovered by inspecting the land.

(iii) *Interests of beneficiaries, if the proprietor is not entitled to the land for his own benefit, but is holding it as a trustee*   These interests should not present a risk to a purchaser. If the proprietor holds as a trustee, this should be disclosed by a restriction on the proprietorship register. The purchaser can then arrange for the beneficiaries' interests to be overreached (if they exist behind a trust for sale or settlement under the Settled Land Act 1925) or otherwise satisfied. Even if there is no restriction on the register to warn the purchaser of the beneficiaries' interests, they may fail against him as being unprotected minor interests.

The danger is the presence of a beneficiary's interest which is not overreached, and which is an overriding interest because the beneficiary is occupying the land (see 3.16).

(b)   Absolute Title to a Leasehold Estate

By virtue of s.9 of the Act a person who is registered as proprietor of a lease with absolute title owns 'the legal leasehold estate, subject to the same rights as those affecting a freehold absolute title, but subject in addition to the covenants and obligations of the lease'.

The registration of an absolute leasehold title amounts to a guarantee not only that the proprietor owns the leasehold estate, but also that the lease was validly granted. Clearly, that guarantee can only be given if the Registrar knows that the landlord had the power to grant the lease. In other words, the Registrar needs evidence of the title to the freehold and to any superior leases. If the superior titles are registered, the evidence of title is in the registry and no further evidence need be deduced to the Registrar. For example, if L is registered as proprietor of the freehold estate with absolute title and grants a thirty-year lease to T, T will be registered as proprietor of the leasehold estate with absolute title.

(c) Good Leasehold Title

If a person is registered as proprietor of a leasehold estate with good leasehold title, his position is the same as a proprietor of a lease with absolute title, but with an important exception. The registration does not guarantee that the lease is valid (s.10 of the Act). A purchaser knows that the proprietor owns the lease, and the purchaser can read the register and inspect the land to discover third-party rights, but the purchaser does not know if the lease is worth anything at all.

Why does an applicant for first registration only obtain a good leasehold title? Look at Example 3 in 3.2. Len cannot be forced by Teresa to give details of his freehold title, unless there is a contract between them that the title will be deduced. When Teresa applies for first registration she will be unable to give details of Len's title to the Registrar.

The Registrar, being unable to investigate the freehold title, cannot guarantee that the lease is valid. He can only give Teresa good leasehold title. Look also at Example 2, where Peter is buying the lease from the personal representative. Terry may have obtained no details of the landlord's title when he was granted the lease. No details can therefore be supplied by the personal representative to Peter. Peter will be registered with good leasehold title.

You can see that a good leasehold title is unattractive both to a purchaser and a purchaser's mortgagee. The problem is discussed in greater detail in Chapter 15.

(d) Possessory Title to a Freehold or Leasehold Estate

A proprietor will be registered with a possessory title when the registrar is not satisfied with the documentary evidence of ownership. This may be because the applicant's title is based on his adverse possession (a squatter's title) or because he has lost his title deeds.

The drawback of a possessory title is that the registration is subject not only to everything to which an absolute title would be subject, but is also subject to any estate or interest that is adverse to the first proprietor's title and that exists at the date of first registration (ss. 6 and 11 of the Act). In other words, the title is subject to the risk that X might pop up and claim that the registered proprietor has not been in adverse possession sufficiently long to extinguish X's estate or interest in the land. X's rights are overriding, so that a purchase from the registered proprietor may also be unable to deny X's superior claim to the land.

(e)   A Qualified Title

An applicant for registration with an absolute or good leasehold title may find that although the title is granted the Registrar wishes to put a qualification on it. This will be because the Registrar has found a particular flaw in it. For example, the Registrar may find that one of the conveyances was a purchase of trust property by one of the trustees. The beneficiaries of the trust could apply to the court to have this conveyance avoided. The Registrar would qualify the title, by stating that registration did not affect the rights of the beneficiaries.

A qualification can only be put on the title with the applicant's consent, but if the applicant refuses he may instead find himself registered with only possessory title. This is no more attractive to a purchaser than a qualified absolute title, as it is subject to *all* pre-registration claims. Qualified titles are rare.

3.7   Upgrading of Title

The rules for upgrading a title are contained in s.77 of the Act, as amended by s.1 of the Land Registration Act 1986.

(a)   A good leasehold title can be upgraded to an absolute leasehold title if the Registrar has satisfactory evidence of the freehold and any superior leasehold title.

Look again at Example 3 in section 3.2. If Len sells the freehold title, the purchaser will have to apply for first registration. Details of the freehold title will then be available to the Registrar. He may register the purchaser from Len as proprietor of the freehold with absolute title, and change Teresa's title to the lease from good leasehold to absolute. Teresa could apply for the upgrading, or the Registrar could upgrade on his own initiative.

(b)   A possessory title can be upgraded to an absolute freehold title, or a good leasehold title, if either:

   (i) the Registrar is given satisfactory evidence of title; or
  (ii) if the title has been registered for at least twelve years and the Registrar is satisfied that the proprietor is in possession.

(c)   a qualified title can be changed to an absolute or good leasehold title if the Registrar is satisfied as to the title.

3.8   The Form of the Register

The register of the title is, confusingly enough, divided into three registers. (In Chapter 5 you will see a rather simplified version of a register of title.) Each registered title has its own title number.

The Property Register

This describes the property, e.g. 1 Smith Avenue. The description usually refers to the Land Registry filed plan. This plan only indicates the general boundaries of the land, but does not fix them exactly (rule 278 of the Land Registration Rules 1925). It describes the estate – i.e. freehold or leasehold. If the estate is leasehold, the register will include brief details of the lease (the date, parties, the term and its starting date).

The Proprietorship Register

This gives the name and address of the registered proprietor. It also gives the class of title, e.g. absolute, possessory, etc. You must realise that the class of title may change with a change of proprietor. O may be registered with an absolute title. If S enters into adverse possession against O, S may eventually be registered as the new proprietor, but possibly only with possessory title.

Any restriction will be entered on the proprietorship register. This is because a restriction reflects some sort of limitation on the proprietor's power to dispose of the land. Cautions are also entered here.

The Charges Register

Here are noted adverse interests such as restrictive covenants, easements and leases (unless the lease is an overriding interest). Also appearing here are registered charges (i.e. mortgages).

3.9   The Land Certificate

As has been seen in 3.6, when Patience applies for first registration of her title, she will send the title deeds to the Registry. When the registration of her as proprietor is completed, the deeds will be returned to her. These deeds no longer prove her title, and provided she has obtained an absolute title, there is no legal reason for preserving them, unless they reveal positive covenants (see Chapter 12). There will also be sent to her a land certificate. This is a copy of the register of title, sewn up in an imposing cover. This, in a sense, now plays the role of the title deeds – i.e. it is evidence of the registered proprietor's title. No transfer of the title, or other dealings, will be registered, unless the application for registration is accompanied by the land certificate. It can be deposited with a creditor to give security for the loan, as can title deeds. The land certificate is not quite the same as the title deeds, however. The register is the real evidence of title. Often the entries in the land certificate are exactly the same as the entries on the register as whenever the land certificate is deposited in the registry, the certificate will be brought up to date with the entries on the register. However, there are some entries which can be put on the register without the land certificate having to go into the Registry. These include cautions, and a notice protecting a spouse's rights of occupation under Matrimonial Homes Act 1983.

3.10   The Charge Certificate

You may know that when an unregistered title is mortgaged for the first time, the lender nearly always takes control of the title deeds. It was felt necessary to reflect this practice in registered conveyancing. If a registered title is mortgaged by deed, the lender can register the mortgage as a registered charge. The application for registration is accompanied by the borrower's land certificate. The land certificate is then retained in the registry and a charge certificate is issued to the lender. The charge certificate will contain a copy of the entries in the register and a copy of the mortgage deed. If the title is mortgaged a second time, the proprietor of the second registered charge will have a second charge certificate.

3.11   Dealings with a Registered Title

The principle is this; that every registrable dealing with a registered title must itself be registered, or it will not pass a legal estate. What does this mean?

The following are registrable dealings:

(a) a transfer of the registered title. This may be on sale or by way of gift.
(b) a transmission of the title, e.g. to a personal representative on the death of the registered proprietor (see Chapter 10).
(c) a grant of a lease out of the registered title, if the lease is for over twenty-one years (see Chapter 16).
(d) the grant of a mortgage or charge by deed.
(e) the grant of an easement (see Chapter 12).

Here is a simple example. Susan owns the freehold estate in Blackacre. The title is registered. Susan sells Blackacre to Petunia. On completion, Susan will hand to Petunia the land certificate and a land registry transfer, executed by Susan. Petunia now owns the equitable interest in the land. She does not own the legal estate. Why not? Because no legal estate will pass until the transfer is registered. So the next step, once the transfer has been stamped with any *ad valorem* stamps necessary, and with the 'particulars delivered' stamp (see 2.16) is to apply for registration of the transfer. She will do this by sending the certificate, the transfer, application form and fee to the District Land Registry. Once Petunia is registered as the new proprietor the legal estate vests in her. There is no time limit for the registration of a dealing with the registered title, but Petunia should apply for registration before the priority period given by her pre-completion search expires (see 7.5).

3.12 Third-party Rights in Registered Title

A registered title can be subject to the same third-party rights (e.g. restrictive covenants, contracts, easements, mortgages, etc.) as unregistered title.

When the registered title is sold, will the purchaser be bound by these third-party interests? Does an owner of the third-party interest have to do anything to protect it?

Third-party interests in registered title fall into two categories, overriding interests and minor interests.

(a)   An Overriding Interest

This is defined by s.3 of the Act as an interest that is not entered on the register, but subject to which registered dispositions are by the Act to take effect. An overriding interest thus binds every purchaser of the title, yet cannot be discovered by reading the register. Most overriding interests are listed in s.70 of the Act and will be dealt with later.

(b)   Minor interests

These are defined by s.2 and s.3 of the Act. The definition creates three categories:

 (i) *Registrable dealings that have not been registered*   So, looking at 3.11, we see that the equitable interest which Petunia acquires at completion is a minor interest until she registers the transfer.
 (ii) *Equitable interests existing behind a trust of the legal estate*   The interest of a beneficiary behind a settlement of the legal estate under Settled Land Act 1925 is a minor interest. The interest of a beneficiary behind a trust for sale of the legal estate may be a minor interest as may the interest of a beneficiary behind a bare trust. (A bare trust exists when the legal estate is held on trust for one adult beneficiary, without any trust for sale being declared. See the case of *Hodgson* v. *Marks* [1971]).

(iii) *Interests that are not created by registrable dispositions and which do not exist behind a trust.*   Into this category will fall restrictive covenants, equitable leases, easements, contracts for sale, options, etc.

Notice that the categories of overriding and minor interest are not mutually exclusive. If a beneficiary behind a trust for sale is living on the property, his interest will be overriding, by virtue of s.70(1)(g) of the Act 1925. (However, the interest of a beneficiary behind a Settled Land Act settlement is always a minor interest, despite occupation. This is laid down by s.86(2) of the Act.)

Similarly, a lease granted for twenty-two years out of a registered title is a registrable disposition. Pending registration, the tenant will have a minor interest but if he goes into occupation, it will be an overriding interest, again because of s.70(1)(g).

3.13   The Need to Protect a Minor Interest

A minor interest, unlike an overriding interest, is at risk. It should be protected by some form of entry on the register. The reason for this can best be given by quoting part of s.20 of the Act.

> In the case of a freehold estate ... a disposition of the registered land or a legal estate therein, including a lease thereof, for valuable consideration, shall, when registered, confer on the transferee or grantee an estate ... subject to the incumbrances and other entries, if any appearing on the register; and ... to the overriding interests, if any, affecting the estate transferred ... but free from all other estates and interests whatsoever.

S.23 is a similar provision dealing with the transfer of a registered leasehold title.

In other words, a transferee for value whether taking an outright transfer, or a mortgage, or a lease, will, when the disposition is registered, take free from any minor interest that is not protected by an entry on the register.

The transferee takes free of the minor interest, even though he knows of its existence. S.59(6) of the Act provides that a purchaser acquiring title under a registered disposition is not to be concerned with any matter or claim (not being an overriding interest) which is not protected on the register, whether he has or has not notice therefore, express, implied or constructive (but see *Lyus* v. *Prowsa Developments Ltd* [1982][*] the facts of which are given in the case notes to this chapter, for circumstances in which a purchaser did take subject to an unprotected minor interest because a constructive trust was imposed on him – when an asterisk appears besides a case for the first time it signifies a case that is mentioned in the case notes).

3.14 Methods of Protecting Minor Interests

(a) Registration

A registrable dealing should be registered. Until this is done, no legal estate is created or transferred.

(b) Notices

A notice is an entry of the interest on the charges register of the title affected. The land certificate must be deposited at the Registry before any notice is put on the register. This is why, generally speaking, the consent of the registered proprietor is needed before a notice can be used. However, we have seen that if the title is subject to a registered charge, the land certificate is retained in the registry. This makes it possible for a notice to be put on the register without the consent of the registered proprietor. The proprietor is told of an application to enter a notice, so he has an opportunity to object. (As an exception to this rule, a proprietor is not, for obvious reasons, told of a spouse's application for a notice to protect his/her rights of occupation under the Matrimonial Homes Act 1983.)

A notice ensures that *if the interest is valid*, any transferee will take subject to that interest. The registered proprietor is, of course, always able to challenge the validity of the interest, as a notice cannot change a void or unenforceable interest into a valid one.

(c) Cautions

If a notice cannot be used, because the land certificate is not deposited at the Registry, a caution must be used. When a cautioner applies for a caution to be entered, the application has to be accompanied by a statutory declaration, briefly describing the interest or right claimed by him. Unlike a notice, the caution itself does not set out the interest. A person reading the register will see merely 'Caution dated 1 April 1989 registered on 6 April 1989 in favour of Avril Printemps'.

The effect of lodging a caution is that the Registrar must inform the cautioner before he registers a dealing with the land. This gives the cautioner an opportunity to assert his claim in a hearing by the Registrar with usually one of three results:

(i) the Registrar registers the dealing, but subject to the interest or rights of the cautioner;
(ii) the Registrar refuses to register the dealing at all;
(iii) the Registrar registers the dealing free of the cautioner's claim.

Theoretically, a caution is not as effective a protection as a notice. A notice ensures that the purchaser will, without more ado, take subject to the protected interest. A caution merely gives the cautioner a right to defend himself against a transferee by disputing the registration. A caution is intended to be used as a temporary form of protection only, for example to defend the cautioner's rights pending litigation between himself and the proprietor. Practically speaking, a caution on the register can paralyse dealings with the title, as no sensible purchaser will pay over the purchase price until the caution is removed from the register. The proprietor is thus forced either to come to terms with the cautioner or to litigate.

Warning Off a Caution   A registered proprietor can apply to the Registrar to 'warn off' a caution. Notice is served on the cautioner, and if he does not object within the time-limit specified in the notice, the caution is cancelled. If the cautioner does object, the dispute will be settled by the Registrar or the court.

(d)   Restrictions

A restriction is an entry on the proprietorship register that reflects the fact that the proprietor's powers of disposing of the land are in some way limited. It ensures that the proprietor complies with certain conditions before any transfer by him is registered. Take, as an example, a proprietor who holds the legal estate on trust for X, an adult. Let us assume that it is a bare trust and not a trust for sale. This would be because no express trust for sale was ever created, and there are no grounds, such as co-ownership of the beneficial interest, for one to be implied.

In unregistered conveyancing, a purchaser for value of a legal estate from a bare trustee would take subject to the beneficiary's interest if the purchase had notice of it. As soon as a purchaser learns of a bare trust, therefore, he should obtain the consent of the beneficiary to the sale.

This is reflected in the restriction that goes onto the proprietorship register if the title is registered. It will say, in effect, that no disposition by the proprietor will be registered unless the consent of X (the beneficiary) is obtained. It is the duty of the proprietor (the trustee) to ensure that this restriction is on the title (but of course, not every person does his duty).

You can see from this example that a restriction may exist as much for the protection of a purchaser as for the owner of the third-party interest, as the restriction ensures that the necessary conditions are fulfilled to clear the third-party interest from the title. To labour the point, you must realise that the absence of the restriction does not prejudice a purchaser if the interest that should have been protected by it is a minor interest. However, failure to enter the restriction will prejudice the purchaser if the interest that should have been protected by it is an overriding interest. The purchaser has been deprived of the warning that there were conditions to be satisfied that *if* satisfied, would have cleared the interest from the title. To return to the example of the bare trust. If no restriction is entered, the purchaser will take free of X's interest if X is not in occupation. The purchaser can plead s.20 of the Act. The purchaser will take subject to X's interest if X is in occupation, as the occupation will make X's interest overriding. A restriction would have ensured that the purchaser either obtained X's consent to the transfer, or did not proceed.

A restriction would have saved the bank (i.e. the purchaser) in *Williams and Glyn's Bank* v. *Boland* [1981]*, but would have saved the parents (i.e. the beneficiaries) in *City of London Building Society* v. *Flegg* [1988]* (see case notes at the end of this chapter).

A proprietor whose powers of disposition are limited does have a duty to apply for the appropriate restriction to be registered. The restriction can also be applied for by a person interested in the land. In some circumstances, the registrar is under a duty to put a restriction on the register, e.g. in the case of co-ownership. Examples of restrictions are given in Chapter 11.

(e) *Inhibitions*

An inhibition prevents any dealing with the land at all. The only common one is the bankruptcy inhibition, which is put in the register when the receiving order is made.

3.15 Overriding interests

Most overriding interests are set out in s.70 of the Act. Only the most common are dealt with here.

(a) *Easements*

To quote s.70(1)(a) of the Act in full:

> Rights of common, drainage rights, customary rights (until extinguished), public rights, profits *a prendre*, rights of sheepwalk, rights of way, watercourses, rights of water and other easements not being equitable easements required to be protected by notice on the register.

The paragraph has been quoted in full, because the wording of it has led to controversy.

It is clear that a legal easement is overriding. Is an equitable easement? S.70(1)(a) excludes equitable easements 'required to be protected' on the register. It is not clear what this means. There is no *requirement* in the Act that equitable easements be protected by an entry on the register, although such protection is possible, using a notice or caution. It may be that 'required' means 'needing', i.e. an equitable easement that needs protection cannot be overriding. In *Celsteel* v. *Alton House Holdings Ltd* [1985] it was held that an equitable easement, openly exercised, is an overriding interest by reason of rule 258 of the Land Registration Rules Act 1925. Therefore, the only equitable easement that needs protection by an entry on the register is one not openly exercised, because such an easement is not an overriding interest. The need to register easements granted out of registered land is discussed in Chapter 12.

(*b*)   *Rights Acquired, or being Acquired under the Limitation Act 1980 (s.70(1)(f) of the Act)*

If a title is unregistered, the effect of a squatter being in adverse possession of land for the limitation period is to extinguish the original owner's title, both to the equitable interest and to the legal estate. If the title is registered, the adverse possession extinguishes the claim of the registered proprietor to the equitable interest. However, because of the principle that only registered dealings can transfer a legal estate, the registered proprietor will retain the legal estate until the register is rectified by entering the squatter as registered proprietor. Until rectification, the original proprietor will hold the legal estate on trust for the squatter.

If the original proprietor sells the title before rectification, the purchaser will take subject to the rights of the squatter. In other words, the transferee will be in no better position than the transferor.

(*c*)   *The Rights of a Person in Actual Occupation of the Land (s.7(1)(g) of the Act)*

This is dealt with in 3.16.

(*d*)   *Local Land Charges (s.70(i)(i) of the Act)*

As local land charges are overriding interests, it is as important for a purchaser of registered title to make a local land charge search, as it is for a purchaser of unregistered title. Details of the search are given in chapter 6.

(*e*)   *Leases Granted for a Term Not Exceeding Twenty-One Years (s.70(1)(k)*

The title to a lease granted for twenty-one years or under is not registrable. The lease however, will be overriding, so that if the landlord's title is registered, any transfer of it will take effect subject to the lease.

In the case of *City Permanent Building Society* v. *Miller* [1952] the word 'granted' was seized on, and held to mean the creation of a legal estate. An informally created lease, taking effect only in equity, cannot, therefore, be overriding under s.70(1)(k). It could be overriding under s.70(1)(g).

It seems that as s.70(1)(k) makes the lease overriding, it will also make overriding any provision in the lease that affects the parties in their relationship of landlord and tenant. This would include an option to renew the lease, but would exclude an option to buy the landlord's reversion, as this is looked upon as a personal covenant. (*Woodall* v. *Clifton* [1905]).

However, such an option could be overriding under s.70(1)(g) (*Webb* v. *Pollmount* [1966].

3.16   Section 70(1)(g) of the Act – Dangerous Occupiers

By virtue of s.70(1)(g), overriding interests include 'the rights of every person in actual occupation of the land, or in receipt of the rents and profits thereof save where enquiry is made of such person and the rights are not disclosed'.

At the start, it must be stressed that s.70(1)(g) does *not* say that occupation *creates* any rights. It is saying that *if* the occupier owns an interest in land arising under ordinary principles of property law, then occupation by the owner of the interest protects the interest and makes it overriding.

Uncle George who has been invited to live with the registered proprietor as a matter of family feeling is not a dangerous occupier, at least not to a purchaser. Uncle has no interest to assert against the purchaser, so his occupation is irrelevant.

However, an Uncle George who has contributed to the original purchase price, or who has paid for substantial improvements to the property and as a result of the work or contribution *owns part of the equitable interest*, is a dangerous occupier. He has an interest to assert, and his occupation makes the interest an overriding one. A purchaser who takes subject to the interest will be faced with the choice of living in the house with uncle, or re-selling the property and sharing the proceeds with him.

S.70(1)(g) makes not only an interest belonging to an occupier overriding, but also an interest belonging to anybody receiving rent from the land. So, for example, if the registered proprietor grants a lease to T, and T sublets to ST who lives on the property, both the sublease and lease are overriding interests.

Section 70(1)(g) can only make an interest overriding if it is one that by its nature is capable of surviving through changes in ownership. Neither a bare licence nor a contractual licence can, for this reason, be overriding interests (see *Strand Securities Ltd* v. *Caswell* [1965]). A licence backed by an estoppel could be overriding.

Although s.70(1)(1)(g) can make an interest overriding it does not otherwise change its character. It is now clear, for example, that the interest of a beneficiary behind a trust for sale remains overreachable, even though the beneficiary is in occupation. Once the interest has been overreached, it cannot be asserted against the purchaser and s.70(1)(g) is irrelevant (*City of London Building Society* v. *Flegg* [1988]).

All interests belonging to the occupier are overriding, not just the interest which entitled him to occupy in the first place. So if a tenant is in actual occupation, not only is his lease overriding, but also an option in the lease for the purchase of the landlord's reversion (*Webb* v. *Pollmount* [1966]).

3.17   The Meaning of 'Actual Occupation'

What does 'actual occupation' mean? In unregistered title, the occupation of land by someone who claims on equitable interest is relevant because it may give constructive notice of the equitable interest to the purchaser. If the purchaser, after diligent enquiry and after inspection of the land, fails to discover the occupation, he will take free of the occupier's interest because he does not have notice of it.

Section 70(1)(g) has no such concept of notice within it. In *Williams and Glyn's Bank Ltd* v. *Boland* [1981] it was said that a person is in actual occupation of the land if 'physically present' there. Lord Scarman in his judgement stressed that the statute had substituted a plain factual situation for the uncertainties of notice. Lord Wilberforce stated that in registered land, if there was actual occupation and the occupier had rights, the purchaser took subject to them, and that no further element was material.

The result of the decision clearly is that a purchaser should make enquiry of any occupier that he discovers on the land, to ascertain if that occupier has an interest in it. The enquiry should be made of the *occupier* not the seller. It is only where enquiry is made of the occupier and the rights are not revealed, that they cease to be overriding.

Yet even if a purchaser makes the most diligent search for occupiers, this may not be enough. Even if an occupier is undiscoverable, (for example, deliberately concealed by the seller) his interest may bind the purchaser, if the occupier can be said to be physically present. It is the fact of occupation that matters, not its discoverability.

The meaning of occupation has recently been discussed by the House of Lords in *Abbey National Building Society* v. *Cann and ors* [1990] (see the case notes to Chapter 11). Mrs Cann claimed that she was in actual occupation on the day that the purchase of the house by her son, financed by a mortgage loan from the Building Society, was completed. On that day she was abroad, but her husband and son began to move her belongings into the house as the seller moved out. Her belongings were on the property for 35 minutes before completion of the purchase.

It was said by Lord Oliver that what was necessary for occupation might vary according to the nature and purpose of the property, but that occupation always involved some degree of permanence and continuity, and not a fleeting presence. A purchaser who before completion was allowed to go in to plan decorations or measure for furniture could not be said to be in occupation.

Mrs Cann's claim that she had been in occupation therefore failed.

3.18   When Must the Occupier be in Occupation?

It has been held that if his interest is to be overriding under s.70(1)(g), the
occupier must be in occupation at the time the title is transferred to the
purchaser (see again *Abbey National Building Society* v. *Cann and ors*,
which are given in Chapter 11). Once the purchaser has taken subject to the
interest, it is not necessary that the owner of the interest remain in
occupation. His interest will continue to bind the purchaser, even though
the owner of the interest then leaves. However, his interest will not bind a
later transferee from the purchaser unless the owner of the interest resumes
occupation before the transfer takes place (*London and Cheshire Insurance
Co. Ltd* v. *Laplagrene Property Co. Ltd* [1971].

3.19   The Undisclosed Trust for Sale

Much of the litigation involving s.70(1)(g) has been in the context of an
undisclosed trust for sale, and is further discussed in Chapter 11.

Case Notes

Williams and Glyn's Bank Ltd. v. *Boland*

[1981] AC 487, [1980] 2 A11 ER 408, [1980} 3 WLR 138, 124 Sol Jo 443, 40 PCR 451.

Mr Boland was the registered proprietor of the family house. His wife had contributed a
substantial sum towards the purchase of the house and as a result owned part of the
equitable interest. Mr Boland, therefore, held the legal estate on trust for sale for
himself and his wife as tenants in common. No entry had been put on the register to
protect the wife's interest. Mr Boland later borrowed money from the bank, and
mortgaged the house to it. The bank made no enquiries of Mrs Boland. Mr Boland
failed to keep up his mortgage payments, so the bank started an action for possession,
with a view to selling the house. Could the bank obtain possession against Mrs Boland,
or was it bound by her interest?

The bank could only be bound if her interest was an overriding one, under s.70(1)(g)
of the Act. Counsel for the Bank raised two arguments in favour of the view that her
interest could not be overriding.

The first was that s.70 defined overriding interests as interests subsisting in the
registered *land*. The interest of a beneficiary behind a trust for sale is traditionally
regarded as being not in the land, but in the proceeds of sale. This is due to what is
known as the equitable doctrine of conversion, based on the maxim that 'equity looks
upon that as done which ought to be done'. As a trust should be carried out, land
subject to a trust for sale is regarded as already sold, and the interests of the
beneficiaries as subsisting in the entirely mythical proceeds of the mythical sale.

The House of Lords nevertheless held that Mrs Boland's interest was capable of
being overriding. It was said to be 'unreal' to describe her interest as existing merely in
the proceeds of sale. Reliance was placed on the earlier Court of Appeal decision in

Bull v. *Bull* [1955] 1QB 234, [1955] 1 A11 ER 253, [1955] 2 WLR 78. In that case, the son held the legal estate on trust for sale, the beneficiaries being himself and his mother as tenants in common. The son brought an action for possession against his mother. It was held that when a house is bought for joint occupation, each tenant in common has the right to be there, and neither is entitled to turn the other out. So an interest of a beneficiary behind a trust for sale, while it may not be technically an interest in land, is something more than an interest in the proceeds of sale.

However, it appears that if the purpose behind the trust for sale is not to provide a home for the beneficiaries, but instead an investment, an interest of a beneficiary will be regarded as being only in the proceeds of sale, and he will not have any right of occupation. In *Barclay* v. *Barclay* [1970] 2QB 677, [1970] 2 A11 ER 676, [1970] 3 WLR 82, a testator devised his house on trust for sale, with a direction that the proceeds be divided among five beneficiaries. One beneficiary wished to continue to live there. The court ordered that he relinquish possession, as his interest gave him no right to occupy the land. The purpose of the trust was that the land should actually be sold, and his interest was only in the proceeds. It follows that if the land had been sold to a purchaser, the interest of the beneficiary in *Barclay* v. *Barclay* could not have been overriding under s.70(1)(g). It would not have subsisted in reference to the land. So the purpose of a trust for sale is significant in deciding whether a beneficiary's interest is capable of binding a purchaser, either under s.70(1)(g), or if the title is unregistered, under the doctrine of notice.

The second argument used by counsel in the Boland case was that Mrs Boland was not in 'actual occupation'. This argument was based on the view that underlying s.70(1)(g) were the old rules about notice, so that the occupation must be such as to make a purchaser suspicious. A purchaser would not be suspicious when he found a wife occupying a husband's house, as the marriage would be a sufficient explanation. This argument was resoundingly rejected. The section was to be interpreted literally. A person is in actual occupation of the house if physically present there.

City of London Building Society v. *Flegg [1988] AC 54, [1987] 3 A11 ER 435, [1987] 2 WLR 1266*

Mr and Mrs Maxwell-Brown, and Mrs Maxwell-Brown's parents, Mr and Mrs Flegg, proposed to buy a house for the four of them to live in. The Fleggs contributed £18 000 towards the purchase price. The title was registered. The legal estate was transferred into the names of the Maxwell-Browns only, who held on trust for sale for themselves and their parents. Later, without the authority of the Fleggs, the Maxwell-Browns mortgaged the legal estate. The payments were not kept up, and the Building Society sought possession of the property. The parents claimed that they had an equitable interest in the house, by reason of their contribution towards its purchase, and that their interest bound the Society as the parents were in actual occupation. It was held in the House of Lords that the parents' interest could not be asserted against the Society, as the mortgage had been created by two trustees for sale and that consequently the interests of the beneficiaries had been overreached. Once the interests of the Fleggs had been overreached, they had no interest left in the land to be overriding.

Note that s.17 of the Trustee Act 1925 provides that a mortgagee lending money to trustees is not concerned to see that the trustees are acting properly. The validity of the mortgage, therefore, was not affected by the fact that the Maxwell-Browns were acting in breach of trust when creating it. The Fleggs could, perhaps, have put a restriction on the register, to the effect that no mortgage by the registered proprietors was to be registered without the Fleggs's consent (see Chapter 11).

Lyus v. *Prowsa [1982] 1 WLR 1044*

Land was sold by S to P expressly subject to X's contract to buy. The title was registered, but X was not in occupation and had not protected his minor interest by any sort of entry on the register. P then sold the land to Q, again expressly subject to the contract.

Q claimed that he was not bound by the contract, as it was an unprotected minor interest. It was held, however, that X could enforce the contract against Q.

The reason given was that P had held the land on a constructive trust for X. The judgement stressed that this was because it had been stipulated between V and P that P should give effect to the contract. No trust would have arisen if the sale had been said to be subject to the contract merely for the protection of V. The Land Registration Act 1925 could not be used as an instrument of fraud, so P could not claim to be released from the trust on the grounds that the contract had not been entered on the register. Q was bound by the trust, because he had bought with notice of it.

The decision has been criticised as having ignored provisions of the Land Registration Act. Section 74 of the Act, for example, states that a person dealing with a registered estate shall not be affected by notice of a trust. So Q should not have been affected by his notice of the constructive trust imposed on P. The decision was approved by the House of Lords, however, in *Ashburn Anstalt* v. *Arnold* [1987].

The same reasoning would apply to a conveyance of unregistered land. X's failure to protect his contract by registering it as a C(iv) land charge would usually ensure that the contract did not bind P, even though the conveyance by V to P said the land was conveyed subject to it. P would, however, be bound if the circumstances justified the imposition of a constructive trust.

Workshop

Attempt this problem yourself, then read the specimen solution at the end of the book.

Problem 1

You act for two brothers, Bill and Ben Brown, who have bought a freehold house, 15 Flowerpot Lane, for £45 000. They bought with the aid of a mortgage loan from the Bleaklow Building Society, for which you also act. The house was conveyed to the two brothers as tenants in common. In the conveyance they covenanted with the seller that no further buildings of any kind would be erected on the land. The transaction was completed yesterday.

1 What steps should you now take to ensure that the brothers will have a good title to the house?
2 What document will finally issue from the District Land Registry?

---

4 Unregistered Title: Third-Party Rights

This chapter serves as a reminder of the principles which decide whether or not a purchaser of *unregistered* land takes subject to a third party interest.

4.1 Is the Third Party's Interest Legal or Equitable?

When deciding whether or not the interest will bind a purchaser, the first question to decide is whether the interest is a legal interest or an equitable one. The reason is that generally speaking a purchaser of an unregistered title will take subject to legal estates and interests, whether he knows of them or not.

Interests capable of being legal include:

(a) A lease. Remember, however, that a lease is *capable* of being legal. In order to be so, it must have been granted by deed. A lease created by signed writing which does not amount to a deed will be equitable only (See Chapter 13 for the rules which now determine whether or not a document is a deed). The exception to this is a lease for 3 years or less at best rent without a premium, and giving an immediate right to possession. This can be created as a legal estate without a deed (Sections 52–4 of the Law of Property Act 1925.) So a periodic lease e.g. a weekly tenancy, will be legal, even though granted informally.

(b) An easement which is either perpetual, or granted for a term of years. (An easement for life can only be equitable.) Again, if the easement is to be legal, it must have been granted by deed.

(c) A legal mortgage or legal charge. However, if the mortgage or a legal charge is not protected by a deposit of title deeds with the lender, it is registrable under the Land Charges Act 1972, and will not bind a purchaser merely because it is legal (see later).

4.2 Is It Overreachable?

Equitable interests do not automatically bind a purchaser. So if faced with an equitable interest, the next questions will be, is the interest overreachable, and was it overreached?

Interests of beneficiaries behind a trust for sale of the legal estate, or behind a settlement under the Settled Land Act 1925 are overreachable. If, for example, the legal estate is vested in two or more trustees for sale, and they all convey, the interests of the beneficiaries will be overreached, and it is irrelevant whether the purchaser knew of their existence or not (see Chapter 11). If the sale had been by a single trustee for sale, the interests would not be overreached, and would bind a purchaser who had notice of them.

4.3 Does the Land Charges Act 1972 apply?

Once you have decided that the equitable interest has not been overreached, the next questions to ask are, was the equitable interest registrable under the Land Charges Act 1972, and if so, was it registered? The principle is that if an interest is registrable, then if it is registered, it will bind a subsequent purchaser. If it is not registered, it will not. Registration is all. Of course, it is not quite as simple as that, and the principle is elaborated in section 4.5.

4.4 Notice

If you are left with an equitable interest that has not been overreached, and is not registrable as a land charge, you come to the well-known rule that the equitable interest will bind anyone who acquires the land with the exception of a *bona fide* purchaser for value of the legal estate without notice of the equitable interest.

Many equitable incumbrances are registrable under the Land Charges Act 1972, and if an interest is registrable under that Act, the concept of notice is irrelevant (see *Midland Bank Trust Co. Ltd* v. *Green* [1981]). The rule about the *bona fide* purchaser covers only those interests that do not fall within the Act. These interests include:

• restrictive covenants created before 1926;
• the interest of a beneficiary behind a trust for sale that has not been overreached;
• an interest created by proprietory estoppel.

If a purchaser wishes to escape such an interest, he must prove that he bought a legal estate for value (this would exclude a donee, someone acquiring property by a gift in a will, and a squatter) without *notice*.

(a) Actual Notice

Notice can be actual, i.e. the purchaser actually knows of the third-party interest. A purchaser may have actual notice of pre-1926 restrictive covenants because they are mentioned in the title deeds, and he reads them. (If he escapes actual notice because of his careless failure to read the title deeds, he will be fixed with constructive notice.)

(b)   Constructive Notice

The purchaser will be treated as having constructive notice of anything he does not know about but would have discovered had he made such enquiries as he ought reasonably to have made. It follows from this that if despite all reasonable conveyancing enquiries the equitable interest remains undiscovered, the purchaser takes free from it.

A purchaser risks constructive notice if he fails to see all the title deeds which he is entitled to see; for example, if he accepts title traced from a document that is not a good root, or accepts title traced from a good root less than 15 years old. He risks constructive notice if he fails to inspect the land.

Occupation   If someone other than the seller is occupying the land, that occupation gives constructive notice of any equitable interest the occupier owns. The occupation is suspicious; it throws doubt on the seller's claim of ownership, and should be investigated. (Do remember that if the occupier's equitable interest is registrable under Land Charges Act 1972, occupation is irrelevant. The interest will only bind the purchaser if it is registered.)

Not only is it possible to have constructive notice of the interest, it is also possible to have constructive notice of the occupation. In other words, if the purchaser, through his failure to make proper inspection of the property, fails to discover the occupier, he has constructive notice of the occupation, and through it, constructive notice of any equitable interest the occupier owns (see *Midland Bank Ltd* v. *Farmpride Hatcheries Ltd* 1980) and *Kingsnorth Trust Ltd* v. *Tizard* [1986].

If the seller is in occupation, but with another, the occupation by that other may also give constructive notice of any equitable interest he owns. It still depends, of course, on the occupier being discoverable by ordinary conveyancing enquiries. It was said in *Kingsnorth Trust Ltd* v. *Tizard* that a purchaser is not under a duty to pry into drawers and wardrobes in a search for signs of occupation. However, it was also said that a purchaser who inspected the property by a pre-arranged appointment with the seller had not made proper enquiries, as the seller had been given an opportunity to conceal signs of occupation. Apparently, according to the judgement, only by calling on the seller unawares, and thoroughly inspecting the property, can a purchaser escape constructive notice.

The case also suggests that if the purchaser has reason to believe that the seller is married, then an enquiry must be pursued as to the possibility that the spouse may have an equitable interest, whether the spouse is in occupation or not.

(c)   Imputed Notice

Any notice, actual or constructive, received by the purchaser's agent (e.g. solicitor, licenced conveyancer or surveyor – see *Kingsnorth Trust Ltd* v. *Tizard* – in the course of the transaction is imputed to the purchaser.

4.5   The Land Charges Act 1972 (formerly 1925)

(*a*)   *Registrable Interests*

The Act permits registration of certain interests affecting the title to unregistered land. Not all the interests registrable under the Act are listed here but only those most likely to be revealed by a search made by a purchaser.

 (i) *A petition in bankruptcy*   This is registered in the register of pending actions. A search certificate will reveal the entry PA(B).
 (ii) *A receiving order in bankruptcy*   This is registered in the register of writs and orders, and a search certificate will reveal the entry WO(B).
(iii) *A land charge class C(i)*   This is a legal mortgage unprotected by a deposit of title deeds with the lender. A mortgage protected by deposit of title deeds cannot be registered as a land charge, the idea being that the absence of the title deeds is itself enough to alert the purchaser to a possible claim against the land.
(iv) *A land charge class C(iii)*   This is defined as an equitable charge not protected by deposit of title deeds. This class includes the purchaser's lien for a deposit paid to the seller or seller's agent, and the seller's lien for any unpaid purchase price provided that he parted with the deeds on completion. It is uncertain whether an equitable mortgage of the legal estate should be protected by being registered as a C(iii) land charge, or as a C(iv) (being a contract for the grant of a legal mortgage).
 (v) *A land charge class C(iv)*   This is defined by the Act as 'a contract by an estate owner or by a person entitled at the date of the contract to have a legal estate conveyed to him to convey or create a legal estate, including a contract conferring expressly or by statutory implication a valid option to purchase, a right of pre-emption or any other like right'.

  (aa) This covers a contract to sell the freehold. It also includes a subcontract. Suppose Sarah contracts to sell Blackacre to Pauline, who immediately contracts to resell it to Rosemary. Pauline can register a C(iv) against Sarah. Rosemary can also register a C(iv), as Pauline is a person entitled to have the legal estate conveyed to her. However, registration of the contract must be not against Pauline's name, but against Sarah's, as the Act requires a land charge to be registered against the name of the estate owner. It is Sarah who owns the legal estate (see *Barrett* v. *Hilton Developments Ltd* [1975]).
  (bb) A contract to assign a lease.
  (cc) A contract to grant a lease.

(dd) An option to buy the freehold or a lease, an option to renew a lease, and an option given to a tenant to acquire his landlord's reversion.

(ee) A right of pre-emption. A right of pre-emption is created, for example, when X contracts that if he wishes to sell the land, he will first of all offer it for sale to Y, before putting it on the open market. By contrast, an option is the right for Y to buy X's land, whether X wishes to sell or not. It was decided in *Pritchard* v. *Briggs* [1980] that a right of pre-emption, unlike an option, does not in itself create any interest in land capable of binding a purchaser. It is a personal right. However, when the circumstances occur which make the right of pre-emption exerciseable, (for instance, in the above example, when X puts the land up for sale) the right of pre-emption ripens into an option. A C(iv) land charge registered when the *right of pre-emption was created* will protect the option, and ensure that the option binds the purchaser.

(ff) A contract by a tenant to surrender his lease before seeking to assign it (*Greene* v. *Church Commissioners for England* [1974]).

(gg) An equitable lease.

(hh) A contract for the grant of a legal easement.

(vi) *Class D(ii)   A restrictive covenant created after 1925* (but not one made between landlord and tenant).

(vii) *Class D(iii)   An equitable easement* If the easement is equitable solely because it was not granted by deed, the correct head of registration appears to be C(iv), as the defective grant is treated as a contract for the grant of a legal easement. It is for the same reason that an equitable lease is registered as a C(iv) land charge. Class D(iii) seems to cover only an equitable easement that is incapable of being legal, e.g. an easement for life.

(viii) *Class F   A spouse's rights of occupation under the Matrimonial Homes Act 1983* Section 1 of the 1983 Act gives a spouse who does not own the legal estate in the matrimonial home rights of occupation in that home. These rights are capable of binding a purchaser, provided (in the case of an unregistered title) they are protected by the registration of a class F charge.

(b)   System of Registration

The system of registration adopted in 1925 was not registration against the land affected, but against the name of the owner of the legal estate who had burdened his land. This is unfortunate as a registration can only be discovered by a search against the right name. For example, suppose that since 1925 the freehold in Blackacre has been conveyed by the following deeds:

1928 a conveyance by A to B
1954 a conveyance by B to C

1969 a conveyance by C to D
1973 a conveyance by D to E

A purchaser from E sees only the 1973 conveyance, as this is fifteen years old. He enquiries of the Chief Land Registrar if any land charges are registered against the names of D and E. The reply is 'no'. Suppose, though, that in 1928, in the conveyance from A, B gave a restrictive covenant to A, burdening the land that B had just acquired from him. A, being the person with the benefit of the covenant, would have hastened to register a D(ii) land charge against B's name. Only a search against B's name will reveal that registration. The purchaser cannot search against B's name because he does not know it, yet the covenant will bind the purchaser, as it is registered. So a purchaser takes subject to all land charges registered since 1925, but only has the opportunity to discover the recent ones.

This is the problem of what is called 'the pre-root land charge'. It is mitigated by:

(i) The practice of every deed mentioning existing incumbrances in the habendum. It is likely that the 1973 conveyance would say that Blackacre was conveyed to E 'subject to the covenants created by a deed dated 29 February 1928 made between A of the one part and B of the other part'. The purchaser can add these two names to his search.

(ii) The duty of the seller to disclose all incumbrances affecting the present title, even those created pre-root.

(iii) The possibility of compensation under s.25 Law of Property Act 1969 (see Chapter 19).

(c) Name?

Although the Act requires registration against the 'name' of the estate owner it does not say what is meant by 'name'. The case of *Diligent Finance Co. Ltd* v. *Alleyne* (1972) established the convenient rule that the name against which registration is to be effected is the name contained in the conveyancing documents.

A registration against an incorrect version of this name will not bind someone who searches against the correct name, and obtains a clear certificate of search. In the Alleyne case, a wife registered a class F charge against Erskine Alleyne. This registration did not bind a mortgagee, who searched against the husband's full name Erskine Owen Alleyne, the version of the name that appeared in the deeds. This shows how the rule in the Alleyne case can catch out a person who cannot see the deeds.

Although a registration against an incorrect version of the name will not bind someone who searches against the correct version, it has been said that it will bind someone who does not search at all, or someone who searches against *another* incorrect version. In *Oak Co-operative Building*

Society v. *Blackburn* [1968] the name against which the land charge should have been registered was Francis David Blackburn. The charge was registered against the name of Frank David Blackburn. The purchaser applied for a search to be made against the name of Francis Davis Blackburn and obtained a clear search certificate. It was held that the purchaser could not rely on the search certificate, but took subject to the charge.

(d)   Effect of Non-Registration

An unregistered land charge is void against a purchaser for value of any interest in the land. Exceptions to this are land charges C(iv), and D(i)(ii) and (iii), which are void against a purchaser for money or money's worth of a legal estate. The only difference in the two types of consideration is marriage, which provides value but not money's worth.

The difference between a purchaser of any interest, and the purchaser of a legal estate is of more significance. An unregistered class F land charge is void against both a legal and an equitable mortgagee. An unregistered estate contract is void for non-registration only against a legal mortgagee.

It seems that once a land charge is void against a later purchaser, it is also void against anyone who claims through the purchaser. For example, suppose that Morgan owns Blackacre, and gives Owen an option to buy it. Two weeks later, Morgan conveys Blackacre to Pritchard. Then Owen registers a C(iv) land charge. Pritchard sells Blackacre to Ross. Does Ross take subject to the option? It was registered before he bought it. However, he probably shares Pritchard's immunity. After all, it means little to Pritchard that he *owns* free of the option if he cannot also *sell* free of it.

(e)   Priority Notice

Any time-lag between the creation of a land charge and its registration is dangerous.

Suppose that X sells the end of his garden to Y, and Y covenants that no more than one house will be built on it. X must register the covenant against Y's name before any later purchaser acquires a legal estate in the land. If Y is buying with the aid of a mortgage loan, the lender will be a subsequent purchaser. The mortgage will be completed a second after the conveyance. It is important that the land charge is registered before the mortgage is created, otherwise the covenant will not bind the lender, and so will not bind anyone to whom the lender sells, if he exercises his statutory power of sale. The land charge cannot be registered until it exists, yet it must be registered the very moment it comes into existence. This can be achieved by X using the priority notice procedure.

X must lodge a priority notice at the Land Charges Registry at least 15 days before completion. This will mean that when the lender makes his pre-completion search, he will discover the notice. After completion X must apply for registration of the land charge within 30 days of the filing of the priority notice. The registration of the D(ii) land charge is then backdated to the moment the covenant came into existence. So it is deemed to be registered before the completion of the mortgage (Land Charges Rules 1974).

(f) *A Search at the Land Charges Registry*

This is dealt with in Chapter 9.

Workshop

Questions needing a knowledge of the Land Charges Act will be asked at the end of later chapters.

---

5 Drafting the Contract

5.1 Introduction

In order to draft the contract, the seller's solicitor must have a thorough knowledge of his client's title, information about the property (almost invariably culled from the client rather than by looking at the property) and must know anything that has been agreed between his client and the purchaser, for example the fact that the sale includes curtains (see 1.3).

5.2 Drafting a Contract to Sell a Registered Title

(a) Introduction

Suppose that you are the solicitor or licensed conveyancer instructed by Harry Mark to sell his house, 232 Main Road. It is clear from the estate agent's particulars and from what Harry tells you, that he owns a small semi-detached house, built about 1900, that fronts onto the road. Harry lives alone there. In response to your questions about the possibility of any neighbours having rights over the property, he tells you that his neighbours, who live at 234, have the right to cross his backyard in order to reach the side entrance which runs between numbers 232 and 230. This side entrance belongs to number 230, but Harry tells you that a right to use it was granted in 1980 to the then owners of 232 and 234, in return for the surrender of a right-of-way across the back garden of 230 to Ship Lane.

The house is mortgaged to Harry's bank, but the bank has told you that the title is registered and you have obtained office copy entries.

Harry wants to take various plants from the garden when he moves, particularly some shrub roses. The purchase price of the house is £72 000 but he is also selling the curtains and the wardrobes. These are not fitted wardrobes, but are being left behind because they are too big to get down the stairs without being dismantled. The price agreed for the curtains and wardrobes is £1,000.

Look at the office copy entries shown opposite.

Office Copy Entries

HM LAND REGISTRY

Title Number K000000

A.   PROPERTY REGISTER

County: Kent   District: Hope's Bottom

The freehold land shown and edged with red on the plan of the above title filed at the Registry registered on 17 October 1951 known as 4 Andrews Cottages, Main Road.

Property now known as 232 Main Road (19.3.81)

The property has the benefit of a right-of-way granted by a deed dated 15 April 1980 made between (i) Express Developments Limited and (ii) Betty Booper.

B.   PROPRIETORSHIP REGISTER

Title Absolute

Proprietor

1.   ~~Betty Booper of 4 Andrews Cottage, Hope's Bottom, Kent, registered on 17 October 1961.~~

2.   Harry Mark of 232 Main Road, Hope's Bottom, Kent, registered on 19 March 1981.

C.   CHARGES REGISTER

1.   17 October 1961 – by an agreement dated 21 February 1961 made between Lilian Hopwood and the County Council of the Administrative County of Kent, a strip of land fronting Main Road comprising three square yards was dedicated as part of the public highway.

2.   19 March 1981 – charge dated 20 January 1981 registered on 19 March 1981 to secure the monies including the further advances therein mentioned.

3.   Proprietor – Midland Bank plc of 19 Pessimist Street, Hope's Bottom, Kent, registered on 19 March 1981.

The property register mentions the right of way over number 230. As this was granted to benefit registered land, the deed granting it was sent to the Land Registry, and the easement was registered in the property register of the benefited land. (If the title to number 230 was also registered, the easement should also appear in the charges register of that title (see Chapter 12). The purchaser will want to see a copy of this deed. We can obtain an office copy of it from the Registry.

There is no mention of the right of way belonging to number 234 over the backyard of our client's house. Remember the age of the property. The right was probably never expressly granted, but arose by prescription, i.e. by virtue of long use. It would have existed as a legal easement when the title to number 232 was first registered, but as there was no documentary evidence of it, no entry was put on the charges register. Nevertheless, it will still be enforceable against a purchaser from Harry, as it is an overriding interest (see 3.15).

Now you can start to draft the contract.

(b)   The Form of the Contract

Look at the form of agreement in the Appendix to this book. This is the standard contract which must be used if you are following the protocol. You are likely to use it even if you are not. It incorporates what are known as the Standard Conditions of Sale (1st Edition). (These supersede the two separate sets of conditions known as the Law Society's Conditions of Sale and the National Conditions of Sale).

The front page of the contract, when completed, will give details of the property, the seller's title to it, and other terms of the bargain. The back page lists the conditions of sale. The conditions are the terms upon which the property is sold. There is a distinction to be drawn between the standard conditions and the special conditions. The standard conditions have been drawn up by the Law Society and the Solicitors' Law Stationery Society Ltd who own the copyright. They are designed to be suitable for both domestic and commercial conveyancing, and cover eventualities likely to be common to most transactions. The special conditions are those written into the contract by the person drafting it, to deal with matters peculiar to that particular transaction (although some special conditions are already printed onto the contract form in a helpful manner).

Read the printed special condition 1. It expressly incorporates the standard conditions into the contract. The Law Society recommends that if the standard conditions are not actually printed on the form of contract, then a copy of them should be attached to it. This will ensure that s.2 of the Law of Property (Miscellaneous Provisions) Act 1989 is satisfied (see 5.10).

(c)   Date and Parties

Still looking at the form, you will see that the first blank to be filled in is the date. *Do not fill this in*. The contract will be dated when the two parts are exchanged, probably with the date of exchange.

The next part to fill in shows the names of the parties. Your investigation of title, and enquiries of Harry have satisfied you that he is the beneficial owner of the legal estate. There seems to be no equitable interest to overreach, and no need for the appointment of another trustee to act with him (see Chapter 11 for circumstances in which the appointment of a second trustee would be necessary). Harry or the estate agents will have told you the purchaser's name.

(d)   The Property

You then have to draft the description of the property. This must be done carefully, for if the seller misdescribes the title (e.g. calls a sub-lease a head-lease) or the property (e.g. says it is 100 acres when it is only 75) he will inevitably break his contract. He will not be able to convey what he has contracted to convey. This particular breach of contract is called misdescription and is dealt with in Chapter 18.

The three things to bear in mind are:

 (i) stating the estate;
 (ii) describing the extent of the property;
 (iii) stating any rights that benefit the property.

So, if number 232 had been an unregistered title, a satisfactory description would have been, 'The freehold property known as 232 Main Road, Hope's Bottom, Kent, together with the benefit of a right-of-way over part of number 230 Main Road, so far as the same was granted by a deed dated 15 April 1980 made between (i) Express Developments Limited and (ii) Betty Booper'. Of course, a copy of the 1980 deed would have to accompany the draft contract, otherwise the purchaser's solicitor would find that part of the description meaningless. No plan would be used. The boundaries of number 232 are well-established and no map is needed to determine them. Most urban properties can be described by postal address alone.

In fact the title to number 232 is registered. This need not make any change to the particulars at all. However, in registered title, it is usual to see the particulars drafted in this way: 'the freehold property situated at, and known as 232 Main Road, Hope's Bottom, Kent, as the same is registered at HM Land Registry with absolute title under Title Number K000000'. This has the advantage of making it clear that the seller is only contracting to convey the land that is registered under the title (if the registered title does not include all the land that the purchaser hoped to buy, the seller cannot be accused of misdescription). An office copy of the entries on the register will accompany the draft contract, and a copy of the 1980 deed. Nothing is said about the 1980 right-of-way in the particulars, as the contract is promising the land described in the property register, and the property register mentions the easement. (Notice that it is in fact never essential to mention easements that benefit the land. They will pass to the purchaser on completion anyway, as being part of the land conveyed. If there is any doubt about the enforceability of the easement against the neighbouring land, the easement should not be mentioned at all, or else the doubt should be made clear in the contract.)

(e)   Burdens on the Property

Look at standard condition 3.1.3. The seller is promising to disclose to the purchaser all adverse interests of which he knows. You know of an adverse interest, i.e. the right of way across the backyard. This must, therefore, be brought to the attention of the purchaser. You will detail it here, saying something like 'a right belonging to the owners and occupiers of number 234, Main Road to walk across the backyard of the Property to and from the side entrance running along the boundary of the Property and number 230, Main Road'. You could also add that there is no documentary evidence of the right of way, but that it has been exercised for many years, and is believed to have arisen through prescription. Now read special condition 2. The sale is now subject to this right of way.

The subject of disclosure of adverse interests is dealt with in greater detail later in this chapter.

(f)   Capacity in which the Seller Sells

Here you state the capacity in which the seller will be expressed to convey in the later conveyance or transfer. There are four capacities in which the seller can say he conveys – i.e. beneficial owner, trustee, personal representative, or mortgagee (s.76 of the Law of Property Act 1925). Your investigation of title has shown that Harry owns the legal estate for his own benefit, so you will state that he will convey as 'beneficial owner'. This is then the capacity which will be stated in the transfer. The point about the statement of capacity is that certain covenants for title will be implied into a conveyance or transfer according to which capacity is stated (see Chapter 19).

(g)   Completion Date

The completion date will be inserted when contracts are exchanged, and is obviously a matter of negotiation between the seller and purchaser. If this clause is not completed, standard condition 6.1.1 provides that the date for completion will be 21 working days after the date of the contract.

Whether the completion date is fixed by a special or by the standard condition, standard condition 6.1.2 states that if the money due on completion is received after 2.00 p.m. on that day, completion is for the purposes of standard conditions 6.3 and 7.3 to be treated as taking place on the next working day. Working days are defined by standard condition 1.1.1 to exclude weekends and bank holidays. So, for example, suppose completion date is Friday, 30 April. The purchase price is not received from the purchaser until 3.30 p.m. on Friday. For most purposes – e.g. the dating of the conveyance or transfer – completion took place on Friday. However, under condition 6.3 the outgoings will be apportioned as if completion took place on Monday, 3 May and the purchaser will under condition 7.3 have to pay interest for late completion.

(*h*) Contract Rate

This clause is used to agree a rate of interest for the contract. This rate of interest is relevant to calculate the amount of interest earned by a deposit (see standard conditions 2.2.3 and 7.2) and the interest payable on late completion (see standard conditions 7.5 and 7.6). The rate of interest can be specified by a special condition. It must not be too high, or it may deter a prospective purchaser from entering into the contract. Remember too that if Harry is responsible for the delay in completion, he will be paying the same rate. The point is to have the contract rate something higher than the rate charged by banks for a bridging loan. This encourages a purchaser to complete promptly, as it will be cheaper for him to obtain a bridging loan than to delay completion. If a special condition is felt necessary, it will probably specify a figure that is something above the base rate from time to time of a chosen bank, e.g. '4 per cent per annum above the base rate from time to time of the Midland Bank plc'.

If a rate is not set by a special condition, standard condition 1.1.1 says that the rate is 'the Law Society's interest rate from time to time in force'. The Law Society will set a rate for this purpose, which will be published in every issue of the *Law Society's Gazette*. It is, apparently, going to be a figure 4 per cent above the base rate of the Law Society's own bank, which is believed to be Barclays. The rate set by the standard condition will, therefore, generally be acceptable, and only peculiar circumstances will make it necessary to set the rate by a special condition.

If conveyancers are prepared to accept the standard condition, it will have the advantage of ensuring that every contract in a chain of transactions will have the same interest rate applying to it. However, this is not always desirable if there is a big disparity in the purchase prices (see Chapter 17).

(*i*) Root of Title/Title Number

A contract only specifies a root of title if the seller's title is unregistered. Your client's title is registered, so you merely state the title number. Had Harry's title been other than absolute, you might have felt it desirable, although not essential, to state the class of title. It would not be essential, because almost invariably office copy entries of the register are sent to the purchaser with the draft contract. The reason that it would have been desirable is that it has been held that if a title is described in the contract merely as registered, the purchaser is entitled to assume that it is registered with absolute title. If the seller is registered only with possessory or good leasehold title, it is true that that will be disclosed by the accompanying copy entries, but a special condition puts the question of disclosure beyond doubt.

If you have already stated the title number and class of title in your description of the property (see b), nothing need be written here at all.

(j)   *The Purchase Price, Deposit and Amount Payable for Chattels*

The purchase price is the amount payable for the land, so in Harry's case it is £72 000. Land includes fixtures. Standard condition 2.2.1 provides for the payment by the purchaser of a deposit of 10 per cent of the purchase price. Unless this is altered by a special condition (it is now quite common for the purchaser to pay less than 10 per cent) the figure here will obviously be £7200.

There is then added the price payable for the chattels (£1000) so the balance payable on completion is £65 800.

It is important for the purchaser that the total of £73 000 to be paid is correctly apportioned between the land and the chattels. One reason is that stamp duty is only paid by the purchaser on the consideration paid for the land. Another reason is that the deposit is 10 per cent of the purchase price paid for the land, not for the chattels.

(k)   *The Agreement*

The front page concludes with the promise of the seller to sell, and the purchaser to buy.

(l)   *Printed Special Conditions*

Now turn to the second page of the form. There is no reason in this transaction to change the four special conditions already printed here.

(m)   *Special Condition 3 – Fixtures and Chattels*

You know that it has been settled between Harry and the purchaser that Harry can remove the roses, but is selling the carpets and wardrobes.

The underlying law is that once Harry has contracted to sell the land, he cannot remove any part of it, unless the contract permits him to do so. Plants are generally part of the land, so the contract must give Harry the right to remove the roses. A dispute can arise as to whether a particular item is a chattel (and not therefore part of the land, so removable before completion unless the contract says otherwise) or a fixture (and therefore part of the land, so not removable). The legal definition of a fixture is that it is a chattel which is fixed to the land and has lost its identity as a chattel and become part of the land. The definition is easy to state, but not to apply. The initial test is that of fixing. If the chattel is fixed to the land or to the house on the land, it is presumed to be a fixture. If not fixed, it is presumed to be a chattel. This test can however, be upset by a finding of intention. An item may not be fixed, yet rank as a fixture because it was intended to become part of the land. A dry stone wall would be a fixture. On the other hand, an item may be fixed yet remain a chattel, because there was no intention that the~chattel should become part of the land, e.g. a tapestry fixed to a wall for display. In other words, there is plenty of scope for argument.

It is always possible to evade argument~by special conditions in the contract. You could have a condition saying that the sale excludes the shrub roses, but includes the carpets and wardrobes. Fine, but this specific condition is of no use when the purchaser bitterly complains that Harry has taken the sundial from the garden. Was Harry justified? Was it a chattel or a fixture?

In its national protocol the Law Society encourages the use of the fixtures, fittings and contents form (set out in the appendix) which lists in detail which items are, or are not, included in the sale. You will have sent this form to Harry for completion or have asked him to complete it at the initial interview. This completed form is then attached to the contract and forms part of it (see special condition 3). Harry will spend a pleasant half-hour filling in the form, stating against each item listed in the form whether the sale includes it, or excludes it. The sundial? It is one of the items noted in the form (garden ornaments). So the dispute will be settled by reading the form to see if Harry said he would be leaving it, or taking it.

(n)   Other Special Conditions

The facts do not seem to justify any other special conditions. The gaps in the agreement – e.g. remedies for late completion – are filled in by the standard conditions incorporated into the contract. Most of the standard conditions are mentioned in other chapters of this book.

Before practising the drafting of another contract, we shall pause to consider the drafting of special conditions relating to the seller's title.

5.3   The Implied Promise as to Title

Although the seller's promise as to his title is the most important of the promises he gives in the contract, you will rarely see the promise expressed in the contract. The parties rely on the fact that the promise is *implied*.

The implied promise is that the seller has a good title to the freehold estate free from incumbrances. Clearly, if he cannot live up to this promise, it must be changed by an express condition in the contract.

It is because of this promise in the contract that it is said that the seller has a duty to disclose latent defects in title. However, this duty of disclosure is perhaps better understood as a *precaution* of disclosure. If there is a flaw in the seller's title, and this is not disclosed to the purchaser before the contract is made, then inevitably the seller is breaking his promise as to title. The purchaser, on discovering the defect before completion, may be able to say that the breach is serious enough to discharge the contract, or may be able to claim a reduction in the purchase price by way of damages. If, however, the seller discloses the defect before the contract is made, the contractual promise is altered. If the defect is disclosed, the purchaser has, by implication, agreed to buy subject to it. The promise by the seller is now 'good title, free from incumbrances, with the exception of this particular matter which has been disclosed to the purchaser'. Disclosure cuts down the seller's promise as to title.

What follows will be easier to understand if you realise that a defect in title may consist of a third-party right enforceable against the land – for example, an easement, covenant or lease. The seller cannot then give title free from incumbrances. Alternatively, it may be what is known as a 'paper' defect – i.e. that there is something wrong with the documentary evidence of title. The deeds may not show that the seller owns the legal estate, or may show that his ownership could be challenged. He would not then have a good title.

What Must the Seller Disclose?

Unless the contract says otherwise, the answer is '*latent* defects in *title*'. So from this we can see that:

(a) *He Need Not Disclose Physical Defects*   There is no implied promise in the contract about the physical state of the property. This is why the purchaser should consider having the property surveyed before he decides to buy. However, a physical defect *may* give the purchaser a cause of action against the seller:

(i)   if before contract the seller states the property is free from physical defect, and the statement is untrue. The purchaser would have remedies for misrepresentation (see Chapter 19);

(ii) if the contract *does* make an *express* promise about the physical state of the property;

(iii) if the property being sold is a leasehold, rather than a freehold estate. The physical defect, if a breach of covenant in the lease, may also be a defect in title (see Chapter 15);

(iv) if the seller has taken active steps to conceal a physical defect before contract. This may amount to fraud;

(v)   if the seller built the house and did it negligently (*Anns* v. *Merton London Borough Council* [1978] and see Defective Premises Act 1977).

(b) *The Seller Need Not Disclose Patent Defects in Title*   A patent defect has been defined by case law as a defect that is visible to the eye or can reasonably be inferred from something that is visible to the eye (*Yandle & Sons* v. *Sutton* [1922]. The logic of this is that as the land discloses the defect to the purchaser, there is no need for the seller to do it. A path across the property might mean that the private right of way along the path would be a patent defect. It was held in the Yandle case however, that a *public* right of way was not necessarily to be inferred from the existence of a pathway. Few defects will be patent. A defect in the paper title will always be latent as it will be discoverable only by looking at the deeds. A lease is a latent defect, even though the tenant is living on the property. In the case of unregistered title, s.24 of the Law of Property Act 1969 makes it clear that the fact that an incumbrance is registered as a land charge under the Land Charges Act 1972, does not make it into a patent defect.

(Do not allow yourself to become confused at this point. Remember we are talking about the responsibility of the seller to tell the purchaser about third-party rights. We are *not* discussing whether or not the rights will bind the purchaser on completion, when registration or occupation might be very relevant).

(c) *The Seller Need Not Disclose Third-Party Rights that Will Not Bind the Purchaser on Completion* They are not defects in title. If the seller is a trustee for sale, he need not disclose the interests of the beneficiaries behind the trust, as he can, by conveying with another trustee, overreach them.

Another example would be an option to buy that has not, in unregistered title, been registered as a C(iv) land charge, or, in registered title, been protected by an entry on the seller's register. The non-registration will make the option void against the purchaser. The same would hold true of unprotected restrictive covenants, although in fact these would have to be mentioned in the contract if an indemnity covenant were required (see Chapter 12).

It should now be made clear that although generally the disclosure of the defect to the purchaser means that he has agreed to buy subject to it, this does, in fact, only apply to an irremovable defect. If a defect is removable – for example, as above – by the appointment of a second trustee, then the purchaser is entitled to assume that it will be removed. This is why it is the duty of the seller to ensure that all mortgages and other financial charges are paid off before completion, even though the purchaser knew of the charges before contract. If, in fact the sale is to be subject to the financial charges, there must be a special condition saying this. (Remember that if it is a financial charge in favour of a local authority, the contract may say that the sale is subject to it, see standard condition 3, discussed later).

Notice two further things about the duty of disclosure:

1. The seller is under a duty to disclose *all* incumbrances, even those he does not know exist. Remember the promise is freedom from *all* undisclosed incumbrances. Therefore, if the purchaser, before completion, discovers a third-party interest over the property which the seller has not told him about, the seller would, in the absence of a condition in the contract, be in breach of contract. It would be no excuse for the seller to say that the non-disclosure was due to his complete ignorance of the interest. The only way that he could escape

liability would be to establish that the interest was a patent, rather than a latent, incumbrance (but notice the effect of standard condition 3, discussed later).

2. In unregistered title, the duty of disclosure covers all defects in the paper title, except a pre-root defect which the seller did not know about. The exception arises from s.45 of the Law of Property Act 1925, which is explained in Chapter 8.

5.4   When Do we Need to Alter the Implied Promise as to Title?

(a)   When We are Not Selling the Freehold, But the Leasehold

It must be made clear that it is a leasehold estate that is being sold. The particulars will generally give details of the lease, and a copy of the lease will accompany the draft contract (see Chapter 15).

(b)   When the Seller Does Not Have a Good Title to the Estate

The seller's promise that he has a good title is not a promise that the title is completely flawless, but that it is a title that will lead to quiet possession of the land, without any real threat of dispute or litigation.

If there is a defect in his title, the first thing for the seller to consider is putting his title into order. If the conveyance to him was void – for example, because it was not properly executed – he may be able to ask for a confirmatory conveyance. He may be able to trace a plan lost from a past deed, or to contact a past mortgagee to obtain a receipt that should have been previously endorsed on a redeemed mortgage.

However when faced with a defect in the paper title that cannot be put right, the last resort of the seller is a special condition which details the defect, and then says that the purchaser cannot raise any objection to the title on that ground. It is a last resort, because if the defect is serious, a purchaser will reject the draft contract, and look for a different property to buy. However, if the defect is there, and cannot be put right, a special condition is the only answer to the problem. A reluctant purchaser might be tempted into the contract by a reduced price, or by arranging insurance against third-party claims.

A condition saying that a purchaser cannot object to some part of the title, or indeed saying that the purchaser cannot object to the title at all, is valid, but only *provided* that the seller is honest. He must disclose defects in the title either that he knows about or that he ought to know about, and then preclude the purchaser from objecting to the title (*Becker* v. *Partridge* [1966]). After such disclosure, the purchaser is bound by the contract, even if the seller's title is not just questionable but non-existent.

This problem of paper defects is peculiar to unregistered title. The only comparable points in registered title would be:

(i) the fact that the registered title is not absolute, but is possessory or qualified. The class of title should be detailed in the contract, and a copy of the entries in the register will accompany the draft contract. The purchaser can be prevented by a special condition from requiring any other evidence.
(ii) The possibility of someone having the right to apply for rectification of the register, e.g. a squatter who has been in adverse possession for over twelve years. This defect, being latent, would have to be disclosed. (Remember that the fact that an interest is overriding has nothing to do with the seller's duty to tell the purchaser about it.)

(c) *When the Seller's Land is Subject to Third-Party Rights (e.g. easements, restrictive covenants, options etc.)*

A special condition in the contract will state that the sale is subject to them. The purchaser, before accepting a term that says the sale is subject to a third-party right, will naturally want details of it, and if it was created by a document, will want a copy of that document. This will be supplied with the draft contract.

5.5 The Effect of Standard Condition 3

Read this condition. How does it alter the position outlined in 5.3?

First, condition 3.1.3 says that the seller must, before contract, disclose to the purchaser all 'adverse interests' that the seller knows about. 'Adverse interests' are defined as:

(a) public requirements;
(b) legal easements;
(c) entries on public registers (e.g. the local land charges register or the register of common land) but *not* entries on the registers maintained at HM Land Registry or the Land Charges Registry;
(d) if the title to the seller's property is registered, overriding interests.

What is a public requirement? It is defined in condition 3.2 as something validly ordered by a body acting on statutory authority. Condition 3.2.2 continues that the purchaser is to bear the cost of complying with any public requirement, whether made before or after contract, and is to indemnify the seller against any liability resulting from it.

Second, the sale is stated to be subject to certain matters (3.1.1) that is:

(a) any matter mentioned in the contract;
(b) *any* adverse interest (i.e. whether disclosed or not);
(c) any matter that would be revealed by the normal pre-contract searches and enquiries (condition 3.1.4).

Third, with these exceptions, the seller *expressly* promises that he is selling free from incumbrances.

So Where does this Leave the Duty of Disclosure?

(a) If a defect in title or a third-party right is mentioned in the contract, there is no controversy. The purchaser agrees to buy subject to it.
(b) If a third-party interest is not an 'adverse interest' but is an incumbrance, there is an express promise for freedom from it. It seems that this promise will only be rebutted by a special condition in the contract; and probably not merely by the purchaser's knowledge of the interest.
(c) If a third-party interest is an adverse interest (as defined) the sale is subject to it. If it is an interest that the seller did not know about, the purchaser has no remedy.
      If it is one that the seller did know about, the contract says that the interest must be disclosed to the purchaser before exchange of contracts.
      It does not seem certain whether supplying evidence of title with the draft contract (which is what the protocol envisages) will amount to disclosure of an adverse interest that is discoverable by reading the evidence. It is not a matter that should be left uncertain, so a special condition should say whether the provision of evidence of title does, or does not, amount to disclosure of adverse interests.

Breaking Condition 3

So in what circumstances could a seller be in breach of condition 3?

(a) If he does not have good title to the legal estate he has contracted to sell, either because his ownership of it is questionable or the *evidence* of his ownership is insufficient.
(b) If there is an adverse interest that the seller knew of, but did not disclose.
(c) If there is an incumbrance which is not an 'adverse interest', which is not discoverable by the sort of pre-contract searches a purchaser would make, and which is not expressly mentioned in the contract.
      You would like an example? Consider the seller's mortgage. This is not an adverse interest, but is an incumbrance, so the seller promises freedom from it (i.e. that it will be paid off on completion) unless the

sale is expressly made subject to it. Another example would be a restrictive covenant. This is not an adverse interest, and is not discoverable by prudent pre-contract searches (because presumably not even a prudent purchaser is expected to do title searches before contract). The seller therefore expressly promises freedom from restrictive covenants other than those mentioned in the contract. This seems to be so, even though the purchaser actually knows of the covenants because copy entries or search certificates are sent to the purchaser with the draft contract, in accordance with the protocol.

5.6 Barring Requisitions

According to standard condition 4.1.1 the purchaser must raise requisitions on title within six working days of the date of the contract or the date of delivery of the evidence of title, whichever is the later. So it is still contemplated by the standard conditions that the purchaser can leave investigation of title until after exchange of contracts, and then object to the title because it is not a good title, or because it is subject to undisclosed adverse interests, or incumbrances not mentioned in the contract.

We have seen in 5.5 that it might be open to argument that if the protocol is followed, disclosure of defects and adverse interests might be treated as having occurred through delivery of the evidence of title. Putting that aside as a debatable issue, if the seller wants to force the purchaser to investigate title before contract he can alter the standard conditions to prevent the purchaser raising requisitions on the evidence of title supplied, once contracts are exchanged. In other words, the purchaser will contract to accept title as deduced pre-contract.

A special condition such as this would not present a purchaser from objecting to the title on the ground of the concealment by the seller of a defect known to him (see 5.4 (b) and *Becker* v. *Partridge* [1966]) or because of a defect not revealed by the evidence of title supplied (Re *Haedicke* v. *Lipski*'s Contract [1901]).

5.7 Drafting a Contract for the Sale of an Unregistered Title

(a) Introduction

While bearing all this in mind, attempt the drafting of a contract for the sale of an unregistered freehold title. You are using the same form of contract incorporating the standard conditions of sale. Your clients are Harry and Martha Hill. The estate agent's particulars and the information given by your clients disclose that the house is a large detached house, standing in two acres of ground. It is in a poor state of repair. There is a public footpath cutting across the far corner of the garden.

You have the following deeds:

(i) a deed dated 1940 conveying the freehold estate on sale, made between B and C as sellers and D as purchaser. It describes the property as being 'Blackacre, in the village of Little Hove and in the parish of St James the Vernacular, in the County of Kent, as the same is bounded to the North by Mr Fitzgerald's property, to the West and South by the park paling of Lord Footscray, and to the East by the London to Folkstone Road'. It also says that Blackacre is more particularly described on the plan attached to a conveyance dated 1 April 1910 and made between A of the one part and B and C of the other part. It says that the property is conveyed subject to restrictive covenants contained in the 1910 deed. (You do not have a copy of this deed.) B and C are expressed to convey as trustees for sale.

(ii) A deed dated 1980, conveying the estate on sale from D to your clients. It describes the property simply as 'Blackacre, Lower Hove, Kent'.

(iii) A mortgage dated 1980 by your clients to the Champagne Building Society.

Notice that you do not have any search certificates against the names of the past estate owners. This means that you cannot be certain that there are not land charges against those names that may have been created by documents that you do not have in your possession.

A cautious solicitor would feel that he did not really know his clients' title without certificates of search, and might now make searches against the names of A, B, C, D, Harry and Martha. (It is certainly always worth thinking about making a search against your own client's name. This might reveal a class F registration (spouse's rights of occupation under Matrimonial Homes Act) and a C(i) or C(iii) (a mortgage unprotected by deposit the deeds, i.e. a second mortgage). It is better to know about these before contract than after, when their existence may mean that your client is in breach of contract). If you are following the protocol, you must do these searches now, anyway, as the certificates must be sent to the purchaser as part of the pre-contract package (see section 1.4). You should have no difficulty in completing the first page of the contract, apart, perhaps, from the particulars.

(b)   Particulars

In unregistered conveyancing, there is often a temptation simply to copy out a description from a title deed. In this case, it would be foolish to use the verbal description in the 1940 deed, as it is clearly now out of date. Also the 1940 deed describes the land by reference to a plan. The plan is lost. For that reason alone, you obviously cannot refer to the plan in the particulars of sale. Even if you had the plan, it would not necessarily form a good basis for the contract description. You would certainly need to confirm that the plan actually represents the present boundaries. In fact, if there is no doubt about where the present boundaries lie, there is unlikely to be any need for a plan to form part of the contract description. (A plan might be vital when a client is selling only part of his property. For example, he might be selling the end of his large garden to a developer. It is necessary to establish the new boundary and a plan is the only way to do it. Of course, the plan must be professionally prepared, and it will be used in the conveyance or transfer as well as in the contract.) In our case, it is probably sufficient to describe the land as the freehold land known as Blackacre, Lower Hove, Kent. (There is no *need* to add, 'and the house built on it' as the house is a fixture and forms part of the land.) The difficulty most often lies in checking that the title deeds are dealing with all the land that is *now* recognised as forming part of Blackacre. Boundaries move. (Look at the problem in the workshop section of Chapter 9.)

(c)   Burdens

The public right of way must be mentioned here. The sale is subject to it (see condition 3.1.2) but the seller must disclose it (see condition 3.1.3).

You must also list the 1910 restrictive covenants.

However, as soon as the purchaser sees a condition in the draft contract saying that the sale is subject to the covenants, he will naturally demand a copy of the 1910 conveyance, to see what they are. We cannot supply him with a copy. The deed appears to have been lost forever. All we can do is add a rider to our condition, saying that no copy of the covenants can be supplied, and that the purchaser can raise no requisition as to what the covenants are, nor as to whether or not they have been broken. Faruqi v. English Real Estates Ltd [1979].

Of course, this is a condition that may deter our prospective purchaser. However, there is nothing else we can do. The purchaser probably need not be unduly concerned with the existence of the covenants if he does not intend to change the existing use of the land. If our clients can confirm that no objection to the existing use has been made by neighbouring landowners in the past, it is unlikely there will be one in the future. The purchaser should be concerned if he intends to develop the land – for example, pull down the house and build a block of flats. This might be breaking the covenants (which binds the purchaser in this case because of actual notice) and a furious neighbour who has the benefit of them may object. One solution for a purchaser who does want to buy the land is to insure against the risk of the covenants being enforced.

(d)   Capacity

To complete the first page of the contract, you must decide in what capacity your clients will be selling. As they co-own the equitable interest in the house, the legal estate will be held by them on trust for sale. The capacity can, therefore, be stated as 'trustees'. It will mean that there will not be implied into the conveyance by the Hills the wide-ranging covenants for title that are implied when a seller conveys as beneficial owner, but only the covenant that the sellers have not themselves incumbered the title (see Chapter 19).

(e)   Root of Title/Title Number

You now have to state how title shall be deduced.

Here, of course, you are dealing with an unregistered title, so what you must do is specify the document with which your evidence of title will start, i.e. the root of title.

If a contract for the sale of an unregistered title says nothing about the commencement of title, the rule is that the seller must start his evidence of title with a 'good root' at least 15 years old. (Again, do not get confused here. For both registered and unregistered title, the promise as to title is the same, i.e. that the seller has a good title to the freehold. Here, however, we are talking about the *evidence* that he must produce to substantiate that claim. As has been seen, in registered conveyancing, the evidence is the register of title. In unregistered conveyancing, the evidence comes usually from the past deeds.) A good root is a document which shows the legal and equitable interest passing from one owner to another, which identifies the land, and which does not itself make the title seem doubtful in any way. Both a conveyance on sale and a deed of gift can be good roots. A purchaser would probably *prefer* to find that the good root is a conveyance on sale, as the purchaser under that conveyance would have investigated the title before he bought. A donee might not have done this. However, if the contract is silent about the start of the title, the purchaser will have to accept a deed of gift as a root of title.

Usually, a contract will not be silent as to the start of the evidence of the title. It will specify the document that is to form the root. Usually, the seller will specify what would have been a good root anyway, and will choose a document that is at least fifteen years old. The reason is that if he proffers a document that is not a good root, or one that is immature, the purchaser may simply say that the condition in the draft contract is unacceptable. There is a risk in a purchaser agreeing to accept evidence starting with a root less than fifteen years old. The risk is that the purchaser misses seeing a section of the title that he would otherwise see, and he may miss a name that he could otherwise search against in the Land Charges Registry.

To illustrate this, suppose that you, as purchaser's solicitor in 1990, see in the draft conveyance a condition that title will be traced from a conveyance dated 1 May 1978 made between John Williams and Albert Black. You notice that the condition does not say whether the conveyance was on sale, or by way of a gift, and the conveyance is only twelve years old.

If the contract had not specified a root, you would have been entitled to one at least fifteen years old. Accepting a root only twelve years old does not mean that you are missing an investigation of three-years ownership. You might be missing considerably more. The conveyance by which John Williams obtained the property might be dated 1930, and it would have been from that that you could have traced title.

Before completion, you will be making a search at the Central Land Charges Registry against the names of past estate owners revealed by the abstract of title. By accepting an immature root, you cannot add the name of the person who conveyed the land to John Williams. If anything is registered against that name, for example, a land charge D(ii) because he (the person who sold to John) burdened the land with restrictive covenants when he bought it, you will take subject to it, and you will have no right to compensation from the Chief Land Registrar (see Chapter 19).

Suppose the conveyance to John was dated 1920, and created restrictive covenants. Again you would take subject to these covenants, even though the later deed might make no mention of them. As they arose before 1926, the covenants are not registrable, but bind people who have actual or constructive notice of them. Your failure to see the 1920 conveyance, when under an open contract you would have been entitled to do so, fixes you with constructive notice of anything you would have discovered had you done so.

To return to the drafting of the Hills' contract, which deed will you specify as the root of title? You know that the purchaser will object if you put the 1980 conveyance forward as a root, as it is not yet fifteen years old. What about the 1940 deed? It *is* fifteen years old. It does show the legal estate and equitable interest passing from Band C to D. (Although B and C, being trustees, may not themselves have *owned* all the equitable interest, they could still passs it to D, because of their powers of overreaching beneficiaries' claims.) It does not disclose anything suspicious about the title. However, it does not by itself describe the property. It refers to the 1910 plan for a better description. Most purchasers, seeing the description in the 1940 conveyance, would instantly demand a copy of the 1910 plan, on the basis that the description in the 1940 deed is inadequate without it. This point of view may not be correct, as the verbal description in the 1940 conveyance might well be a sufficient description, but the point in drafting a contract is to anticipate difficulties.

So, if you had a copy of the 1910 deed, you would have a choice. You could still state that the root of title is the 1940 deed, but supply a copy of the 1910 plan with the draft contract. (Strictly speaking, you should supply a copy of the entire 1910 conveyance, so the purchaser can check if the plan is said to describe the land in detail, or merely provide a general identification.) Or, you could state that the 1910 conveyance is itself to be the root of title.

In this case, it would scarcely matter which course you adopted. It would have made a difference if there had been documents of title between 1910 and 1940 as they would not have to be abstracted if the root were the 1940 conveyance, but would have to be abstracted if it were the 1910 conveyance.

However, you do not have a copy of the 1910 conveyance. So nip objections in the bud. Say in the contract that title will be traced from the 1940 deed, and that no copy of the plan on the 1910 conveyance can be supplied, and that the purchaser shall not be entitled to ask for it. There seems to be no need here for any clauses to be added on the second page.

Notice that nothing is said in the contract about the disrepair of the property. There is no duty on the seller to disclose physical defects, and standard condition 3.1.5 states that the purchaser accepts the property in the physical state it is in when the contract is made.

5.8   Other Conditions that it Might be Necessary to Add to a Contract

(a)   Deposit

Standard condition 2.2 provides for a 10 per cent deposit to be paid on exchange of contracts by the purchaser to the seller's solicitor as stakeholder. We have already considered the possibility that a purchaser might ask to pay a smaller deposit (see section 2.3). The point here is the capacity in which the deposit is held by the solicitor. A stakeholder holds a deposit as agent for both seller and purchaser, so cannot release it to either until the contract is discharged. Usually the contract will be discharged by the successful completion of the contract, when the deposit is released to the seller. It is possible for the contract to be discharged (i.e. terminated) by one party breaking the contract. If the breach is the purchaser's, the seller is entitled to call for the deposit to be forfeited to him. If it is the seller who has broken the contract, the purchaser can ask for the deposit to be returned to him. While the contract still exists, the deposit is frozen.

The exception to this is standard condition 2.2.2. This applies when the seller is buying another house. The seller would like to use the deposit paid on his sale to finance the deposit he must pay on his purchase. This is possible, as the condition provides that the deposit may be released to the seller to be used *for that purpose only*. If the seller would like to have the use of the deposit before completion for some other purpose, the standard condition does not permit this. A special condition would have to be substituted saying the deposit is to be paid to the seller's solicitor as agent for the seller. This change is likely to prove unpopular with the purchaser. A deposit paid to a stakeholder is safe if the seller goes bankrupt, as the trustee in bankruptcy has no better right to the deposit than the seller, i.e. usually, only if and when the sale is completed. A deposit paid to an agent of the seller is not safe; it belongs to the seller. To recover it, a disappointed purchaser would have to prove in the bankruptcy. The only safeguard is that if a deposit is paid to a seller or seller's agent, the purchaser has a lien on the seller's land for its recovery. The lien is in the nature of an equitable charge, so the purchaser is a secured creditor. However, the lien offers no comfort if there are prior mortgages that exhaust the value of the property.

You must also consider the need for a special condition if the deposit is to be held by someone other than the seller's solicitor. A special condition must provide for this, and state in what capacity the deposit is to be held. It seems that a deposit paid on exchange of contracts to the seller's estate agent will be held by him as agent for the seller unless the contract says otherwise. (Note that 'solicitor' for the purpose of the standard conditions is defined to include a licensed conveyancer.)

At common law a stakeholder is entitled to keep any interest earned by the deposit. Higher standards are, however, expected of a solicitor. The Law Society has recommended (*Law Society's Gazette*, 29 April 1987) that interest earned by a deposit should belong to the client, not the solicitor. Standard condition 2.2.3 reflects this, as it provides that on completion the deposit is to be paid to the seller with 'accrued interest' (this term is defined in standard condition 1.1).

What if, as events turn out, the deposit has to be returned to the purchaser? The purchaser will then receive accrued interest paid by the seller – see standard condition 7.2.

(b) Sale of Part

We have seen that if the seller is selling only part of his land, the drafting of the particulars will require care. He must also consider the grant and reservation of easements, and the giving or imposition of restrictive covenants. This topic and the effect of Standard Condition 3.4 are considered in Chapter 12.

(c) The Need for an Indemnity Covenant

This is considered in Chapter 12.

(d) Sale Subject to an Existing Tenancy

Unless the contract *expressly* makes the sale subject to the tenancy, standard condition 3.3.1 promises vacant possession to the purchaser. If the land is to be sold subject to an existing tenancy, this should be stated in the special conditions, for example, 'the sale is subject to the weekly periodic tenancy of the top floor, the tenant being Mr Alex Brown'. A copy of the tenancy agreement has to be supplied to the purchaser with the draft contract (condition 3.3.2). The purchaser is then treated as entering into the contract with full knowledge and acceptance of the terms of the tenancy.

The sale may be to the sitting tenant himself. If this is so, the tenancy will probably end on completion, as it will merge into the freehold that the purchaser has acquired. However, this is a matter for the purchaser. The contract will still say that the sale is subject to the purchaser's own tenancy, and that as he is the tenant, he is taken to buy with full notice of terms of the tenancy.

The purchaser must, of course, read the tenancy agreement. He must not lose sight of the fact that if it is a residential tenancy, the agreement will not in fact reflect all the rights of the tenant. These may be considerably increased by statute.

If the tenancy was created before 15 January 1989 it may be protected by the Rent Act. This Act gives the tenant considerable security of tenure, and may limit the amount of rent that can be recovered from him.

If the tenancy was created on or after 15 January 1989, the Housing Act 1988 will apply, and the tenant will have some degree of security of tenure, but little rent protection.

Standard condition 3.3.7 emphasises that the purchaser must satisfy himself as to whether the tenancy is protected by either Act and as to what rent is legally recoverable.

(*e*)   *Sale of a Matrimonial Home when the Legal Estate is Owned by only One of the Spouses*

This is dealt with in Chapter 11.

(*f*)   *Sale of a Leasehold Estate*

Additional matters to be borne in mind when drafting a contract for the sale of a leasehold property are dealt with in Chapter 15.

(*g*)   *Absence of title deeds*

If the title is unregistered, and the seller bases his title on adverse possession, or while having documentary evidence of his title does not have either the original or a marked copy of every title deed, he should alter standard condition 4.2.3 and 4.2.4.

5.9   Conditional Contracts

The seller and the purchaser may agree to the sale of the property, but 'subject to' some matter being first of all settled. This qualification can have different results:

(a)   It may mean that there is no contract at all. The phrase 'subject to contract' nearly always has this effect.
(b)   It may simply be one of the terms in a concluded contract. In this sense, it is possible to say that the contract is 'subject to' the purchaser paying the price, or 'subject to' the seller making good title. In *Property and Bloodstock Ltd* v. *Emerton* [1967], the contract was expressed to be subject to the seller obtaining his landlord's consent to

the assignment of the lease. It was held that this was a promise by the seller as to title. It did not create a 'conditional contract' in the sense that the phrase is used in the next paragraph.

(c) It may create a conditional contract. This term is used here to mean a concluded contract, but which cannot be enforced by either party until a condition is fulfilled. If the condition is not fulfilled within its time limit, both parties are released from the contract.

If the parties wish to create a conditional contract, they must make their intention clear, and must ensure that the condition is sufficiently certain.

A condition is void for uncertainty if it is impossible for the court to decide the circumstances in which it could be said to be fulfilled. If the condition is void, the contract is void. If the contract is to be conditional on planning permission, for example, the condition should give details of the permission being sought, and whether or not it will be fulfilled by an outline planning permission, or by one with conditions attached.

A contract subject to the results of a local land charge search and additional enquiries should say that it depends on the results being satisfactory to the purchaser or his solicitor acting reasonably. This is a standard that can be objectively tested by the court. (See *Janmohamad* v. *Hassam* (1976) and *Smith and Olley* v. *Townsend* [1949]).

5.10 Formalities for the Creation of a Contract for the Sale of Land

Nothing has been said as to the legal formalities until this late stage, because if the usual conveyancing procedures are followed, the formalities will inevitably be observed.

Section 2 of the Law of Property (Miscellaneous Provisions) Act 1989 states that a contract for the sale or other disposition of an interest in land must be in writing. The contract must incorporate all the terms which the parties have expressly agreed. It will incorporate the terms if it actually contains them or if it refers to some other document which contains them.

The contract must be signed by or on behalf of each party to the contract.

If, in the usual way, contracts are prepared in duplicate with a view to exchange, s.2 will be satisfied if *both* copies incorporate all the agreed terms, and if each party signs one copy, even though they sign different copies.

The result of s.2 is that there can no longer be an oral contract for the sale of land. Under the previous law (s.40 of the Law of Property Act 1925) an oral contract was unenforceable. Now, there can be no such thing as an oral contract.

Interest in land is defined to include an interest in the proceeds of sale of land – i.e. an equitable interest existing behind a trust of sale of the legal estate.

Section 2 does not apply to a contract to grant a lease for a term not exceeding 3 years at best rent without a premium nor to a contract made at auction. At auction, the contract comes into existence at the fall of the auctioneer's hammer. Both seller and purchaser are in fact then invited to sign a written contract, but the contract exists without the writing.

Section 2 provides that the document must incorporate all the terms agreed between the parties, so that if one party can point out that a head of agreement is *not* contained in the written contract, the contract becomes void. One answer to this could be rectification of the contract on the ground that the written document by mistake does not express the true agreement of the parties (see *Joscelyne* v. *Nissen* [1970].

Workshop

Attempt this problem yourself, then read the specimen solution at the end of the book.

Problem

(This problem is best attempted after you have read Chapter 11.)

You have been instructed to act for Ada Faulkener in the sale of her cottage. You have borrowed the title deeds from Doom Building Society, Ada's mortgagee. There is a memorandum on the conveyance to Ada to the effect that part of the garden was later sold by Ada to a neighbour in June 1980. You did not act for Ada then. You have taken the precaution of obtaining a land charges search against her name. The search reveals a D(ii), a C(i) and an F land charge registered against her name, all apparently affecting the cottage. None of the entries can be explained by the documents in your possession. What action will you need to take in respect of the matters disclosed by your search and when?

N.B. An exercise in drafting a contract is set at the end of Chapter 12.

---

6 Pre-contract Searches and Enquiries

6.1 Introduction

You now know that a seller has a duty either implied or expressed in the contract to disclose certain defects in his title to the purchaser. Much information which might affect the value or the enjoyment of the property, and make it unattractive to the purchaser is not within this duty of disclosure. He should seek out this information before contract. As the seller is not under a duty to disclose it, it is too late for a purchaser to discover it after the contract, as there will be no breach of contract to offer him a remedy.

The solicitor for the purchaser therefore always makes, or ensures that he has the results of, what are known as the 'usual' pre-contract searches and enquiries. They are called 'usual' because they are applicable to nearly every transaction. There are also 'unusual' searches which might have to be made because of the property's location. A purchaser's solicitor who fails to obtain the usual searches, and whatever other searches are considered necessary as a matter of good conveyancing practice, will have failed in his duty to his client.

Again we revert to the protocol. The *seller's* solicitor, if following the protocol, will be making the pre-contract searches, and supplying the results to the purchaser's solicitor as part of the pre-contract 'package' (see section 1.4). Keep this in perspective. The protocol states that the searches are to be done by the seller's solicitor solely because this will save time, particularly if, as the protocol hopes, the seller consults his solicitor as soon as he decides to put his house on the market. The protocol, of course, produces the result that the expense of the searches falls on the seller rather than the purchaser. The search fees are not light. If there is a chain of transactions, a person in the middle of the chain will see no difference, as the fees which he bears as seller he now escapes as purchaser. The Law Society in its introduction to the protocol has said that it would deplore a situation in which a solicitor who had agreed to use the protocol made a habit of advising clients to opt out of the requirement for the seller to make the searches on the grounds only of saving the expense. Such a practice, the Society says, could have a knock-on effect in a chain and would destroy the advantage of speed in conveyancing transactions which can be the result of the seller making the search.

The fact remains that whoever *does* the searches, it is the responsibility of the purchaser's solicitor to decide if the searches are adequate, if the replies are satisfactory, and if any necessary ones have been omitted. That it is the seller who actually puts the searches in train is a matter of procedure; the rule remains '*caveat emptor*' for matters that do not fall within the seller's duty of disclosure.

6.2 The 'Usual' Searches and Enquiries

(*a*) *Enquiries of the Seller (The Property Information Form)*

Making the Enquiries There have been until the introduction of the protocol and perhaps will continue to be, many standard lists of enquiries to be asked by the purchaser of the seller. At one time the Oyez form reigned supreme, but in recent years has been challenged by others. The number of questions grew steadily and the answers given by the seller's solicitor became increasingly non-committal and unhelpful. To quote from the Law Society's introduction to the protocol:

> if any one part of the conveyancing process over the past years has caused criticism within the profession it has been the use of ever-lengthening forms of enquiries before contract, some being a repeat of those included in the standard form and others being irrelevant to the particular transaction or relating to the structure or condition of the property.

The seller's solicitor will now complete the property information form from information given by his client, and send it to the purchaser's solicitor as part of the pre-contract package (see section 1.3(c)). The form reads as a series of questions and answers. Why? To quote again from the Law Society:

> the property information form continues to be set out as replies to a series of standard questions. Since the seller's solicitor will be providing this information it might be seen as more logical at a future date to develop this as a simple statement of information without the question and answer format. However there are two reasons for retaining this. First it is a system with which the profession is familiar and secondly, it is hoped that even in those instances where for any reason the protocol is not being followed the buyer's solicitors will still use the property information form rather than revert to other forms for raising enquiries before contract.

The form is in the Appendix for you to read. Below are a few of the questions for discussion.

(i) Question 4 asks if the property has the benefit of any guarantees. This might cover guarantees given after damp or timber treatment or in respect of double glazing. A purchaser should ensure that the benefit of the guarantees is expressly assigned to him on completion.

According to the protocol, if there are any such guarantees, the seller's solicitor should obtain copies of them and send them to the purchaser's solicitor with the property information form.

This enquiry may also reveal the fact that the house is protected by the National House Building Council's Scheme. This scheme covers houses, bungalows flats or maisonettes built by a builder or developer who is registered with the Council. The scheme protects a purchaser for ten years against the developer's failure to build the house properly and against structural defects. It is backed by insurance cover. The original purchaser must ensure that he has the protection of the scheme and that he receives the necessary documentation, i.e. offer of cover form, the booklet which explains the scheme and the warranties that are given by the developer, and the 'ten year' notice, which is issued by the NHBC and which brings the scheme into operation. Anyone who buys within the ten year period should ensure that these documents are handed over to him.

(ii) Question 5 asks what services (e.g. gas and electricity) the property has and the routes taken by the pipes, wires, etc., and whether they have to cross anybody else's land to reach the property. The point of this is to investigate whether any necessary easements exist.

(iii) Question 8 asks the names and ages of any person in actual occupation of the land, and what legal or equitable interest such an occupier has. Having read Chapters 3 and 4 you know why a purchaser is concerned about anybody other than the seller occupying the land. The age of the occupier is relevant because it is suggested that if the occupier is so young that he cannot be considered as independent of his parent, the child is not in actual occupation for the purposes either of constructive notice, or s.70(i)(g) of the Land Registration Act 1925. An answer denying that anybody else is in occupation is usually accepted in practice, unless the purchaser knows better, but an untruthful denial by the seller that Uncle George is in occupation does not clear any interest that Uncle might have from the title, although there would be a cause of action against the seller. (This is elaborated in Chapter 11.)

(iv) Question 10 is checking on compliance with planning requirements (see section 6.5).

(v) Question 11 asks if the sale is dependent on the seller buying another property, and if so, whether he needs and has arranged a mortgage loan to finance the purchase. This is to check if there is likely to be a delay before the seller is in a position to exchange contracts. The seller's solicitor owes a duty of confidentiality towards his client, and must not reveal these details without his consent.

The protocol also recommends that the purchaser's solicitor tell the seller's solicitor about the position of the purchaser's own sale, and the progress of his mortgage arrangements to finance the purchase, but again only if the purchaser consents.

Having received the pre-contract 'package' the purchaser's solicitor may make additional enquiries but according to the protocol only those specific additional enquiries which are required to elucidate some point arising out of the documents submitted or which are relevant to the particular nature or location of the property or which the purchaser has expressly requested, but omitting any enquiry, including one about the structure of the building, which is capable of being ascertained by the purchaser's own enquiries or survey or personal inspection.

If the sale is of a leasehold property, the purchaser's solicitor must also be sent a completed 'additional property information form'. This is discussed in Chapter 15.

Replying to the Enquiries　Imagine now that you are the seller's solicitor. The replies to the questions on the form are the seller's. You formulate and sign the replies as his agent. So there are two reasons why you must ensure that the replies are correct.

The first is that an incorrect answer may mean that the seller can be held liable for misrepresentation (see Chapter 19).

The second is that if it is due to your carelessness that the answer is wrong, you will be liable to your own client for any loss you cause him. In *Sharneyford Supplies Ltd* v. *Edge* (Barrington Black Austin & Co [a firm], third party) [1987] an enquiry was raised as to the existence of tenancies. The solicitor for the seller, *without consulting his client*, said that the tenants had no security of tenure. The purchaser successfully sued the seller when the tenants were found to be irremovable, and the seller's solicitors were ordered to indemnify their client. It has also been suggested (see *Wilson* v. *Bloomfield* (1979) that the seller's solicitor might owe the purchaser a duty of care in framing the answers. If this is the case, the *purchaser* could sue you for negligence.

(b)　The Local Land Charge Search

Each district authority (or for Greater London, each London Borough or the Common Council of the City of London) maintains a register of local land charges affecting the land within its area. It is difficult to define a local land charge, except to say generally that it is something designated as a local land charge either by the Local Land Charges Act 1975 itself or by some other Act. They are matters affecting land that are public matters, rather than private ones, and are registrable either by the district authority itself, or some other statutory body. Their name is legion, but they include:

(i)　*Financial charges*　Examples would be charges to recover the cost of street works, or the cost of emergency repairs to unsafe buildings, or to recover some forms of improvement grant.

(ii) *Planning matters* These include conditions imposed after July 1977 on planning permissions, enforcement notices actually in force, tree preservation orders.

(iii) *The listing of buildings as being of special architectural or historic interest* This listing restricts demolition and alteration of the building, and so can remove any development potential from the land (see *Amalgamated Investment and Property Co. Ltd* v. *John Walker & Sons Ltd* [1976].

It is not clear to what extent the existence of a local land charge will constitute a defect in the seller's title. A financial charge and probably an order requiring demolition of the property will be a matter of title and therefore fall within the seller's duty of disclosure. (In this context, consider the case of *Rignall Developments Ltd* v. *Halil* * [1987].) If a local land charge, or other local authority matter, is not a defect in title, it does not have to be disclosed. These rules are affected by the standard conditions. Consider again standard condition 3.

As many local land charges are not matters of title, and so not within the seller's duty of disclosure and as standard condition 3 makes the sale subject to all of them anyway, the purchaser will ask the authority to make a search of the local land charges register *before* he enters into the contract. The official search certificate will list any land charges registered at the date of the certificate, but the certificate is not conclusive nor does it give the purchaser any priority period. (See Local Land Charges Act 1975.) The purchaser will take subject to all charges in existence at the date of the search, whether revealed by the certificate or not, and subject to all charges coming into existence after the date of the search. What the certificate does do is give a limited right to compensation. A purchaser who relies on an official search certificate before entering into a contract can claim compensation if he is adversely affected by a land charge that existed at the date of the search but was not registered, or by a charge that was registered but was not disclosed by the search certificate. (A purchaser who relies on a *personal* search of the register can claim compensation only in respect of a local land charge that existed, but was not registered.)

To claim compensation the purchaser need not have ordered or made the search himself. It is sufficient if he or his solicitor had notice of the contents of the search certificate before exchange of contracts (s.10 of the Local Land Charges Act 1975). This is why the protocol is able to require the seller's solicitor to make the search. Notice, however, that no compensation is payable in respect of local land charges that come into existence after the date of the search, so certificates become increasingly useless with age.

In connection with the introduction of the protocol, the Law Society has arranged a Search Validation Scheme. This protects a purchaser for six months from the date of the search against new entries being registered against the property. The protection comes from an insurance policy backed by the Lombard Continental Insurance plc and Eagle Star. At the time of writing (1990) the premium is £10 if the property's value does not exceed £250 000, and £20 if it does not exceed £500 000. The insurance can be taken out by either seller or purchaser, as an alternative to repeating the search.

It is usually pointless for a purchaser to repeat a local land charge search after contract but before completion, because, if any new matter has arisen, standard condition 3 will have thrown the burden of it onto the purchaser anyway. However, the purchaser's intended mortgagee may ask for the search to be repeated, and may withdraw or reduce the loan if anything adverse is discovered.

It is because the certificate is not conclusive that Enquiry 3 on the property information form asks the seller if he has received any notices or communications from the local authority or other statutory body.

(c)   The Additional Enquiries of the District Authority

The district authority will know much that will not be revealed by the local land charge search, for the simple reason that the information is not registrable as a land charge. This information can be extracted from the authority by raising additional enquiries. There is a standard form of enquiries, approved by local authorities. The form is divided into two parts. The first contains questions that are always answered by the authority. The authority will only answer those questions in the second part which the enquirer has initialled, and for which he has paid an extra fee. The enquirer may also add further questions of his own devising, but the authority can refuse to answer these.

Examples of Part I Enquiries

(i) *Roads*   The Authority is asked if the road and paths giving access to the property are maintained at the public expense, and if not, whether the authority has passed a resolution to make up the roads, etc., at the cost of the frontagers. It is also asked if it has entered into any outstanding agreement relating to the adoption of any such road or path, and if any such agreement is supported by a bond.

If you are buying a house that is reached by a road that is not maintained by the local authority, the following problems arise;

(aa) *Easements*   Does the house have easements over the road, so that the purchaser will have the right to walk and, if relevant, drive over the road without relying on someone's permission?

(bb) *Maintenance*   At the moment, is anyone under an obligation to repair the roadway? The answer may be 'no', as the owner of land subject to a right of way does not generally have a duty to keep the way in repair. Sometimes, there is an agreement between the people who use or own the road to maintain it.

(cc) *Future expenses* Has the local highway authority resolved to 'make up' the road? Under the Highways Act 1980, the local authority can pass a resolution to 'make up' a road not previously maintained at the public expense. When the road has been repaired to a suitable standard it is 'adopted' by the authority and from then on will be maintained out of public funds. This sounds like good news to the owners of houses reached by the road. The drawback, however, is that the authority can apportion the cost of the work that brings the road up to standard in the first place among the owners and occupiers of premises which have a boundary adjoining the road. This can involve an owner in considerable expense. The owner (and his successors) can be sued for debt by the authority, and in addition the amount due is a charge on the property and registrable as a land charge.

A developer building estate roads will normally enter into an agreement with the authority under s.38 of the 1980 Act. The developer promises the authority to build the estate roads to a certain standard. The authority agrees that once the roads are completed, it will adopt them. The developer may be selling the completed houses before the roads are adopted. If he breaks the agreement, and does not build the roads to the required standard, the authority can do the work, and charge the houseowners. So the purchaser will find that he is having to pay a substantial amount towards the creation of the road. The developer may have covenanted in the conveyance to the purchaser that he would complete the roads, but the problem has probably arisen in the first place because of the developer's insolvency.

To avoid the problem, the s.38 agreement is supported by a bond, given by, for example, an insurance company. The insurance company promises the authority that if the developer does not make up the roads, the cost of the authority doing it will be paid by the insurers. This does not remove all risk, as if the sum promised under the bond is insufficient to cover the costs of the roads, there will again be a charge to the frontagers.

So a purchaser of a house on a new estate where the roads have not yet been adopted, will want to be satisfied as to the existence of the s.38 agreement, and as to the existence and adequacy of the bond.

(ii) *Sewers* The authority is asked if the property is served by a sewer maintained at the public expense.

In the case of a new building estate, there may be an agreement between the developer and the authority under the Public Health Act 1936, similar to the agreement under the Highways Act. The authority is asked to disclose the existence of any such agreement and supporting bond.

(iii) *Land Registration Act* The authority is asked the date that the area became one of compulsory registration.
(iv) *Various planning matters* designed to gauge the authority's planning intentions for the area.

(d)   Search in the Public Index Map, and Parcels Index

This search is usually only relevant when the purchase is of unregistered title. It is made at the District Land Registry that serves the area in which the land lies. It will reveal:

 (i) whether the title is unregistered, or registered. It is apparently possible for it to be forgotten that a title has been registered, and for subsequent owners to deal with it as if it were unregistered. None of these unregistered dealings will have passed the legal estate. It may also warn the purchaser that there has been a previous sale of part of the land dealt with by the title deeds.
 (ii) if the title is registered, the title number, and whether the title is freehold or leasehold.
(iii) any caution against first registration. This can be lodged by anyone who fears that an application for first registration will prejudice his rights over the land. The effect of the caution is that the Registrar must inform the cautioner of any application for first registration. The cautioner then has an opportunity of claiming that his interest should be noted on the register, or perhaps that registration should not take place at all.

(e)   A Search in the Land Charges Register against the Seller's Name

This will only be relevant when buying an unregistered title. It is usually unnecessary to make a search of the central land charges registry before contract, as any registered land charge should be disclosed by the seller (See section 5.3 of this book, s.24 of the Law of Property Act 1969 and standard condition 3).

If the seller's solicitor is following the protocol, a search against the seller's name and against the names of the other estate owners revealed by the evidence of title will have been supplied to the purchaser as part of the pre-contract package (see section 1.4).

If the protocol is not being followed, and the purchaser's solicitor is not given evidence of title before exchange of contracts, it is impossible to make the search pre-contract. The purchaser's solicitor does not know the names of the estate owners. However, in these circumstances, a cautious purchaser might consider making a search before contract against the seller's name. It might give early warning of his bankruptcy, or the registration of a Class F land charge. The purchaser might then decide that the least troublesome thing to do would be to buy a different house.

(f)   Inspection of the Property

The property should be inspected before contract

 (i)   to look for physical defects (see section 6.4).
 (ii) to look for patent defects in title (see section 5.3).
(iii) to look for dangerous occupiers (see sections 3.16 and 4.4).

This inspection is far more likely to be done by the purchaser, than by his solicitor.

6.3   The 'Unusual' Searches

There are searches that will be made only for certain localities (for example, areas where minerals have been won, or limestone or salt extracted) or particular problems (for example, where the land is cut by a rail line or a canal). Details of the searches required can be found in specialised textbooks on conveyancing searches.

One of the more common is an enquiry of the area office of British Coal, when buying land in a coal-mining area. Information will be obtained as to the whereabouts of existing workings, plans for new workings, whether a claim for subsidence has already been made, and whether any compensation has been paid. (A full account of coal-mining enquiries is given in the *Law Society's Guardian Gazette* of 27 September 1989).

6.4   The Survey

As the contract promises nothing about the physical condition of the property, it is sensible for a purchaser to have the property surveyed before he agrees to buy it. He can instruct a surveyor to carry out a full structural survey. Even this cannot guarantee the complete soundness of the property, as inspection is limited by problems of access to floorboards, rafters, etc. The cost of a full survey is currently about £400 for a three-bedroomed house, and few purchasers commission one. A cheaper alternative is a house-buyer's report, which comments on the condition and value of the property, and lists visible serious defects.

If the purchaser is borrowing money to buy the house, the prospective lender will instruct a surveyor to carry out a valuation report. The Royal Institute of Chartered Surveyors stresses that this is not a survey. Its purpose is only to value the property to decide if it offers sufficient security for the loan. Some lenders let the purchaser see this report, others do not, although in all cases it is the purchaser who pays for the inspection to be carried out. Well over three-quarters of house-buyers rely on this report alone. Whether or not the purchaser sees the report, he assumes that the lender would not lend unless the report was satisfactory. The House of

Lords had recently held that on the purchase of a 'modest' house, the lender's surveyor owes a duty of care to the purchaser and cannot protect himself from liability for negligence by a disclaimer of responsibility (see *Smith* v. *Eric S. Bush* [1987]*, and *Harris* v. *Wye Forest District Council* [1987]*.)

6.5   Town and Country Planning

Planning matters feature in the preliminary enquiries, the local land charge search and the additional enquiries of the district authority. For this reason a brief outline of planning law is given here.

(*a*)   *Development of Land*

Note: A reference in this section to 'the Act' is a reference to the Town & Country Planning Act 1990.

Planning permission is needed for the development of land (s.57 of the Act). Development is defined as:

(i)   the carrying out of building engineering, mining or other operations in, on, over or under the land;

(ii)   the making of any material change of use of any buildings or other land (s. 55 of the Act).

Buildings and Other Operations   It is clearly development to build a house or to extend an existing house. It is development to add a garage, or a potting shed. It is development (because it is an engineering operation) to make an access way from the house to the highway.

However, the Act expressly provides that internal or external improvements or alterations to a building are not development if they do not materially affect its external appearance (s.57(2) of the Act).

Change of Use   A *material* change of use is development. As a guideline, a change in the kind of use will be material, but a change in the degree of use will only be material if it is substantial. Thus, to change the use of a house from residential to a business use would require planning permission. For an owner-occupier of a house to take in a lodger would not be a material change of use, but for the owner-occupier to turn his house into a boarding-house probably would be.

It is specifically provided that it is a material change of use if a single house is used as two or more separate dwellings. This point is of concern to a purchaser of a flat created by the conversion of a house (s.55(3) of the Act).

It is not a material change of use if a building or land within the curtilage of a dwelling house is used for any purpose incidental to the enjoyment of the house as such. That is why no permission is needed to start using an existing outhouse as a garage. (Remember it *is* development to build a new garage.)

To assist in the decision of whether or not a change of use is material, there exists the Town and County Planning (Use Classes) Order 1987. This specifies various classes of use. For example, Class A1 is use for the purpose of most sorts of shop. Class A2 is use for the provision of financial or professional services to the visiting public (e.g. the offices of Building Societies, or banks). Class B1 is use as an office other than as in Class A2.

A change of use from one use to another is not development, provided that both uses are within the same class. A change from use in one class to a use outside that class may be development. It will depend on whether the change is considered to be material. For example, to change from a clothes shop to a grocery store will not be development, as both uses are within class A1. Similarly, a change from an accountant's office to a solicitor's office will not need permission, as both uses are within Class B1. A change from a clothes shop to use as a branch office of a Building Society would need permission as it would be a change of use that would be considered material.

(b) Applying for Planning Permission

 (i) If you are not sure whether the proposed activity constitutes development, you can apply to the local planning authority for a decision on the point (s.64 of the Act).

 (ii) If planning permission is needed, you must consider whether express permission is needed, or if the General Development Order can be relied on.

(iii) The Town and Country Planning (General Development) Order 1988 (as amended) itself gives planning permission for certain developments.

For example:

Part I Class A – development within the curtilage of a dwelling-house This includes enlarging a house, (subject to limitations on the volume and the height of the extension), and building a new garage (subject to limitation on size and situation). If the proposed development is outside the limitations imposed by the order, express planning permission will be needed. Class I also permits the erection of greenhouses, sheds, chicken-houses, etc.

Part II Class A – minor operations These include erecting fences (subject to limits on height) or painting the outside of the building.

Before relying on permission given by the general development order, you must check if an 'article 4' direction exists. This will be revealed by the additional enquiries of the local authority. The local planning authority can direct that all or any of the permissions granted by the General Development Order shall not apply to the whole or part of its area. For example, the authority may withdraw the permission granted for the erection of chicken-sheds. Anybody wanting to build one would then have to apply for express planning permission.

(iv) If express planning permission is needed, the application must be accompanied by detailed plans. If the applicant does not own the land, he must certify that he has notified every owner of the land. 'Owner' includes an owner of the freehold, and anyone owning a lease with seven or more years to run. (s.66 of the Act).

(v) If you propose to build on land and want to check that there is no objection in *principle* to the development, you can apply for outline planning permission. This commits the authority to allowing that type of development while allowing it to control any matter that is expressly reserved in the outline permission for later approval, such as the exact siting of the buildings, or their appearance. This procedure avoids the delay and expense of preparing detailed plans, when the application in fact never had any chance of success. (Outline planning permission is not available for a proposed change of use.)

(vi) The planning authority must give written notice of its decision within 2 months of the application. If the decision is not made within this period, the applicant can, if he wishes, treat the failure to give a decision as a refusal of permission, and appeal to the Secretary of State (ss.78 and 79 of the Act).

Once a planning permission has been given, it enures for the benefit of the land, so that a purchaser of land will acquire the benefit of existing permissions. That is why one often sees a house advertised for sale with the benefit of a planning permission. However, a purchaser must remember that planning permissions do lapse (see next paragraph).

Duration of Planning Permission

(i) A planning permission is subject to a condition that development will be begun within five years of the date of the grant or whatever period is specified by the authority. If development is not begun, the permission lapses.

(ii) An outline planning permission is subject to a condition that application for approval of the reserved matters be made within three years of the grant of the outline permission and that development be begun within either five years of the grant of the outline planning permission, or two years of the approval of the reserved matter, whichever is the later. (Sections 91 and 92 of the Act).

(c)   Enforcement of Planning Control

(i) If development is carried out without permission, or is in breach of a condition imposed on the planning permission, the local planning authority can issue an enforcement notice (s.172 of the Act). The notice has to be served on the owner and on the occupier of the land, and any person who has a property interest in the land which might be affected by the notice. The notice is first of all issued; it may then be served not more than 28 days after its issue. It will specify a date on which it is to become effective, and this must be at least 28 days from the date of service.

(ii) *Time limits for service*

  (aa) If the breach consists of an unauthorised building, mining or engineering operation, the notice must be served within four years of the breach.

     The four-year rule also applies to an unauthorised change of use *from* any building to use as a single dwelling-house.

  (bb) If the breach consists of any other unauthorised change of use occurring after 1963, there is no time limit for the service of the notice. (An unauthorised change of use which occurred before 1964 cannot be challenged by an enforcement notice. The use is not a legal use, but no action can be taken in respect of it. If a person wishes to have proof that a use started before 1964, he can apply to the authority for an 'established use' certificate. The authority must give this certificate if the case for it is proved.)

(iii) Failure to comply with an enforcement notice is a criminal offence, and there is liability for fines and other financial penalties. In addition, if the enforcement notice specifies steps such as the demolition of an unauthorised building, or reinstatement of the land to its previous condition the authority can enter onto the land and do the work itself, recovering the expense from the owner of the land (s.178 of the Act). This means that if a purchaser buys land that had, say, a garage built on it by the seller without planning permission, it is the purchaser (as the current owner) who will have to pay the authority's costs of demolition. The purchaser will be able to recover this expense from the seller (see s.178 of the Act). The authority cannot enter onto land to force discontinuance of an unauthorised use.

(d)   Planning and the Property Information Form

Having digested all this, we can return to the property information form and question 10 on it.

The protocol requires the seller's solicitor to send with the property information form all planning decisions and building regulation approvals that the seller possesses. If he is buying a new house, the purchaser will want a copy of the planning permission for its erection. He will also want a copy of the building regulations consent given by the Local Authority under the Public Health Acts.

Even if he is not the first purchaser of the house, he will want to see a copy of the planning permission, as he will want to check not only that permission was obtained to build the house, but also if conditions were imposed on the permission, and if these conditions have been met. He will also require details of any further building on the land, or any improvements or alterations made in the previous four years. You can now see why the enquiries are confined to this period. If a garage (or indeed, the house) was built or altered more than four years ago, no enforcement notice can be served; and although there is generally no time-limit in respect of changes of use, the four-year time-limit does apply if the change is to a single dwelling-house. Of course, if you are buying business property, you do need to confirm that the existing use is either authorised, or covered by an 'established use' certificate.

If the purchaser is hoping to acquire the benefit of an existing permission for future development, he will want to check that the permission has not lapsed, or will not shortly lapse. If the purchaser intends to enlarge the house under the authority of the general development order, he must ask for details of any previous extensions carried out. The point is that the *original* volume of the house can only be increased within specified limits, so previous additions may already have exhausted those limits. If the house has been in existence since 1 July 1948, any enlargement since that date will be relevant.

(e)   *Building Regulation Approval*

Apart from planning permission, a purchaser of a new house, or of a house recently substantially altered, needs evidence that the Building Regulations were met. The purpose of these regulations is to ensure that houses are safe and provide a decent living standard. Major alterations must comply with them, but smaller improvements such as conservatories are exempt.

Building Regulations approval must be obtained from the local authority.

Case Notes

Smith v. *Eric S. Bush [1989] 2 WLR 790*

In this case, a firm of surveyors was instructed by a building society to carry out a visual inspection of a house and to report on its value. The surveyor noticed that two chimney-breasts had been removed, but failed to check if the chimneys had been left adequately supported. His report said that the house needed no essential repairs.

The application form for the mortgage loan and the valuation report both contained a disclaimer of liability for the report's accuracy, both on behalf of the building society and the firm of surveyors. The borrower, Mrs Smith, was warned that the report was not a full survey, and that she should seek independent advice. The building society supplied her with a copy of the report, and in reliance on it she bought the house. One chimney collapsed. She sued the surveyors for negligence, who relied on the disclaimer.

Harris v. Wyre Forest District Council [1989] 2 WLR 790

In this case, the Council lent money to Mr and Mrs Harris. It instructed one of its employees to value the property. The application form for the mortgage said that the valuation report was confidential, and that the Council accepted no responsibility for the value or condition of the house by reason of the report. The Council's valuer recommended minor repairs. Three years later it was discovered that the house suffered from serious structural faults. The Harrises sued the Council, as being responsible for the negligence of its employee. They had not seen the report, but had assumed, when the Council continued with the loan, that it must have been favourable.

It was held in both cases that a valuer instructed by a prospective lender to carry out a valuation of a house at the 'bottom end' of the market to decide if it offered sufficient security for the loan, owed a duty of care to the borrower to exercise reasonable skill and care in carrying out the valuation, if he realised that the borrower would probably buy the house in reliance on the valuation, without having an independent survey.

It was stressed that this principle applied on the purchase of a 'modest home', when there was great pressure on a purchaser to rely on the valuation report, because he might be unable to afford a second survey fee. Lord Griffiths expressly reserved his position in respect of valuations of industrial property, large blocks of flats, and very expensive houses. In these cases, it would be more reasonable to expect the purchaser to arrange his own full structural survey.

In neither of these two cases had the surveyor exercised reasonable skill and care as, although only a limited appraisal was expected, it was by a skilled professional person, and each surveyor was guilty of an error which the average surveyor would not have made.

It is possible for a surveyor to disclaim liability for negligence, but the disclaimer would be ineffective under s.2(2) of the Unfair Contract Terms Act 1977 unless it was fair and reasonable to allow reliance on it, under s.11(3) of the Act. Since a surveyor was a professional person, whose services were in fact paid for by the borrower, it would not be fair and reasonable for him to rely on a disclaimer. Also, the disclaimer was unfair in that it was imposed on a person who had no power to object to it.

Rignall Developments Ltd v. Halil [1987] 3 WLR 394

The property was subject to a local land charge. It was a financial charge to recover an improvement grant made by the district authority. The seller knew that this charge existed. The property was sold by auction. One of the conditions of sale was that the purchaser was deemed to have made local searches and enquiries and that the property was sold subject to anything that might be revealed thereby.

After contract, the purchaser learned of the charge, and refused to complete. The seller argued that the condition in the contract prevented the purchaser from objecting to the charge. However, the validity of the condition depended on the seller disclosing any matter she knew of, and as she had not disclosed the charge she could not rely on the condition (see section 5.4). It was, therefore, her duty to remove the charge by paying the local authority.

It was argued as that s.198 of the Law of Property Act 1925 says that registration of a charge amounts to actual notice for all purposes, registration was equivalent to disclosure. (You will remember that this argument could not have been used had it been a *central* land charge, but s.24 of the Law of Property Act 1969 does not apply to local land charges.)

It was held that where there was such a condition, and the seller knew of the charge, s.198 could not discharge her duty of expressly disclosing the existence of the charge.

Workshop

Attempt these problems yourself, then read the specimen solutions at the end of the book.

Problem 1

Your client tells you that he has signed a written contract to buy 'Fools Paradise', a freehold house at the price of £90 000. He shows you a copy of the contract. It incorporates the standard conditions. He entered into the contract without having made or seen any local land charge search certificate or answers to additional enquiries. He has now discovered that the house is burdened with a financial charge in respect of the cost of road works prior to the adoption of the road on which the house fronts. The charge existed before he signed the contract, but he tells you he knew nothing of it. Advise him.

Problem 2

You have been consulted by Mr David Jones who proposes to purchase a semi-detached house which was built sixteen years ago on a small private residential estate. The house occupies a corner site on the edge of the estate and the side road is a private unmade road. Mr Jones is particularly attracted to this house because the present owner built a very large garage five years ago at the bottom of the garden and fronting onto the side road. Since that time he has been using the garage for repairing motor vehicles and Mr Jones wishes to do the same. The present owner has said that he has been using the garage for this business since it was built although he admits that he did not get planning permission either to build the garage or to use it for business purposes.

(a) Explain the issues, other than planning matters, with which you will be concerned in your perusal of the contract, the property information form, the searches and the evidence of title, in the particular circumstances of this case.
(b) Can the Local Planning Authority require the garage to be demolished?
(c) If the garage is not demolished, can the Local Planning Authority prevent its continued use for business purposes?

(This question is based on one in the Law Society Summer paper 1983).

Problem 3

Joan is thinking of buying a house, but she would need to build an extension to provide a bedroom for her elderly mother. The seller's solicitor has provided her with the pre-contract package in accordance with the protocol. It includes the local land charge search certificate and the replies to the additional enquiries. They are four months old.

1. If Joan decides to buy, will she need to repeat the search and enquiries?
2. Will she need ·planning permission for the extension?
3. If she does need express planning permission, when should she apply for it?

7 Deducing and Investigating a Freehold Registered Title

7.1 Deduction of title

As we have seen, the seller promises in the contract that he has a good title to the freehold estate, free from incumbrances (other than those, if standard condition 3 applies, that are 'adverse interests' or that are mentioned in a special condition). At some stage the seller must prove that he does indeed have that title. He must 'deduce' his title, i.e. give evidence of it. Traditionally title was deduced after contract. If the seller's solicitor is following the protocol, title will be deduced *with* the draft contract.

So we are now considering what evidence of title the seller must produce, if he is contracting to sell a registered freehold title.

7.2 Section 110(1) of the Land Registration Act 1925

In the case of a registered title, s.110 of the Land Registration Act 1925 stipulates that the seller *must* supply the purchaser with

- a copy of the entries on the register;
- a copy of the filed plan;
- copies or abstracts of documents noted on the register of title;
- an authority to inspect the register.

Note

(a) The Land Registration Act 1988 will come into force on 3rd December 1990, and as a result the register of title will no longer be private. It will then be unnecessary to give the purchaser an authority to inspect the register.

(b) S.110 only requires the seller to provide *a* copy of the entries on the register. So the seller could merely photocopy the contents of his land certificate. This would provide the purchaser with details of the register of title as at the date when the land certificate was last compared with the register. This date is printed inside the cover of the certificate, and the purchaser would need to be told this date, for the purpose of his pre-completion search.

Alternatively, the seller can provide the purchaser with an office copy of the register, filed plan, etc. (and this is made obligatory by standard condition 4.2.1). Office copies are obtained from the District Land Registry. They are dated and are as admissible in evidence as to the state of the register at that date as is the register itself.

It is preferable for the seller's solicitor to obtain *up-to-date* office copy entries for his own sake. He might be caught out if he relies on the land certificate when drafting the contract. A caution, and a notice protecting a spouse's rights under the Matrimonial Homes Act 1983 can be entered on the register without the Land Certificate being put on deposit at the Registry, and so will not appear on the Land Certificate.

(c) Subsection (1) of s.110 cannot be altered by the contract. These documents *must* be supplied by the seller.

7.3 Section 110(2) of the Land Registration Act 1925

This provides that the seller must provide 'copies, abstracts and evidence (if any)' in respect of matters as to which the register is not conclusive.

Remember that the register is not conclusive:

(a) as to overriding interests. If an overriding interest exists, the effect of standard condition 3 is that the sale is subject to it, but the seller should have disclosed it if he knew of it. The purchaser would at the draft contract stage have been given whatever documentary evidence existed, and may have been excluded by a special condition in the contract from requiring any other evidence.
(b) in the case of a possessory title, as to matters affecting the pre-registration title. The seller may have no evidence as to this title, and again a contractual condition would prevent the purchaser from asking for any.
(c) in the case of a leasehold title, as to the provisions of the lease and in the case of a good leasehold title, as to the validity of the lease. The points are dealt with in Chapter 15.

7.4 Investigation of Title

The protocol requires the copies of the register, etc., to be sent to the purchaser with the draft contract, so some of the matters dealt with below would in fact have been dealt with before the purchaser decided to enter into the contract.

Suppose that as the purchaser's solicitor, you have the office copy entries and filed plan in front of you. Read them.

(a)   The Property Register and Filed Plan

(i) Check the title number, estate and description of the property against the contract details. Care will be needed if there have already been sales of part of the land originally comprised in the title. The property register will indicate that part of the land has been sold off, and the filed plan will have been amended. Check that the seller is not contracting to sell land he has already transferred to someone else.

(ii) Check any reference to appurtenant rights. If the property register includes an appurtenant right, such as an easement, as part of the description of the property, you can be certain that the easement exists. The registration indicates ownership of the easement just as it indicates ownership of the estate to which it is appurtenant. If the register merely says that right is 'claimed' by the proprietor or that a deed 'purports' to grant the easement, the register is not conclusive as to its existence. The existence of the easement should be proved by the proprietor, unless the contract says otherwise.

(b)   The Proprietorship Register

(i) Check that the seller is the person who is registered as proprietor. Suppose he is not? The solution may be that:

(aa) the seller is the personal representative of the dead registered proprietor (see Chapter 10).

(bb) the seller is the trustee in bankruptcy of the registered proprietor (see section 9.10).

(cc) the seller is a trustee for sale, who has been appointed, but who has not been registered as proprietor (see Chapter 11).

However, the solution may be that the seller has contracted to sell a legal estate that is in fact vested in someone else.

The principle here is that a seller shows good title only by establishing that he owns the legal estate, or that the legal estate is owned by someone who can be *compelled* by the seller to convey it to the purchaser. This is illustrated by the case of *Elliott* v. *Pierson* [1948] in which it was held that the seller had proved a good title to the freehold when he established that it was owned by a limited company which he controlled. If he had not had control of the company he would not have made good title, even if the company had been willing to convey to the purchaser. This would not have created any difficulty if the purchaser had been equally willing to accept a conveyance by the company, but the flaw in the seller's title would have given a reluctant purchaser the opportunity to treat the contract as discharged.

(ii) Look for restrictions. Either the seller must have the restriction removed before completion, or he must comply with it. Otherwise, the transfer to the purchaser will not be registered.

(iii) Cautions. If a caution is discovered on the register, do not accept an explanation of why the protected interest is in fact void, and so could not be asserted against the purchaser. Insist that the caution must be removed from the register before completion.

(c) *The Charges Register*

(i) Are there any entries on the charges register of incumbrances that are not mentioned in the contract?

(ii) Registered charges. Unless the contract expressly says otherwise, a purchaser is entitled to a title free from any mortgage. There are two usual methods by which a registered charge can be removed from the register.

(aa) *through its redemption* – i.e. the loan is repaid. The seller will be using part of the purchase price to pay off the mortgage. In the case of registered title the evidence that the mortgage loan has been repaid is Land Registry form 53 executed by the mortgagee (see s.35 of the Land Registration Act 1925). In essence, the form says that the proprietor of the registered charge admits that the charge has been discharged.

In an ideal world, this form would be handed to the purchaser on completion. However, some banks and building societies refuse to seal form 53 in advance of payment, so it is not available at completion. The solicitor acting for the purchaser is often prepared to accept what are called 'the usual undertakings' from the solicitor acting for the mortgagee, who will usually also be the seller's solicitor. The undertakings are guarded in form, because the solicitor will only undertake to do things that are within his own control. So he will not undertake that form 53 will be sealed. He will only undertake that he will forward the money necessary for redemption to the mortgagee, and that if and when the form 53 is sent by the mortgagee to him, he will send it on to the purchaser.

The purchaser accepts these undertakings, because it causes too much fuss and delay to object to an established practice. However, a purchaser does not have to accept the undertakings, and should not do so if there is a possibility that the execution of form 53 might be delayed. The undertakings should not be accepted, for instance, if the mortgagee is a private person. A building society does not die, or go on an extended holiday. A private mortgagee might. Form 53 must be available at completion.

An undertaking should only be accepted from a solicitor or licenced conveyancer. If the seller is acting for himself, an undertaking from him should not be accepted, and the form 53 should be available at completion.

If part of the land in the title is being transferred, and the mortgagee is releasing only the part being transferred from his mortgage, form 53 will say that the mortgage is discharged as regards the part of the land identified by the plan accompanying form 53. This plan would also be executed by the mortgagee.

(bb) *through being 'overreached'*. The proprietor of a registered charge has a statutory power of sale. (s.101 of the Law of Property Act 1925 and s.34 of the Land Registration Act 1925).

The power arises when, under the terms of the mortgage, the money is due and owing. This means that someone purchasing from a registered chargee must read the mortgage. He may, in an old-fashioned mortgage, find a promise to repay on a specified date, usually six months from the date of the mortgage. It is on this date that the money is technically due, and the power arises. Other mortgages may say that the money is repayable on demand (in which case evidence is needed that the mortgagee has requested repayment), or that the money is deemed to be due as from the date of the mortgage. The only check that a purchaser need make is that the power exists and has arisen. The power should only be used by the mortgagee when it has become exercisable. It may become exercisable under s.103 of the Law of Property Act 1925 (because of failure to repay capital, pay interest, or because of a breach of a provision in the mortgage) or under the terms of the mortgage. Some mortgages exclude s.103 and specify the defaults on which the power of sale becomes exercisable, or even say that the power becomes exercisable without default as from the date of the mortgage. Whatever the mortgagee may say, this question of exercisability is an internal matter between the mortgagee and mortgagor (s.104 of the Law of Property Act 1925). Someone purchasing from the mortgagee need not enquire as to whether the power of sale is exercisable, and will get a good title from the mortgagee even if it is not. (However, it is said that a purchaser who learns that the power of sale is not exercisable should not complete, as he will not get a good title.)

Equally, a mortgagee when selling must take reasonable precautions to obtain the true market value at the time of sale. Failure in this duty to the mortgagor will not invalidate the sale to a purchaser who is innocent of fraud or collusion. The mortgagor must sue the mortgagee for damages.

The power is to sell the mortgagor's legal estate, free from the mortgage of the mortgagee who is selling and from any mortgage later in priority. These mortgages cease to be claims against the land and become instead claims against the purchase money paid to the mortgagee who sold. The mortgages are not cleared from the title through their redemption, so the purchaser will not receive forms 53 in respect of them. Even if the purchase price is not enough to repay the mortgages, the purchaser takes free of them. They no longer affect the land. Therefore, a purchaser from the proprietor of the first registered charge will receive on completion a transfer signed by the mortgagee, and the mortgagee's charge certificate. When the transfer is registered, all registered charges will be cancelled.

A mortgagee has no power to overreach a mortgage which has priority over his own. Therefore, if the seller is the proprietor of say, the second registered charge, there is a choice. The sale must either be subject to the first mortgage, (unlikely) or the mortgagee who is selling will redeem the first mortgage.

(d) Overriding Interests

These, of course, will not be discovered from looking at the entries on the register. Any known to the seller should have been disclosed in the contract. If any overriding interest not disclosed by the contract and known to the seller is discovered before completion, the seller has broken his contract. (This is assuming standard condition 3 applies to the contract).

A transfer signed by the seller's attorney   This is discussed in 9.4.

7.5   The Pre-Completion Search: Form 94

This is the final step in the investigation of the seller's title.

The purchaser has evidence of the state of the title up to a certain date. If he was given office copy entries, it is the date of the office copies. If he was given a copy of the entries in the Land Certificate, it is the date that the certificate was last officially compared with the register.

The object of the pre-completion search is to bring the purchaser's information up to date. The search form, (Land Registry form 94A if a purchase of all the land in the title, 94B if a purchase of only part) consists in essence of an enquiry addressed to the Land Registrar, as to whether any adverse entry has been made on the register since one of the two dates mentioned above. On 3rd December 1990 the register of title ceases to be private, and the authority of the registered proprietor to make the search is no longer needed.

On receipt of the search form, the Registry will issue an official search certificate, saying whether or not adverse entries have been entered on the register since the date specified in the search form. This official search certificate gives a purchaser a priority period of 30 working days (i.e. excluding weekends and bank holidays) the first day of which is the date of delivery of the search at the Registry. Any entry made on the register during this period is postponed to the purchase, provided the purchase is completed, and an application to register the purchaser's title is delivered to the registry, before the period expires. So a purchaser is protected against last-minute registrations made after the date of his search.

It is important to apply for registration before the period expires, as otherwise anything that was being postponed to the purchase (e.g. an application to enter a caution) will cease to be postponed, so that when the purchaser does eventually apply for registration, the registration will be subject to it.

The priority period cannot be extended by another search. The second search will simply give a different priority period, and can only postpone applications made after the second search, but not ones made after the first search but before the second.

Subject to this limitation, a second search is worth making. It will give the second priority period, and will also reveal if an adverse entry has been put on the register since the date of the first search.

The priority period protects a purchaser. 'Purchaser' includes a prospective mortgagee or tenant. A search made by a prospective transferee acquires a priority period for the transferee, but not for the transferee's mortgagee. A search by the prospective mortgagee, however, does give a priority period both to the mortgagee and to the transferee. In other words, if Jane is the solicitor both for Bill, who is buying the house, and for the Larkshill Building Society who is lending Bill the money to do it, Jane will make only one search, on behalf of the Building Society. The priority period given by the search will protect both Bill and the Society against last-minute entries on the register, provided the application to register the transfer and the mortgage is delivered to the registry before the 30 days expire. (This is the effect of the Land Registration (Official Searches) Rules 1990).

A search certificate is not conclusive in favour of the purchaser, so if it is wrong (for example, if it fails to reveal an adverse entry) the purchaser will take subject to the entry. He will, however, be able to claim compensation from the registrar (s.83(3) of the Land Registration Act 1925).

7.6   Other Pre-Completion Searches

(a)   At the Companies Registry

If the registered proprietor is a limited company, it appears unnecessary to search the company file at the Companies Registry.

(i) *Fixed charges* A fixed charge will not bind the purchaser unless protected by an entry on the register of the title at HM Land Registry, even though it is registered at the Companies Registry (s.60(1) of the Land Registration Act 1925).

(ii) *Floating charges* A floating charge will not bind a purchaser unless protected by an entry on the register of title. If it is so protected, the purchaser will need to obtain a certificate of non-crystallisation signed by the company secretary, or, preferably, by the owner of the floating charge. This certificate should be dated as at the date of completion.

(iii) A company going, or gone, into liquidation. It is suggested (see Ruoff and Roper - Registered title) that there is no need to search for this purpose, because so long as the company remains registered proprietor, it has the ability to transfer the legal estate, provided there is no caution on the register.

(b) *A Bankruptcy Search in the Land Charges Registry Against the Name of the Purchaser*

This search has nothing whatsoever to do with the investigation of the seller's title, but is added to the list of pre-completion searches for the sake of completeness.

If the solicitor for the purchaser is also acting for the purchaser's mortgagee, it is his duty, as the mortgagee's solicitor, to discover if the purchaser is, or is about to become, insolvent. This can be done by making a search against the purchaser's name at the Land Charges Registry, to see if there is a PA(B) or WO(B) registered (see sections 4.5(a) and (b)). This is not a title search, and it has nothing to do with the seller's ownership of the property being sold. It is a status search, to prevent the mortgagee lending money to a bankrupt. It is done by sending to the Land Charges Registry a search form K16, which asks the Registrar to search only for bankruptcy entries against the names listed.

Of course, this search is not necessary if the loan is not to the purchaser of a registered title, but to the existing registered proprietor. In the latter case, entries as to the bankruptcy of the proprietor will appear on the register of title, and will be revealed by the Land Registry Search.

Workshop

Attempt this problem yourself, then read the specimen solution at the end of the book.

Problem

You are acting for William and Mary Thompson, who are buying a freehold dwelling-house, number 34 Holly Avenue, at the price of £34 000. They are obtaining an advance of £30 000 from the Best Building Society (for whom you act) by way of an endowment mortgage. The seller is the Z Finance Company Ltd, which is selling as second mortgagee free from incumbrances, the first mortgagee being the Y Building Society.

List the documents you will send to the Best Building Society after completion.

---

8 Deduction of Unregistered Title

8.1 Form of Evidence

In the case of an unregistered title, a seller deduces his title by providing evidence of what his title deeds say. At one time, he would have sent the purchaser an abstract of the deeds. This amounted to a précis of their contents, prepared in a stylised form. Nowadays, the simplest method of letting a purchaser know the contents of deeds is by sending him photocopies of them. The photocopy deeds must be accompanied by an epitome i.e. a chronological index of the accompanying deeds. The epitome should state whether each original deed will itself be available on completion, and whether it will be handed over then to the purchaser. In this book, 'abstract' is used to mean both the traditional abstract and the epitome.

8.2 What Deeds and Other Documents Should be Abstracted?

The abstract will start with the deed that the purchaser is entitled to see as the root of title. Usually there will have been a term in the contract specifying what deed this is to be. If not, the document must be one that is a good root of title at least 15 years old (see section 5.8(e)). The abstract may start with an earlier document in circumstances in which the purchaser is entitled to see a pre-root deed (see section 8.3(e)). Having started with the root, the abstract must then give details of every deed, document or event that passes the legal estate from owner to owner, and eventually to the seller. Notice again that he must establish either that he owns the legal estate, or that it is owned by someone who can be compelled by him to convey it to the purchaser. This has been discussed in the context of registered title in section 7.4(b).

8.3 Which are Not Abstracted?

(a) An abstract should not contain *information about equitable or other interests that will be overreached by the sale*, and so will not affect the purchaser. So, for example, on a sale by trustees for sale the purchaser need not be given information about the interests of the beneficiaries. On a sale by a mortgagee, the purchaser need not be given details of mortgages later in priority than that of the seller's.

(b) *A lease that has expired by effluxion of time*   For example, if a lease was granted in 1975 for ten years, and the tenant left at the end of the term in 1985, the purchaser need not be given a copy of that lease. If the lease ended by any other means, the purchaser should be given whatever information is available to prove its termination, so if the tenant surrendered the lease in 1980, the purchaser should see a copy of the lease, and of the deed of surrender.

(c) *Birth, death' or marriage certificates*   These are matters of public record, and the strict rule is that if a purchaser wants a copy he can get one for himself. What the purchaser must be given is the information he needs to do this, e.g. the date of the marriage. In fact, if the seller has these certificates, it would be churlish of him to refuse the purchaser a copy.

(d) Strictly, *equitable mortgages should be abstracted*, so that the purchaser can check on their redemption. Remember though, that an equitable mortgage can be created with little formality. So equitable mortgages are not usually abstracted. If however, an equitable mortgage is protected by the registration of a C(iii) land charge, the registration should be cancelled, otherwise the purchaser is alerted to the existence of the mortgage, and will need evidence of repayment of the loan.

Any legal mortgage created after the root of title should be abstracted, together with any relevant vacating receipt.

A legal mortgage created before the root of title, but discharged at a date after the date of the root of title should be abstracted, together with any vacating receipt. If it was not redeemed or otherwise discharged until after the date of the root of title, it is part of the post-root title, no matter when it was created.

A legal mortgage created and discharged earlier than the date of the root of title need not be abstracted.

(e) *Pre-root deeds and documents* Generally, a purchase has no right to see any deeds or documents that are dated earlier than the root of title.

Section 45 of the Law of Property Act provides that 'a purchaser shall not:

(i) require the production, or any abstract or copy of any deed, will or other document, dated or made before the time prescribed by law, or stipulated, for the commencement of the title, ...;

(ii) require any information or make any requisition, objection or enquiry, with respect to any such deed, will or document, or the title prior to that time ...'.

This section prohibits the purchaser from making any objection to the soundness of the pre-root title. It is as if there were an express term in the contract itself preventing the purchaser from raising requisitions on title. We have seen that any such contractual stipulation is valid only if the seller has shown good faith, i.e. has revealed to the purchaser any defect he knows about or ought to know about (see section 5.4). The same is true of the s.45 interdiction. So the purchaser can object to the pre-root title if he establishes the existence of a defect that was known to the seller at the time of contract and not disclosed. For this reason, a seller cannot use the section to escape his duty of disclosure. Any pre-root defect known to the seller should be expressly disclosed, and the purchaser expressly prohibited from raising a requisition in respect of it. Further, an incumbrance that is still enforceable is a matter of the post-root title, even though created pre-root.

There are four exceptions to s.45, when a purchaser can insist on seeing a pre-root document. The first three are laid down by s.45.

(i) a purchaser can see a power of attorney, no matter what its date, if it authorised the execution of a document that is part of the title;

(ii) a purchaser can see a document no matter what its date which created an interest or obligation which still subsists, if one of the documents on the title conveys the land subject to the interest;

(iii) a purchaser can see a document which creates a trust, if one of the documents on the title is disposed of by reference to that trust. This does not however apply to a trust deed of a settlement by way of trust for sale, or one governed by the Settled Land Act 1925, the reason being that the equitable interests created by those sorts of trust deeds should be cleared from the title by being overreached. So this exception is only likely to apply to a conveyance by a trustee of a bare trust at the direction, or with the consent, of the beneficiary.

(iv) the fourth exception comes not from s.45 but from the definition of a good root, i.e. that it must describe the property that is being conveyed. If the root of title describes the property it is conveying by a reference to a description in an earlier deed, or to a plan in an earlier deed, it is possible that a purchaser can either insist on a copy of the deed being produced, or can claim that the root of title is not a good root, as not containing an adequate description.

These rights of a purchaser can be removed by a special condition in the contract, with the exception of the pre-root power of attorney. Section 125(2) of the Law of Property Act 1925 makes it impossible for the purchaser's right to any power of attorney affecting his title to be excluded by the contract.

(f) *Past land charge search certificates*   These are not documents of title, and the purchaser is not entitled to the results of past searches. However, if the seller has any, it is courteous to send copies to the purchaser, as it may save him from repeating searches against the names of past estate owners. The protocol requires the seller's solicitor to provide a certificate of search against 'appropriate' names which must mean the names of all the estate owners revealed by the abstract.

8.4   Verification of the Abstract

The abstract or epitome is only *prima facie* evidence of the seller's ownership of the property. The abstract might be inaccurate, omit vital documents or memoranda, or, of course, be a complete fabrication. Either at or before completion the purchaser must see the original deeds.

If the seller will be retaining the title deeds, it is usual for the purchaser's solicitor to 'mark' the abstract (or the copy deeds, in the case of an epitome) i.e. to write on it the fact that it has been examined against the original, and that the abstract is correct. This statement is signed by the solicitor, who adds the date, and sometimes the place where the examination was made. In later transactions the marked abstract or marked deeds may be acceptable as evidence of title, without recourse to the original deeds. However, a solicitor who relies on a marked abstract or marked copies which then turn out to be inaccurate, might be accused of negligence. (The protocol requires the seller's solicitor to mark any copy or abstract of a deed that will not be given to the purchaser on completion before sending the copy or abstract as part of the pre-contract package).

8.5   Retention by the Seller of Deeds at Completion

On completion, a seller must generally hand to the purchaser all title deeds in his control. The seller can, however, retain the title deeds if he is also retaining part of the land to which they relate (s.45(9) of the Law of Property Act 1925). In such a case the purchaser should:

(a) mark the abstract as examined against the original deeds (if not already done);
(b) ensure that a memorandum of sale of part is endorsed on the conveyance to the seller;
(c) ensure that the conveyance to him contains an acknowledgement and undertaking in respect of the retained deeds.

It will often be wise for a seller of part to retain a copy of the conveyance to the purchaser with his deeds. It will identify exactly what part was sold and disclose any easements or covenants given by the purchaser in favour of the retained land.

Workshop

Attempt this problem yourself, then read the specimen solution at the end of the book.

Problem

You are acting for Patrick O'Connor who is selling his freehold house. You have the documents listed below:

1. 4 July 1970 – a conveyance on sale from A to B, said to be subject to covenants contained in a deed dated 1950.
2. 4 July 1970 – a mortgage given by B to the Foundation Building Society, with a receipt endorsed on it dated 30 September 1973 executed by the Society.
3. 6 July 1970 – a lease by B to T for 30 years.
4. 20 September 1973 – land charges search against B and O'Connor.
5. 30 September 1973 – a conveyance on sale from B to O'Connor, subject to the 1950 covenants.
6. 30 September 1973 – a mortgage given by O'Connor to the Roof Building Society.
7. 9 February 1975 – a surrender of lease by T to O'Connor.

(a) When you are drafting the contract, which document will you specify as the root of title?
(b) What documents will you abstract when deducing title to the purchaser?

9 Investigating an Unregistered Title

9.1 Introduction

When investigating an unregistered title, we are looking for a flaw in the soundness of the seller's claim to own the legal estate, and for any third-party right that will bind the purchase after completion but to which the sale has not been made subject by the contract. This is easier said than done.

It does not matter for present purposes whether we are investigating the title before exchange of contracts or after. In the former case we will ask for any defect to be put right before we agree to buy; in the latter case we shall raise a requisition on the basis that the seller has not proved that he has the title promised in the contract. Of course, if we agree by a special condition in the contract to accept the title as deduced, we must investigate the title before exchange of contracts, as our power to object to the title after contract will be very limited (see Chapter 5).

We will start by considering the basic points of the root of title, the stamping of the title deeds, the identification of the property, execution of the deed, and the 'missing link'.

Suppose we are acting for Paula Prentiss, who is contracting to buy the freehold of Sandy Cottage from Ian Lane.

We receive an epitome of title, accompanied by the photocopies of two documents.

9.2 The First Document of Title

The first document is a deed of conveyance on sale dated 3 June 1971, and this deed is now going to be considered.

(a) The Root of Title

If the contract does not specify what document is to be the root of title, we will consider our right to have title traced from a good root at least 15 years old, and we will check that this conveyance satisfies the definition of a good root (see section 5.8(e)). Our contract doubtless specifies from what document title is to be traced, so the question as to whether this document is adequate as a root is considered before accepting the contractual condition. We will be wary of any condition compelling us to trace title from an immature root. The 1971 conveyance appears to be a good root, and is, of course, over 15 years old.

(b)   Stamping

(i) If the 1971 deed is not properly stamped, that is a defect in the seller's title. A document that is not properly stamped cannot be produced in court, and a title that cannot be defended in court is not a good title. If the deed is not properly stamped, we shall insist that the seller have it stamped. (We can do this even though there is a condition in the contract saying that no objection can be raised to an insufficiency of stamps, as the condition is void, by virtue of s.117 of the Stamp Act 1891).

As the conveyance is on sale, we would expect to see the 'particulars delivered' stamp. We also need to check that the conveyance bears the correct *ad valorem* stamps. The difficulty is that the thresholds for stamp duty have changed over the years, as have the rates of duty. In the past, rates of stamp duty were graded, so the certificate of value (see section 2.17) was used not just as now, to claim total exemption from duty, but also to claim a reduced rate, e.g. 0.5 per cent rather than 2 per cent. So it is possible for a conveyance to have a certificate of value and also *ad valorem* stamps. Details of past rates of duty should be kept to hand, so that the stamping of past conveyances and other documents can be checked.

One thing must always be wrong, namely the absence from a conveyance on sale of both a certificate of value and *ad valorem* stamps. Total exemption from *ad valorem* stamp duty could only ever be claimed through a certificate of value. If the conveyance contained no certificate, *ad valorem* duty was payable at the then full rate, no matter how low the consideration.

(ii) *A Note about Particular Documents* In the past, not only conveyances on sale had to be stamped *ad valorem*. A deed of gift was also liable, the duty being calculated on the value of the land. A certificate of value could be used to claim a nil or a reduced rate. The deed had to be sent into the Stamp Office for the duty to be adjudicated, so the deed should bear a blue adjudication stamp. A deed of gift made on or after 25 March 1985 was liable for a 50p deed stamp. A deed of gift made after 30 April 1987 bears no stamp duty, provided it is certificated (see section 2.17).

An assent under seal was liable for a 50p deed stamp if made before 25 March 1985.

Mortgages and vacating receipts (with the exception of a building society receipt) were liable to stamp duty if made before 1 August 1971.

(c)   The Parties to It

Suppose the seller in the 1971 deed is John Smith, and the purchaser is Alice Hardy. John is a mystery to us and will remain so. We may never know how he obtained the legal estate, as that can only be revealed by investigating the pre-root title.

(d)   The Parcels Clause

We are hoping to establish that the land conveyed in the 1971 deed did include the land that Ian has contracted to sell to our client. Under an open contract, the seller must prove that the property he has contracted to sell is the same as that being dealt with by the title deeds. This obligation does not appear to be altered by the standard conditions, although condition 4.3.1 absolves the seller from having to prove the exact boundaries of the property or the ownership of the boundary forces.

The proof usually comes merely from the description in the deed, i.e. that it says it is conveying Sandy Cottage. If the deed did not make it clear that it was dealing with Sandy Cottage, further evidence would be needed, for example, a declaration from Ian that the land has been occupied since 1971 under the authority of the title deeds without challenge from anyone.

(e)   Incumbrances

Reading the parcels clause in the 1971 conveyance might reveal the reservation of an easement not disclosed in the contract but known to the seller. Reading the habendum might disclose incumbrances already existing before 1971 but not mentioned in the contract.

(f)   Execution of the deed

The formalities for execution of a deed by an individual changed on 31 July 1990 when s.1 of the Law of Property (Miscellaneous Provisions) Act 1989 came into force. The new formalities are set out in Chapter 13, where the drafting of a deed is considered. The old formalities are set out here, as they remain important when checking the due execution of a past title deed.

A deed executed before s.1 of the 1989 Act came into effect had to be signed and sealed by its maker, and delivered as his deed (s.73 of the Law of Property Act 1925). If these formalities were not observed, the document was not a deed, and could not create or convey a legal estate (s.52 of the Law of Property Act 1925).

We are unlikely to query the authenticity of a signature on a deed. In theory we could ask Ian to provide evidence that what purports to be John Smith's signature is indeed that very thing. In practice we would not do that. Anyway, in respect of the 1971 deed, any requisition by us would be countered by Ian quoting the rule that a deed or document 20 years old proves itself, provided it is produced from proper custody and there are no suspicious circumstances. A suspicious circumstance would be a startling difference between two signatures both purporting to be that of John.

Section 73 did also require a seal. The days of personal seals are long past, and a seal became only a red wafer disc to be obtained from any law stationer. However, it was still essential that a seal be on the conveyance *before* the maker signed. So if the 1971 conveyance does not bear a seal, evidence is needed that a seal was in position at the time of execution. If a seal was never there, nor anything such as a printed circle which might have served as a seal, then the document is not a deed, and could not have conveyed the legal estate (see *First National Securities* v. *Jones* [1978]; and *TCB Ltd* v. *Gray* [1986]).

The delivery of a deed is a matter of intention. A deed is delivered when it is signed by the maker with the intention that he shall be bound by it. If a person signs and seals a deed, it is inferred from this that the deed is also delivered, so we will not call on Ian for evidence that John delivered the deed.

9.3   The Second Document of Title

We now turn to the second and final document of title. This is a conveyance on sale dated 1 March 1987.

(a) We again check stamping.

(b) We again consider the parties, looking particularly for the 'missing link'. If in 1971 the property was conveyed to Alice Hardy, we expect to see Alice Hardy conveying it in 1987. Suppose for the sake of argument, that we find that the seller in the 1987 deed is, in fact, Christopher Camp. We need an explanation. Perhaps Alice had died, and Christopher was her personal representative. If so, we would ask for a copy of the grant of representation, identifying Christopher as executor or administrator, and would turn to Chapter 10. Alternatively Alice might have gone bankrupt, and Christopher was the trustee in bankruptcy, in which case we would ask to see a copy of the certificate of appointment of Christopher as trustee.

If the ownership of the legal estate had not passed to Christopher by operation of law, then it must have passed by conveyance. In the absence of such a conveyance, the title is bad. The legal estate remained in Alice, and only she had power to convey it to Ian. To put his title right, Ian must either procure a conveyance by Alice to himself, or prove to us that he can compel Alice to convey the property directly to our client (see sections 7.4(b)).

(c)   *The Parcels Clause*

We expect to see a description similar to that in the 1971 deed, or at least linked to it. For example, the 1971 deed might talk about 'Farmer Giles's 10-acre field', but (we hope) also refer to an annexed plan which shows that the field covered the site of what is now Sandy Cottage. The 1987 deed may talk about Sandy Cottage forming part of the land 'conveyed by the 1971 deed'.

(d)   *Incumbrances*

We are again looking to see if the 1987 deed created new incumbrances not disclosed in the contract.

There now follows a list of diverse points to be considered on investigating the title. The list is not complete, and must be read in conjunction with Chapters 10, 11 and 12.

9.4   Execution of a Deed by a Company

Again, the formalities for the execution of a deed by a company changed on 31 July 1990, but this time by virtue of s.130 of the Companies Act 1989, brought into force on that day. The present formalities are set out in Chapter 13. The previous formalities are set out here.

If a conveyance was executed by a limited company, the execution was valid if the conveyance was executed in accordance with the company's articles of association. If the company's articles incorporated Table A of the Companies Act 1985, its articles provided for a deed to be executed by the affixing of the company seal by the authority of the directors in the presence of a director and the secretary, or the presence of two directors.

By virtue of s.74 of the Law of Property Act 1925, if the company seal had been affixed in the presence of the secretary and director, the deed was deemed to have been duly executed, even if in fact the articles demanded different formalities. Further, a purchaser could assume that the deed had been executed so as to satisfy s.74 if there was on the deed a seal that purported to be the company seal, and signatures that purported to be that of secretary and director. So a purchaser could take these matters at face value.

It follows from s.74 that the company was bound by its deed executed in accordance with the section, even though the seal was affixed without the authority of a resolution from the board of directors (*D'Silva* v. *Lister House Development Limited* [1971] Ch 17 [1970] 1 All ER 858).

9.5   Execution of a Document by an Attorney

(a)   *Power of Attorney*

A seller who will, for example, be out of the country when the sale of his property is to be arranged, may authorise someone else to sign all the necessary documents on his behalf. If it is to confer the power to execute a deed (i.e. sign as well as deliver) the authority must itself be given by deed. The authority is called a power of attorney. We will call the seller, who confers the power, the principal, and we will call the person on whom the power is conferred, the attorney.

(b)   Scope of the Power

A purchaser, before accepting a conveyance or transfer signed by the seller's attorney, must consider whether the attorney has the necessary authority under the terms of the power to sign the conveyance. This is decided by reading the power, and seeing what acts it does authorise.

A power may be specific, i.e. may authorise the attorney to do only those things which are enumerated in the power. A power 'to do all things, and execute all documents connected with the sale of 10 Cherry Avenue' is clearly useless if an attorney seeks to establish his authority to execute a mortgage of 10 Cherry Avenue.

Alternatively, a power may be general. The power may say simply that the attorney is appointed in accordance with s.10 of the Powers of Attorney Act 1971. This confers on the attorney authority to do on behalf of his principal anything that can lawfully be done through an attorney. So this attorney can execute a mortgage or conveyance of 10 Cherry Avenue, or of anything else that the seller owns beneficially.

(c)   Revocation of the Power

The purchaser must also consider the possibility that the power had been revoked before the attorney executed the deed. Most powers of attorney are given solely because the principal is not able himself to sign the documents. The attorney has no proprietary interest in the land that is to be conveyed. This type of administrative power can be revoked by the principal at any time. It is also automatically revoked by the death of the principal, or by his bankruptcy or mental incapacity.

By contrast, the attorney may have an interest in the property to be conveyed, and the power might have been given to protect that interest. An example would be a power of attorney given to an equitable mortgagee authorising him to execute a legal mortgage in his own favour. This type of power is called a security power, and can be made irrevocable. Section 4(1) of the Powers of Attorney Act 1971 provides that if a power of attorney is *expressed* to be irrevocable and is given to protect a proprietary interest of the attorney, then so long as the attorney has that interest the power is not revoked by any event, nor can it be withdrawn by the principal unless the attorney consents.

(d)   Protection for the Purchaser from the Attorney   But for the 1971 Act

(and earlier Acts) the rule would be that if the power had been revoked before the attorney executed the conveyance or transfer, the conveyance would be void. Section 5 of the Powers of Attorney Act protects the person dealing with the attorney from the possibility of previous revocation of the power. It provides that even if the power has been revoked, the transaction by the attorney is nevertheless valid, provided that the person dealing with the attorney (i.e. the purchaser from the principal) did not know of the revocation. So it is not the fact of revocation that matters, so much as whether or not the purchaser from the principal *knew* of the revocation. (It must be remembered that knowledge of a revoking event – for example, the death of the principal – amounts to knowledge of the effect of that event, i.e. the consequent revocation of the power.)

Section 5 also provides that if the power is *expressed* to be irrevocable and is *expressed* to be given by way of security, the person dealing with the attorney is entitled to assume that the power can only be revoked with the consent of the attorney. Knowledge of the donor's death would in such a case be irrelevant. The person dealing with the attorney does not receive this protection if he knows that the power was not in fact given by way of security. The Powers of Attorney Act 1971 applies to all powers of attorney whenever created but only to transactions completed by the attorney on or after 1 October 1971. For the validity of transactions completed before that date, the effect of ss.123 – 128 of the Law of Property Act 1925 must be considered.

(e) Evidence of the Power

On completion, the attorney will not part with the deed creating the power if it is a general power, or if it authorises any disposition other than that to the purchaser. What he will give the purchaser is a facsimile copy (e.g. a photocopy) certified by the solicitor as being an accurate copy. This copy is then conclusive evidence of the contents of the original power. This means that anyone later investigating title need never see the original power; he need only see the copy, which will be handed from purchaser to purchaser with the title deeds.

(f) Protection of Later Purchasers

We can see that the validity of the title that the attorney gives to the person dealing with him may depend on whether or not that person knew of a revocation of the power. There are two occasions when it is conclusively presumed in favour of any subsequent purchaser that the person dealing with the attorney did not know of a revocation.

One is where the transaction between the attorney and the person dealing with the attorney is completed within 12 months of the date of the power. The other is where the person dealing with the attorney makes a statutory declaration before or within 3 months of the subsequent purchase that he did not at the material time know of the revocation of the power (s.5(4) of the 1971 Act).

Example An example might help. Vimto has agreed to sell Blackacre to Pedro. Vimto gives his solicitor, Alexis, a power of attorney to execute a deed of conveyance and to complete the transaction.

Alexis executes the deed and completes on 1 October 1989. The conveyance to Pedro will be valid unless Pedro knew that Vimto had by then revoked the power, or became bankrupt or insane or had died.

Pedro later sells to Quentin. Quentin can conclusively presume that Pedro did not know of any revocation, provided that the power came into effect in the 12 months preceding 1 October 1989. Quentin will *not* raise any requisition as to Pedro's knowledge. He will simply compare the date of the power and the date of the conveyance. If the 1989 conveyance was executed by Alexis more than 12 months after the date of the power, Pedro will be asked to make the statutory declaration.

Again, the requisition to Pedro is not 'did you know of any revocation?' but is 'supply the statutory declaration'. Pedro may be lying in his teeth when he makes the declaration, but the title he gives to Quentin will be sound.

(g) *A Power of Attorney Delegating a Trust*   Section 25 of the Trustee Act 1925 (as amended by s.9 of the Powers of Attorney Act 1971) provides that a trustee (including a trustee for sale) can by a power of attorney delegate the exercise of his trust and powers for up to 12 months.

The power of attorney must be executed in the presence of a witness, and notice of it must be given to the other trustees.

A trustee cannot delegate to his fellow-trustee if there are only the two of them. One of three or more trustees can delegate to a fellow-trustee. Nor can a trustee use the statutory form of power of attorney under s.10 of the Powers of Attorney Act 1971 even if the trustee is also a beneficial owner (see *Walia* v. *Michael Naughton Ltd* [1985]).

So if A and B own the legal estate on trust for sale for themselves as beneficial co-owners:

 (i) A cannot appoint B as his attorney;
 (ii) If A appoints X as his attorney, the power must be in the form prescribed by the Trustee Act 1925, otherwise it will be void.

(h)   *The Application of these Rules to Registered Title*

Although this chapter is on the subject of unregistered title, this is a convenient time to consider the application of these rules to a registered title.

A transfer by the attorney of the registered proprietor will again be valid, provided that the person dealing with the attorney did not know of the revocation of the power. The transferee will then apply for registration of the transfer. It is now the *Registrar* who is concerned as to whether the transferee did or did not know of any revocation. Therefore, if the transfer did not take place within 12 months of the power, the Registrar will require the transferee to provide the Registrar with a statutory declaration that at the time of completion the transferee did not know of the revocation of the power. If the power is a security power, the transferee must declare that he did not know that the power was not in fact given by way of security, and did not know of any revocation with the attorney's consent. The power, or a certified copy of it, must also be filed (Rule 82 of Land Registration Rules 1925, as substituted by Land Registration (Powers of Attorney) Rules 1986).

This declaration must also accompany an application for first registration.

(*i*)   *The Enduring Powers of Attorney Act 1985*   The purpose of this Act is to enable a principal to appoint an attorney whose authority will not be revoked by the principal becoming mentally incapable. The power must be created while the principal is of sound mind, and so long as he remains mentally capable the power operates as an ordinary power of attorney. It may confer a general authority on the attorney, or empower him to do only those things specified by the power. It must be in a prescribed form (see the Enduring Powers of Attorney (Prescribed Form) Regulations 1990 SI No. 1376). It must, for example, contain an express statement that the principal intends the power to continue notwithstanding any later mental incapacity, and the principal must confirm that he has read this statement. The power must be executed by the principal and the attorney in the presence of a witness.

When the donor becomes mentally incapable, the attorney is under a statutory duty to register the power with the court, and his authority to deal with the principal's property is suspended until the power is registered. Once the power is registered, the principal cannot revoke the power unless he recovers mental capacity *and* the court confirms the revocation. The power, although not revoked by the mental incapacity of the principal, is revoked by his death or bankruptcy.

The risk for the person dealing with the attorney is not so much the risk of *revocation* of the power, as of its invalidity, or its suspension through non-registration. The Act contains provisions to protect the person dealing with the attorney against such possibilities. The protection depends on the ignorance of these matters. Subsequent purchasers have the benefit of a conclusive presumption that the transaction between the attorney and the person dealing with him is valid if either it took place within one year of the date of the power, or the person dealing with the attorney makes a statutory declaration that he had no reason to doubt the existence of the attorney's authority to enter into the transaction.

As an exception to the rule set out in (g), a power under the 1985 Act will delegate any powers which the principal had as a trustee, even though the attorney is the sole fellow-trustee. So, if A and B were co-owners of land, a power given by A to B under the 1985 Act would enable B to sell the property effectively on his own (although in the name of A and B) and by himself to give a good receipt for the purchase price (s.3(3) of the Enduring Powers of Attorney Act 1985).

9.6   Clearing a Mortgage off the Title

In unregistered title, there are three usual ways of removing a mortgage from the title.

(*a*)   *Redemption*

The purchaser is entitled to evidence that the mortgage loan has been repaid. Section 115 of the Law of Property Act 1925 provides that a receipt for all the money due under the mortgage endorsed on the mortgage and executed by the lender will discharge the mortgaged property from all interest and principal secured by the mortgage. The section also provides that the receipt should name the person making the payment. When investigating the discharge of the mortgage, you need to check that the person named in the receipt as making the payment was the person who then owned the mortgaged property. If he was, the receipt does discharge the mortgage. If he was not, the receipt does not discharge the mortgage; instead it transfers ownership of it from the original lender to the person named as making the payment. This is why care is needed in dating the receipt. Suppose that Bella owns Blackacre, which is mortgaged to the Northlands Bank. She contracts to sell Blackacre free of the mortgage to Catherine, and the sale is completed on 6 March. Part of the purchase price is used to pay off the Bank. The Bank endorses the receipt on the mortgage deed and names Bella as having made the payment. It is correct to name Bella rather than Catherine as the arrangement in the contract was that the mortgage was to be discharged by the seller before Blackacre was conveyed to Catherine. The receipt must be dated either 6 March or earlier. If it is dated 7 March, Bella is not at that date the owner of the land. The receipt transfers the mortgage from Northlands Bank to Bella. Although in theory Bella would have taken a transfer of the mortgage, probably nothing would have to be done to clear the title. If the conveyance to Catherine said that Bella's title was 'free from incumbrances', Bella would be estopped from asserting the mortgage (see *Cumberland Court* (Brighton) Ltd v. *Taylor* [1964].

A receipt will not operate as a transfer if the receipt provides otherwise.

A building society will use the form of receipt allowed by the Building Societies Act 1986. This merely acknowledges receipt of the money. It does not name the person making the payment, and cannot operate as a transfer.

The seller's mortgage   As has already been mentioned, banks and building societies sometimes refuse to endorse the receipt in advance of completion. The purchaser's solicitor may accept undertakings as discussed in section 7.4(c).

(*b*)   *By Release*

This is discussed in Chapter 13.

(c) By Overreaching

This is discussed in section 7.4(c). A purchaser will not see a receipt on the mortgage of the mortgagee who is selling, nor on any subsequent mortgage. In unregistered title, the power of sale is implied into any mortgage by deed (s.101 of the Law of Property Act 1925).

9.7 Establishing a Title by Adverse Possession

A seller can establish that he has a good title by proving adverse possession. However, he must establish not only that he (and possibly his predecessors) have been in possession of the land, but also that the possession has extinguished the title of the true owner (see Re *Atkinson and Horsell's* contract [1912]). This means that the title of the true owner must be deduced, and the extinction of that title must be proved. It is not sufficient merely to prove possession, for however long, as the effect of the possession cannot be gauged unless it is known whom the possession has been against. If, for example, the land is subject to a ninety-nine year lease, possession for over twelve years may have extinguished the tenant's title to the lease, but will not have extinguished the landlord's title to the reversion, as time does not start running against a landlord until his right to possession arises at the end of the lease.

It will often be impossible for a seller to prove the title of the true owner, and a special condition in the contract will be required, limiting the evidence of title to, for example, a declaration by the seller that he has been in undisputed possession of the land for however long it is. If the condition specifies what evidence of title will be supplied, the seller will be in breach of contract unless he supplies that very evidence. In the case of *George Wimpey & Co Ltd* v. *Sohn* [1987] the sellers promised in the contract to give the purchaser a statutory declaration that they had been in undisputed possession of the land for twenty years. However, the sellers could not make the declaration, as their possession had been disputed. The sellers then claimed that they had been in adverse possession for twelve years, and had thereby extinguished the title of the true owners. The purchaser could refuse this title, as he had not been given the evidence of title he had been promised.

9.8 Minors

It is not usual to raise a requisition as to the age of a purchaser under a past title deed. This is because there is a *presumption* that a party to a deed is adult. If, however, it becomes known that land was conveyed to a minor then the following principles apply:

(a) A minor cannot hold a legal estate, either beneficially or as a trustee.

(b) If land is conveyed to a minor for the minor beneficially, he does obtain the equitable interest. The legal estate remains with the transferor, who holds it in trust for the minor. The transferor is under an obligation to create a settlement on the minor under the Settled Land Act 1925 (s.27 of the Settled Land Act 1925). It will be necessary to do this if the land is to be sold while the minor is still under 18. This will mean drawing up a trust deed, and a vesting deed, transferring the legal estate to the trustees of the settlement. They can then convey it, and overreach the minor's equitable interest.

If the minor has reached 18, there is no need to create a settlement. The transferor can execute a confirmatory conveyance of the legal estate.

(c) If the legal estate is conveyed to an adult and a minor as beneficial co-owners, the legal estate will vest only in the adult. He will hold it in trust for sale for himself and the minor. He can overreach the minor's interest by appointing a second trustee for sale (see Chapter 11).

9.9   A Voluntary Conveyance

A deed of gift can be set aside under the Insolvency Act 1986. A donee has therefore a voidable title. Under s.339 of the Insolvency Act 1986, a trustee in bankruptcy can apply to have the deed set aside if made within the two years prior to the presentation of the petition in bankruptcy. If the two years are past, but five years have not yet passed, it can be set aside providing the donor was insolvent at the time of the gift, or became insolvent as a result. It will be up to the trustee to prove the insolvency, unless the donee was an associate of the donor (as defined by s.435 of the Act) e.g. a spouse, in which case there is a rebuttable presumption of insolvency.

However, s.342 provides that the gift cannot be set aside if this would prejudice an interest in the property acquired in good faith without notice of the relevant circumstances.

Rider   It is doubtful if s.342 offers a purchaser of an unregistered title any protection if the purchaser buys from the donee within two years of the gift. The purchaser is bound to know that the seller acquired the property by way of gift, simply by reading the conveyance to him, so will have notice of the 'relevant circumstances'. The solution, pending the promised amendment of the Act, is to arrange title insurance. (If a registered title is given away, the donee will be registered as the new proprietor. The purchaser will not know that the transfer was by way of gift, so will be protected by s.342).

9.10 Bankruptcy of the Seller

Bankruptcy proceedings are started by the presentation of the petition in bankruptcy, usually by a creditor. If the court is satisfied that the debtor is unable to pay his debts it will make a bankruptcy order. This has the effect of vesting the bankrupt's property in the official receiver. This would be followed by an appointment of a trustee in bankruptcy. When the trustee is appointed, the bankrupt's estate vests in the trustee and it is his duty to collect and distribute the bankrupt's assets (ss. 305 and 306 of the Insolvency Act 1986).

As soon as the court makes the bankruptcy order, any disposition by the bankrupt made between the time of the presentation of the petition and the time when his assets vest in his trustee in bankruptcy is void (s.284 of the Insolvency Act 1986). Therefore, a conveyance made by the bankrupt in this period would be void. So a purchaser who is alerted as to the presentation of the petition will not accept a conveyance from the seller, but will await the appointment of the trustee and take a conveyance from him. This may mean delay, and a purchaser who is unwilling to accept the delay could terminate the contract by serving a completion notice (see Chapter 18). If the purchaser suffers loss through the delay he will have to prove in the bankruptcy. If he ends the contract, he will also have to recover his deposit. There will be no difficulty if this is held by a stakeholder. If it had been paid to the seller's agent the purchaser would have to prove in the bankruptcy, unless he can rely on his lien (see section 5.9(a)).

It is possible for the trustee in bankruptcy to disclaim the contract and as a result cease to be under any obligation to fulfil it. However, it is unlikely that the seller's trustee would do this. The equitable interest in the land would have vested in the purchaser as a result of the contract and disclaimer of the contract would not restore this interest to the trustee, who would, therefore, lose both property and price.

The purchaser should be alerted to the bankruptcy of the seller by the pre-completion search. If the title to the bankrupt's land is unregistered, the petition in bankruptcy is registrable under the Land Charges Act 1972 in the register of pending actions and the order in bankruptcy is registrable in the register of writs or orders. If the title to the bankrupt's land is registered under the Land Registration Act 1925, when the petition is presented *and* it is ascertained that the bankrupt does own the registered land, a creditor's notice will be registered in the proprietorship register. When the order in bankruptcy is made, a bankruptcy inhibition is entered preventing the registration of any disposition other than by the trustee (s.61 of the Land Registration Act 1925).

It is very unlikely, in the case both of unregistered and registered title, that the registration will not be made, as the registration is applied for by the staff of the Bankruptcy Court on the filing of the petition in bankruptcy. If it should happen, however, a purchaser would as the result of the non-registration take the property free from the claims of the creditors and of the trustee in bankruptcy (see s.6 of the Land Charges Act 1972 and s.61 of the Land Registration Act 1925).

9.11   Bankruptcy of the Purchaser

The trustee in bankruptcy could disclaim the contract if it is unprofitable (s.315 of the Insolvency Act 1986). Otherwise, he will have to complete it.

Section 284 of the Insolvency Act 1986 again presents a danger. A payment by the purchaser of the purchase price will be a disposition and therefore void, so that the trustee could reclaim the purchase price. The seller might be able to claim the protection of s.284(4) which provides that a payment received by a person before the order in bankruptcy is made, in good faith, for value and without notice that the petition has been presented, shall be valid.

9.12   The Purchaser's Pre-completion Search – The Last Stage in the Investigation of Title

(*a*)   The Search at the Central Land Registry

A search should be made against the name of every estate owner revealed by the abstract of title. The search form (K15) must:

 (i) Specify the name against which the search is to be made. If variations of a name appear in the abstract, a search should be made against every variation of the name, e.g. Edward Smith, Edward John Smith, Eddie Smith, Edward Smyth.
 (ii) Specify the county in which the land is situated. This means not just the county in which the land is now, but also any county in which it has been during the period covered by the search. The difficulty can be illustrated by looking at Sidcup. The postal address of a house in Sidcup is Sidcup, Kent. But Sidcup is in the London Borough of Bexley, not in Kent. It was however in Kent until the creation of Greater London in 1965.
(iii) Specify the years to be searched. For example, if Edward Smith bought the house on 1 June 1960, and sold it on 12 August 1964, the form would specify 1960 to 1964 inclusive.

The registry will issue an official search certificate, saying either that there is no adverse entry against the name or that an entry does exist:

e.g: Edward Smith
Dii No 40 dated 1 June 1960
Land at Greenstairs, Kent

If the purchaser's solicitor finds an unexpected entry, he can ask the seller's solicitor to certify that the entry does not affect the land contracted to be sold. (This could be because it affects other land in the county owned by this Edward Smith, or because the registration is against a different Edward Smith.) If either solicitor feels doubt on the matter, he can obtain an office copy of the entry on the register, and from this find the name and address of the person who owns the benefit of the interest that has been registered.

Advantage of an Official Search Certificate

(i) The official search certificate gives the purchaser a priority period of 15 working days from the date of the certificate. If the purchaser completes his purchase within that period, he will take free of any entry made on the register after the date of the search and before completion. Purchaser is defined to include someone who takes a lease or a mortgage. It also presumably includes anyone who claims through the purchaser. So suppose Vera owns a freehold house. She arranges to borrow money, and to grant a mortgage of her house in return. On the Monday before the completion of the mortgage, the lender obtains a certificate saying there is no entry against Vera's name. On Tuesday, Vera's husband Horatio registers a class F land charge. The mortgage is completed on the Friday. The mortgage is not subject to Horatio's rights of occupation. If Vera fails to keep up her mortgage payments, the mortgagee may exercise his statutory power of sale. The purchaser from the mortgagee also takes free from Horatio's rights. (Remember, however, that the search certificate does not protect against a last-minute registration that is made pursuant to a priority notice - see section 4.5.)

(ii) The certificate is conclusive (s.10(4) of the Land Charges Act 1972). This means that if the Registry staff makes a mistake, so that the certificate fails to reveal the D(ii) registration against the name of Edward Smith, the purchaser will take free of the covenants leaving the incumbrancer to the chance of redress from the Chief Land Registrar. There is no statutory right to compensation in these circumstances, which seems strange, but it seems that an action against the Registrar for negligence would be possible. However a purchaser can only rely upon the certificate if his application for the search was in order. If the D(ii) is properly registered against the name of Edward Smith, a certificate issued in the name of Edward Smyth, because that was the version of the name supplied by the purchaser, confers no protection against the registration. The purchaser will take subject to the covenants (see section 4.5).

Section 10(6) states that there is no liability on the part of the registry staff for a discrepancy between the particulars in the application for the search, and the search certificate itself. So if the purchaser searches against the name of Edward Smith, and receives a certificate saying there is no registration against the name Edward Smyth, the purchaser must realise that this certificate is not reliable, and ask for the search to be repeated. So when reading a certificate of search, you must ask yourself, 'Is this the name I asked for the search to be made against?'

Past Search Certificates   As a matter of courtesy, the seller's solicitor usually sends with the abstract of title any past search certificates that exist. If the protocol is being followed, the seller's solicitor must supply search certificates against the names of past owners revealed by the evidence of title. The purchaser's solicitor needs to check on the reliability of any such certificate. He must check that the search is against the correct name, that it covers the period of estate ownership and that completion took place within the priority period given by the search. Try problem 1 in the workshop section.

(b)   If the Seller (or a Past Owner) is a Limited Company, is a Search of the Companies Registry Necessary?

A search at the companies registry in the file of the company concerned may be essential. A fixed charge created by a company before 1 January 1970 could be protected against a purchaser *either* by its registration at the companies registry, *or* (if unprotected by deposit of title deeds) by its registration as a land charge. Therefore, a clear land-charge search certificate against the company's name does *not* clear away the possibility of there being a pre-1970 fixed charge capable of binding a purchaser on completion. A fixed charge created by a company after 1969 and unprotected by deposit of title deeds must be registered as a land charge if it is to bind a purchaser for value.

A floating charge created by a company at whatever date is not registrable as a land charge. The purchaser will require a certificate of non-crystallisation signed by the company secretary, or better, by the chargee, to be handed over at completion.

A search must also be made for evidence of the commencement of winding-up proceedings. In a winding-up by the court, any disposition of the company's property after the commencement of the winding-up is void (s.127 of the Insolvency Act 1986). The winding-up of a company by the court is deemed to commence at the time of the presentation of the petition for winding up (s.129(2) of the Insolvency Act 1986). The *order* for the winding-up will be filed in the company's file, but the petition is advertised in the *London Gazette*, so a search must also be made in the *London Gazette*.

It is also important to discover the appointment of an administrator or administrative receiver.

The company's file can only be searched personally, so this will be done either by the solicitor, or by a law agent instructed by the solicitor. The search gives no priority period, so should be done only shortly before completion.

(c) *A Bankruptcy Search at the Central Land Charges Registry against the Name of the Purchaser*

This has been explained in section 7.6(b). It is made on behalf of the mortgagee who is lending money for the purchase. It has nothing to do with the seller's title, and has been added here simply to complete the list of pre-completion searches.

(d) *Repetition of Local Land Charge Searches*

The solicitor acting for the purchaser's mortgagee may have instructions to repeat the local land charge search before completion if it is by then more than, say, 3 months old. This applies equally to registered title. Use of the Law Society's Search Validation Scheme would be an alternative (see section 6.2(b)).

Workshop

Attempt these problems yourself, then read specimen solutions at the end of the book.

Problem 1

You are investigating an unregistered freehold title. The seller Anthea Grumble has supplied you with a search certificate. The date of the certificate is 1 June 1969. It reveals that the search was against the names of William Faulkner and Anthea Grumble, and says that there were no subsisting entries against these names. She also supplies you with a copy of the conveyance dated 1 July 1969 by which William Faulkner conveyed the property to her. Does the search have to be repeated against these two names?

Problem 2

Alan Brown is acting for Vesta Smith, who is selling Rosedene, a large property in the village of Leadlode. The title is unregistered. The conveyance to Vesta, dated 1940, describes the property as the 'piece of land together with the dwelling-house standing thereon known as Rosedene, as the same is for the purpose of identification only outlined in red on the plan annexed hereto'. Alan used this description in the contract, and a copy of the 1940 plan and deed were sent with the draft contract to Paula Prentiss, the purchaser, for approval. Paula looked at the plan, and has told Alan that it does not show the current boundaries of Rosedene. She feels that the site of the large water-garden and summer-house is not, according to the plan, part of the property conveyed by the 1940 deed. What should Alan do?

Problem 3

You are investigating the title to Blackacre. The abstract of title gives you details of the following deeds:

1. 1 October 1973 – a conveyance on sale from Agnes to Bertha.
2. 4 December 1979 – a power of attorney given by Bertha to Sarah, her solicitor, authorising Sarah to execute all documents and deeds connected with the sale of Blackacre.
3. 23 December 1980 – a conveyance on sale from Bertha, executed by Sarah as Bertha's attorney, to Charles.
4. 14 March 1981 – grant of letters of administration to the estate of Charles, the administrator being Delia. Delia is the seller.

Is this title in order?

Problem 4

This question is taken from the Law Society Examination Winter 1985.

Your firm acts for James Brown who has just contracted to purchase 23 Chestnut Grove from the West Building Society. The contract incorporates the standard conditions. The Building Society is selling the property in exercise of the power of sale given by a mortgage dated 24 June 1982 executed in their favour by Donald Smith. The root of title is a conveyance on sale dated 6 July 1974. The XY Building Society is to lend Mr Brown £20 000 towards the purchase price of £25 000 and your firm has been instructed to act for them. You have taken over the conduct of the transaction from a colleague who is on holiday and you have just received the replies to his requisitions on title which include those shown below.

(a) Comment on these requisitions and the replies and briefly explain whether or not the replies are satisfactory. If not, state what further action is necessary and whether or not this can be left until your colleague returns from holiday.
(b) List and briefly explain the steps you will take up to the completion of the transactions once you are satisfied with the replies to the requisitions on title.

Requisitions on title

1. The conveyance of 23 August 1974 is insufficiently stamped and this must be rectified before completion.
2. A land charges search has revealed a C(i) entry against Donald Smith registered on 10 September 1982. This must be discharged on or before completion.
3. Please supply a copy of the plan annexed to the conveyance dated 4 March 1960 to which reference is made in the conveyance of 6 July 1974.

Replies to requisitions on title

1. See the special condition in the contract prohibiting requisitions on stamping of documents.
2. The Purchaser is not concerned with this.
3. This plan is annexed to a pre-root conveyance and the purchaser is not entitled to a copy.

10 Personal Representatives: The Passing of the Legal Estate on Death

10.1 The Death of a Sole Beneficial Owner

Suppose that Albert is the sole owner of the legal estate in Blackacre, and he owns it for his own benefit – i.e. not as trustee for someone else. When Albert dies, Blackacre will be owned by his personal representative. His personal representative may be his executor, i.e. the person appointed by Albert in his will to manage his affairs. If Albert has not appointed an executor, his personal representative will be the person, probably a member of his family, who applies to the probate registry for a grant of letters of administration. Both executors and administrators are known as personal representatives, and their statutory powers of disposing of Albert's assets are the same. The powers include a power of sale (s.39 of the Administration of Estates Act 1925).

10.2 Buying from the Personal Representative

If you are buying Blackacre from Albert's personal representative, when investigating his title you must check his identity, the number of personal representatives, and if any memoranda are endorsed on the grant.

(a) The Identity of the Personal Representative

Look at the grant of representation to confirm the identity of the personal representative. The grant is the only evidence that is acceptable.

An executor would actually have become the owner of Albert's property as soon as Albert died, as his position of executor derives from his appointment by the will. Despite this, you must not complete the purchase until the executor has obtained a grant of probate of the will, naming him as executor. The grant is conclusive evidence of his status. The will is *not*. (Remember the will may turn out to be void, or to have been revoked by a later one. Of course, the will may be challenged after probate has been granted, and as a result, the grant of probate itself revoked, but a dealing with an executor who has obtained a grant usually remains valid despite the later revocation of the grant, s.37 and s.55(1)(xviii) of the Administration of Estates Act 1925). It is possible to enter into the contract with the executor before probate, but the grant must be obtained before completion.

An administrator would not have become the owner of Albert's property, nor would he have any powers over it, until he had obtained the grant of letters of administration. The point is that it is *the grant* which makes him the administrator. Therefore, both contract and completion should wait until the grant is obtained.

(b)   The Number of Personal Representatives

The grant may be to a single personal representative. If so, it is perfectly safe to deal with him alone. He can on his own give a good receipt for the purchase money (s.27(2) of the Law of Property Act 1925). (Do not confuse a personal representative with a trustee for sale. A receipt must be given by at least two trustees for sale, but personal representatives and trustees for sale are different animals.)

The grant may be to two or more personal representatives. The authority of personal representatives to *convey* is joint *only*, i.e. they must *all* execute a conveyance or assent if it is to be valid (s.68 of the Administration of Estates Act 1925). (Their authority to *contract* to convey is several, i.e. they can act independently of one another, so in theory, if A and B are the two personal representatives, A could sign the contract alone, and thereby bind himself and B to convey.)

(c)   Memoranda Endorsed on the Grant

When looking at the grant, check that no statement has been written on it, to the effect that Blackacre has already been transferred by the personal representative to someone else. If there is such a memorandum, if you have any sense you will realise that the personal representative can no longer transfer Blackacre to you. Completion will not take place, and you will turn hurriedly to Chapter 18 to consider remedies for breach of contract.

If there is *no* such memorandum, this is probably for the simple reason that the personal representative has *not* already disposed of Blackacre to someone else and that is why he now feels free to convey it to you.

However, the interesting thing is that if the personal representative *has* already disposed of the legal estate to someone else (let us call him Ben), and Ben has failed to put a memorandum warning of this on the grant, then, in some circumstances, when the personal representative later conveys to you, you *will* get the legal estate, and Ben will lose it.

The reason for this is s.36(6) of the Administration of Estates Act 1925. There is now set out a simple, and *so far as it goes*, accurate version of s.36(6) – if a personal representative conveys the legal estate in Blackacre to a purchaser for money, and the conveyance contains a statement that the personal representative has not made any previous conveyance or assent in favour of someone else and the purchaser relies on that statement, then the conveyance will vest the legal estate in the purchaser, despite the fact that the personal representative has already passed the legal estate on to a beneficiary of the will or intestacy, provided that the beneficiary has not by then put a memorandum about the disposition to him on the grant. The disposition to the beneficiary is overridden. The personal representative cannot override any earlier disposition to another purchaser for money, be he a purchaser from the personal representative himself, or from the beneficiary. So the' protection given to a purchaser from a personal representative by s.36(6) is really very narrow.

If you think this through slowly, the following points will occur to you:

1. any sensible beneficiary, having had the legal estate vested in him by the personal representative, will immediately insist on a memorandum about it being put on the grant. This makes it impossible for him to lose the legal estate to a later purchaser for money from the personal representative. Section 36 gives the beneficiary the right to insist on this. The memorandum does not have to be in any particular form; it will probably say something like 'By an assent dated . . . , Blackacre was transferred by the personal representatives named in this grant to Ben Brown.'

2. any sensible purchaser who is buying from a personal representative will:
   - when drafting the conveyance to himself, put in a statement (usually a recital – see section 13.2(b)) that the seller (i.e. the personal representative) has not made any previous assent or conveyance in respect of the property being conveyed. Without this statement, s.36(6) does not apply.
   - on completion, ask to see the original grant to check there is no memorandum on it. He must see the original, and not allow himself to be fobbed off with an office copy, which for this purpose is useless;
   - after completion, put a memorandum on the grant about the conveyance to himself. This is said to be good conveyancing procedure, in all circumstances. It certainly is in the case of a sale of part of the land owned by the deceased, when the personal representative is retaining the deeds. In this case, a memorandum about the sale should be endorsed either on the conveyance to the deceased, as in any sale of part, or on the grant. However, failure on the part of a purchaser from the personal representative to put a memorandum of the sale on the grant cannot prejudice his title by virtue of s.36(6). Remember that a personal representative cannot override a previous conveyance to a purchaser for money, and if you are still in doubt look at problem 3 at the end of this chapter.

3. s.36(6) is perhaps relevant only to unregistered title. If the title is registered, the problem will be solved by provisions of the Land Registration Act 1925. Again for an explanation, look at problem 3.

10.3   The Use of an Assent

Once the personal representative has the grant, he can convey the legal
estate. Nothing further is needed if he intends to convey in the capacity of
personal representative. The contract will say that he *will* convey as a
personal representative, and the conveyance will say that he *does* convey as
a personal representative. No assent will be needed.

An assent is needed (a) to transfer ownership from the personal
representative to a beneficiary, or (b) to change the capacity in which the
personal representative holds the estate.

(a)   To Transfer Ownership from the Personal Representative to a Beneficiary

This is an area where it is easy to become confused, and it really may be
helpful to look first of all at the pre-1926 law, and then to realise the nature
of the changes made by the Administration of Estates Act 1925.

Suppose that Albert died in 1924. His will appointed Edward as his
executor, and gave the legal estate in Blackacre to Ben. On Albert's death
two titles to Blackacre were created. Ben had a title to Blackacre by virtue
of the gift in the will. That is why, if Ben had decided to sell the property,
the will would have appeared on the abstract. However, the death also gave
the executor a title to Blackacre, for the purpose of administering the
estate. This meant that if, for instance, money had to be raised to pay the
deceased's debts, Edward could have sold Blackacre, and so defeated Ben's
title. The title of the executor was the better or 'paramount' title. If it had
become clear that the executor would not need to sell Blackacre, he could
have allowed the gift to the beneficiary to take effect. In other words he
could have 'assented' to the gift. The use of the word 'assent' for what the
executor was doing made sense before 1926 as it means 'consent'. The
executor consented to the gift, and so released his own superior title to the
property. As the assent was not in any way a conveyance to the beneficiary,
it could be informal, and the mere fact that a beneficiary was allowed to
take possession could indicate assent to the gift. When you consider the
nature of a pre-1926 assent, it becomes clear why an administrator could
not assent when the deceased died intestate. There was no gift to which to
assent, so the administrator would convey the legal estate to the beneficiary
by deed.

In 1925, the Administration of Estates Act made considerable changes.
An assent made after 1925 is quite different from an assent made pre-1926,
and it is a pity that this was not made quite clear by giving a different name
to the thing.

On a death after 1925, no title is conferred by the will on the beneficiary.
This is why a will of a person who dies after 1925 no longer appears on the
abstract of title to prove change of ownership of the legal estate. The title
belongs only to the personal representative. If he conveys the legal estate to
a purchaser, he will use a deed of conveyance or a land registry transfer. If

a sale is not necessary, the personal representative will wish to vest the legal estate in the person entitled to it under the terms of the will or under the intestacy rules. The document that he will use is what is now called an assent. You can see now how an assent has changed its character. It is now actually a document of transfer, passing ownership from the personal representative to the person in whose favour the assent is made. As it does transfer ownership, it can no longer be allowed to be informal; and it can be used by administrators as well as executors, because it no longer depends upon there being a gift in a will.

Form of a Post-1925 Assent   Section 36(4) demands that an assent that relates to a *legal estate* in land be in writing, be signed by the personal representatives (i.e. it need not be delivered as a deed) and name the person in whose favour it is made.

An assent says something like 'I Alice Grace as the personal representative of May East as personal representative assent to the vesting in fee simple of Blackacre in Ann Hyde and I acknowledge the right of Ann Hyde to production of the probate of the will of May East and to delivery of copies thereof. Signed this 4 day of July 1989.'

The assent is by deed if the beneficiary gives a covenant to the personal representative, e.g. an indemnity covenant.

So an abstract of title tracing a change of ownership of the legal estate by virtue of death would now, for example, give details of the following deeds and events:

1 January 1960 Conveyance of Blackacre by W to X.

1 January 1980 Statement that X died on this date.

1 July 1980 Grant of probate to Y + Z.
> [If you were buying from Y + Z as personal representatives, the abstract would end here.]

1 January 1981 Assent signed by Y + Z, saying that they assent to the vesting of Blackacre in Ben.

1 January 1981 A memorandum of the assent endorsed on the grant of probate.

On this basis would we be happy to buy from Ben? Yes, because on the evidence we have here, Ben could convey to us as beneficial owner. If there were no memorandum on the grant, we would have cause for concern (see problem 3).

Points which Might Occur to You

(i) Do we need to see X's death certificate? Realistically, the answer is 'no'. A grant of probate of his will, or a grant of letters of administration to his estate is usually taken as being satisfactory evidence that X really is dead.

(ii) How do we know that Ben was the right person to be given the legal estate? We do not know, and we will not usually enquire. The reason for this is s.36(7) of the Administration of Estates Act 1925, which says that the assent itself is 'sufficient evidence' that the assent has been made to the correct person, and has been made upon the correct trusts, if any. So we can take an assent at face value. That is why we are safe in buying from Ben, and why we will assume he is a beneficial owner, as the assent makes no mention of the legal estate being transferred to him on any sort of trust. If we did have reason to suspect that Ben were not the person entitled to have the legal estate passed to him, or that he ought to be holding it on some sort of trust, *then* we could no longer take the assent at its face value, and we would have to enquire about its correctness. If we did not do this, we would risk being fixed with constructive notice of other beneficiaries' rights. This is because s.36 says that the assent is 'sufficient' evidence, but it does not say it is 'conclusive' evidence. So no enquiry is made *unless* we have cause for suspicion (see Re *Duce* and *Boots Cash Chemists (Southern) Ltd's* Contract [1937]).

(iii) What if the title were registered? The use of the assent is exactly the same. The events would be, for example:

(aa) X is registered proprietor.

(bb) X dies. There is a grant of representation to Y + Z. They have a choice, so,

(cc) *either* Y + Z register themselves as the new proprietors, by producing an office or certified copy of the grant to the Chief Land Registrar. Y + Z could then sign the assent in favour of Ben.

or Y + Z could choose not to be registered. Indeed, there is little point in the personal representatives registering themselves as proprietors if they intend to assent to a beneficiary, or convey to a purchaser, within a reasonable time. Y + Z could sign an assent to a beneficiary, who could register himself by producing a copy of the grant, and the assent, and the land certificate.

(b)   *To Change the Capacity in which the Personal Representative Holds the Legal Estate to that of Trustee for Sale, or Beneficial Owner*

Suppose that Albert's will says 'I appoint X and Y as the executors and trustees of this my will. I give Blackacre to X and Y to hold on trust for sale, the proceeds of sale to be held by them on trust for my widow for life, and after her death for my daughter Sara absolutely.'

On Albert's death, Blackacre vests in X and Y as *personal representatives*. If they have to sell it, that is the capacity in which they will convey. When X and Y have administered the estate, they will be ready to change their capacity to that of trustees for sale. They must change their capacity as the final step in the administration of that asset, as there can be difficulties if a personal representative dies with property still vested in him as such (see section 10.4). Re *King's Will Trusts* [1964] decided that s.36(4) of the Administration of Estates Act 1925 (which demands a written assent) applies not only when a personal representative is actually going to transfer ownership of the legal estate, but also when he is going to retain it but wishes to change the capacity in which he holds it. So in order to become trustees for sale, X and Y must sign a written assent in their own favour, e.g. 'We X and Y hereby assent to the vesting of Blackacre in ourselves, upon trust for sale.' Until this written assent is made, there is no change of capacity, and X and Y continue to hold the legal estate as personal representatives.

A similar case would arise if Albert's will said 'I give all my property to X, and appoint him the executor of my will.' X holds the legal estate in Blackacre as personal representative. He does not hold it as beneficial owner until he signs a written assent in his own favour. It is important that this is done if he intends to keep Blackacre, as if he dies with the legal estate still vested in him as personal representative, his own personal representatives may not be able to deal with Blackacre at his death (see problem 2). Even if he intends to sell Blackacre, although he could convey as personal representative, a purchaser might prefer to take a conveyance from him as beneficial owner, rather than personal representative as wider covenants for title would be implied (see Chapter 19), and if the purchaser persists in this point, an assent will again be necessary.

10.4 The Death of a Personal Representative

A personal representative is himself mortal. If he dies before he has finished administering the estate, there may be difficulties if he is the sole personal representative.

Suppose that Albert dies, and X and Y are his personal representatives. Albert's assets are vested in X and Y jointly, so that if X dies, Y will have the whole of Albert's property vested in him alone, and he can happily continue administering Albert's assets as the sole surviving personal representative. So X's death, although a serious blow to his many admirers, has not caused any difficulty in the administration of Albert's estate.

Suppose now that Y dies, while still in the course of administering the estate, so that on his death there are still assets vested in him as personal representative.

The difficulty now is that Albert has run out of personal representatives. The estate can only be administered by new personal representatives *of Albert*. Where will these new personal representatives come from? There are two possibilities:

1. That there exists what is known as a 'chain of representation' under s.7 of the Administration of Estates Act 1925. It may save you from error

if you think of it as a chain of *executorship*. Section 7 provides that on the death of a sole, or last surviving proving executor, *his* proving executor takes over his unfinished executorship. The chain only forms through *proving executors* (i.e. who obtain probate. It is a general rule that executors who are appointed by the will but who do not obtain probate can be ignored.) It only forms through the death of the last proving executor to die. It is best explained through an example. Suppose Albert dies, and Betty and Carol obtain probate of his will. If Betty dies before all of Albert's assets are administered, you do not consider the chain of executorship at all. Albert still has an executor, and Carol will simply carry on alone. Betty's personal representatives do not come into the picture at all. On Carol's death, as she is the last surviving executor of Albert, you will look to see if any of her executors obtain probate of her will. Suppose she has appointed David as her executor, and he obtains probate. The effect of s.7 is that when David becomes Carol's executor, he automatically becomes Albert's executor as well, with power to dispose of his assets. He does not need a further grant to Albert's estate.

If Carol had died without appointing an executor, so that David had been her administrator, having applied for a grant of letters of administration, then David would not acquire any power over Albert's assets. Remember, it has to be a chain of *executorship*.

2. If a chain of executorship does not exist (for instance, as in the last example, if either Betty and Carol, or David, were administrators) the only way that Albert could acquire a new personal representative is by a new grant of representation to his estate. This would be a grant of letters of administration (if relevant, with will annexed) '*de bonis non administratis*' – that is, it gives the person who obtains the grant the power to deal only with the unadministered part of Albert's estate. Who will be entitled to this grant? It depends on the Non-contentious Probate Rules 1987. Their effect can be summed up very briefly by saying that the grant will be to a person who is in some way entitled to the assets. The grant must be made to create the new personal representative. Without it, no one has power to pass title to the assets.

Workshop

Attempt these problems yourself, then read specimen solutions at the end of the book.

Problem 1

You have contracted to buy an unregistered title from Eric. He has contracted to convey it as beneficial owner, and to trace title from a conveyance on sale dated 1 April 1970. The abstract gives details of the following documents:

1 April 1970 Alan conveys as beneficial owner to Bertha.

1 April 1982 Bertha dies.

1 April 1983 Grant of probate to Charles and David, the executors of Bertha's will.

1 April 1985 Conveyance on sale by David to Eric. Is Eric's title acceptable?

Problem 2

We have contracted to buy Blackacre from Fred. The abstract gives details of the following transactions:

1 April 1975 Alice conveys Blackacre as beneficial owner to Bill.

1 April 1980 Edward conveys it as personal representative to Fred.

The recitals in the 1980 conveyance make the following statements to explain why Edward is the seller:

 (i) that Bill died in 1977, and a grant of letters of administration was made to his wife Carol;

 (ii) that Carol died in 1978, and a grant of probate of her will was made to Edward.

Was Edward able to convey Blackacre to Fred in 1980?

Problem 3

Consider the following abstract of title:

1970 Albert conveys Blackacre to Bryn as beneficial owner.

1972 Bryn dies.

1973 Grant of probate of his will to Cathy and Drew.

1974 An assent, signed by Cathy and Drew, in favour of Elaine.

1980 Elaine conveys to Fred.

Should we raise a requisition on Fred's title?

11 A Sale by Trustees for Sale

11.1 How Do You Know the Sellers are Trustees for Sale?

Suppose you are buying an unregistered title. You are buying it from Abel and Bertha. You read a copy of the conveyance to them. A clause in it says 'the purchasers declare that they hold the property hereby conveyed on trust to sell the same (with power to postpone sale), and to hold the net proceeds of sale, (and pending sale, the income of the land) on trust . . .'. It does not require a great mental effort to deduce from this that Abel and Bertha hold the legal estate as trustees for sale. The trust to sell is expressly declared.

Suppose instead that you read the conveyance and it says 'the seller . . . hereby conveys . . . Blackacre to hold unto Abel and Bertha in equal shares'. This also tells you that Abel and Bertha hold the legal estate as trustees for sale. Why? It is because they co-own the beneficial interest. When two or more purchasers co-own the equitable interest, then if no express trust for sale of the legal estate is declared, the legal estate vests in them on an implied trust for sale (ss.34 – 36 of the Law of Property Act 1925). They will always hold the legal estate as joint tenants, whether they hold the equitable interest as joint tenants or tenants in common.

If the conveyance had been to Abel, Bertha, Charles, Deirdre and Edna in equal shares, the difficulty would have arisen that although the equitable interest is owned by five people, a legal estate can only be held by four. The legal estate would vest in the first four adult co-owners named in the conveyance (s.34 of the Law of Property Act 1925). So although the conveyance simply says that the land is conveyed to the five people, it has the same effect as if it read 'to A B C and D on trust to sell, proceeds of sale to be held by them on trust for A B C D and E equally'. You can see from this that if you were buying the legal estate, you would need a conveyance signed only by A B C and D. E does not own the legal estate. He is sacrificed in the interests of limiting the number of estate owners, but he has not lost his share of the beneficial interest, which is what really matters.

Now suppose that the title is registered. When Abel and Bertha bought from the then registered proprietor, the transfer would either have declared an express trust for sale, or have disclosed the circumstances which gave rise to an implied trust for sale, e.g. the co-ownership of the beneficial interest by the two of them. Abel and Bertha, as the trustees for sale, are entitled to apply to the Registrar to have themselves registered as proprietors. As they are trustees for sale they are under a duty to apply for a restriction to be entered on the register. (The one exception to this is where they hold on trust for sale for themselves as beneficial joint tenants – see later). The restriction will read 'No disposition by a sole proprietor of the land (not being a trust corporation) under which capital arises is to be registered except under an order of the Registrar or of the court' (Land Registration Rules 1989).

If they do not apply for the entry of the restriction, the Registrar is nevertheless under a duty to enter it whenever it is clear to him that a trust for sale exists (s.58(3) of the Land Registration Act 1925).

The restriction reflects the fact that a sale by a sole trustee for sale has no overreaching effect, so should not be accepted by the purchaser.

If Abel and Bertha, under an expressly declared trust for sale, hold on trust for people other than themselves, they will only have those powers to deal with the legal estate which statute gives them (see s.28 of the Law of Property Act 1925). They have a power of sale, but only limited powers of leasing and mortgaging. It is a principle of registered conveyancing that the registered proprietor has *unlimited* powers of disposition, unless an entry on the register says otherwise. If their powers are limited, they should apply for a further restriction to be entered on the register, preventing the registration of unauthorised leases or mortgages.

It is possible for a conveyance or transfer to trustees to increase their powers to deal with the legal estate to those of a sole beneficial owner, i.e. their powers become unlimited. If this has been done, this second restriction will not appear on the register.

If Abel and Bertha are holding a trust for sale for *themselves* as *tenants in common*, the first restriction, preventing a sale by the sole survivor, will appear on the register, again reflecting the fact that a ˜sole trustee cannot make good title. However, as in this case the trustees are also the only beneficiaries, their powers of dealing with the legal estate are unlimited, as what they cannot do by reason of their powers as trustees, they can do by virtue of their beneficial ownership. The second restriction will not, therefore, appear on the register.

If Abel and Bertha hold on trust for themselves as beneficial joint tenants, there will be no restriction at all on the register. This reflects the fact that the sole survivor of Abel and Bertha will be able to sell by herself/ himself, without any need to appoint another trustee.

Note that a trust for sale can be created by will, and is implied on an intestacy. The vesting of the legal estate in the personal representatives, and later in the trustees for sale, is dealt with in Chapter 10.

11.2 Who Are the Current Trustees?

If you are buying a legal estate that is held by trustees for sale, the first obvious question to ask yourself is 'who are the current trustees?' In unregistered conveyancing, the original trustees are identified by reading the conveyance which created the trust for sale. In registered conveyancing, the original trustees will have been registered as the registered proprietors. Of course, trustees, like all mortal things, are transient. They come and go. The important thing is to check that when a trustee goes, he parts with all his interest in the legal estate, and that when a new trustee arrives, the estate is vested in him.

11.3   Changes of Trustees

(a)   Death of a Trustee Leaving At Least One Trustee Behind

Suppose that Alice, Beryl and Catherine are the three trustees when the trust for sale first arises. The legal estate is vested in them jointly, no matter how they, or anyone else, might share the equitable interest. If Alice dies, the legal estate remains vested in the surviving trustees. (Remember that it is a characteristic of a *joint* tenancy, as opposed to a tenancy in common, that when a joint tenant dies, the surviving joint tenant(s) continue to own the entire interest.) Beryl and Catherine, therefore, can convey the legal estate. As there are two trustees for sale, the effect of the conveyance will be to overreach the equitable interests, so that they become claims against the purchase price. The only thing that the purchaser has to check is that Alice really is dead. (If she is still alive, a conveyance or transfer by Beryl and Catherine alone will be void; see later.) This is done by seeing a copy of her death certificate.

Note that in registered conveyancing, Beryl and Catherine could have had Alice's name removed from the proprietorship register by sending to the Registrar a copy of the death certificate (Rule 172, Land Registration Rules 1925). They need not do this. They can prove Alice's death to a purchaser from them by a copy of the death certificate, and when registering the transfer the purchaser will send to the Registrar the Land Certificate, copy of death certificate, and the transfer signed by Beryl and Catherine.

Appointment of New Trustee   Should Beryl now die, Catherine will be left as sole trustee, owning the legal estate. She cannot sell alone, as a conveyance by a single trustee has no overreaching effect, so another trustee must be appointed to act with her. (As an exception to this general rule, she could sell alone if she and Alice and Beryl had been not only joint tenants of the legal estate, but also the only joint tenants of the beneficial interest; see later.)

Who Can Appoint this New Trustee?   An expressly created trust for sale may give a particular person a power to appoint new trustees. Otherwise, for both express and implied trusts for sale, it is the surviving trustee(s) who can appoint the new one (s.36 of the Trustee Act 1925). In other words the new trustee will be appointed by Catherine.

Method of Appointment   In unregistered title, a trustee can be appointed by writing, but a *deed* of appointment should be used. This is to take advantage of s.40 of the Trustee Act 1925, which provides that if a new trustee is appointed by deed, the deed vests the trust property in the people who become, or are, the trustees after the appointment, without any need for a separate conveyance. For example, Catherine can execute a deed saying that she appoints Deirdre to be the second trustee. The effect of that will be that the legal estate will be vested in Catherine and Deirdre.

If the title is registered, the appointment of Deirdre as a new trustee will not in itself vest the legal estate in her. The legal estate will vest when, after seeing the appointment, the Registrar adds Deirdre's name to the proprietorship register. The appointment can be carried out by Catherine executing a Land Registry transfer to herself and Deirdre. Notice that if Deirdre is appointed solely for the purpose of selling the land, it is not necessary that her name be entered on the register before completion. The purchaser will be registered as proprietor by including in the application copies of the death certificates of Alice and Beryl, the appointment of Deirdre, and the transfer signed by Catherine and Deirdre.

(b) Death of the Sole, or Last Surviving, Trustee for Sale

Suppose Catherine dies, without having appointed another trustee? There are three ways in which title could now be made to the legal estate:

 (i) Section 36 of the Trustee Act 1925 provides that on the death of a sole trustee, her personal representative(s) can appoint new trustees. So suppose Catherine's executor is Dorothy, then Dorothy could appoint Edna and Florence as new trustees of the trust. Edna and Florence could then convey the legal estate to a purchaser.

 (ii) Sections 18(2) and (3) of the Trustee Act 1925 provide that on the death of a sole trustee, her personal representatives can actually carry out the trust, i.e. stand in for her and convey the legal estate to a purchaser. However, because the personal representatives, when they do this, are acting in the role of trustees for sale, rather than as personal representatives, there must be at least two of them if the conveyance is to overreach the equitable interests. So, in the above example, Dorothy could not sell the property herself; she could only appoint the new trustees. If Catherine had left two executors, say Dorothy and Deborah, they could themselves exercise the trust by conveying the legal estate under s.18(2).

 (iii) If Alice, Bertha and Catherine had been holding on trust for themselves as beneficial joint tenants, then Catherine's personal representative(s) could make title, relying in unregistered conveyancing on the Law of Property (Joint Tenants) Act 1964, or in registered title, on the absence of any restriction on the register (see later).

(c) Retirement of a Trustee

A trustee might wish to retire from the trust whilst still alive. For example, Alice, Bertha and Catherine might be partners in the running of a grocery business. The shop premises would be owned by them jointly on trust for sale. They would probably own the equitable interest as tenants in common. Alice might wish to retire from the partnership and Bertha and Catherine agree to buy her out. Alice must divest herself of all interest in the legal estate, otherwise, if Bertha and Catherine later wish to sell it, Alice would have to be traced to her retirement home, as her signature to the conveyance or transfer would be needed. If the title to the shop is unregistered, the retirement will be by deed and the effect of s.40 of the Trustee Act 1925 will be that the legal estate will vest in Bertha and Catherine. If the title is registered, the simplest procedure is again for the three registered proprietors to sign a transfer in favour of Bertha and Catherine. On registration of the transfer, the name of Alice will be removed from the register.

11.4 How Many Trustees Are There?

Having identified your current trustees, you must now consider how many there are.

If there are two or more, you must remember that their powers are joint. In other words *all* the trustees must sign the conveyance or transfer. If the legal estate is vested in three trustees, you will not obtain it if only two of these three trustees convey it to you. If there are three registered proprietors of the registered title, all three must sign the Land Registry transfer. Otherwise it is totally void.

If the conveyance is by all the trustees, and there are at least two of them, a conveyance (or mortgage) by them will overreach the interests of the beneficiaries, which become claims only against the purchase price (ss.2 and 27 of the Law of Property Act 1925). If there is only one trustee for sale, then generally, as has been said, a second trustee for sale must be appointed. A conveyance by a single trustee will pass the legal estate to the purchaser, but will not overreach the equitable interests.

11.5 Consents

It is possible for the person creating the trust for sale to say that the trustees can only sell if they first obtain the consent of some person named by the settlor.

For example, a wealthy testator may in her will give her property to her husband for his lifetime and provide that on his death the capital is to go to the children. As a life interest is being created, the legal estate in any land will have to be settled. The testator will usually choose a trust for sale so the legal estate will be held by trustees for sale on trust for the husband and children. (If a trust for sale is not created, the land will be settled under the Settled Land Act 1925.) The power of sale is, therefore, exercisable by the trustees, but the testator may wish to ensure that her husband will have some control over whether or not the family home is sold. One solution is to appoint the husband as one of the trustees. The will may also say that the husband's consent must be obtained to any sale.

If there is a requirement that a consent be obtained, the purchaser from trustees must ensure that the consent is obtained, otherwise he will not get a good title. (In registered conveyancing the need for consent will appear as a restriction on the register.)

However, s.26 of the Law of Property Act 1925 may make life easier for the purchaser. First, it says that if the person whose consent is necessary is under age, or mentally incapable, the purchaser need not obtain that consent. Second, if that still leaves the purchaser faced with the task of obtaining more than two consents, only two need be obtained. The provision does not exist to make life easier for the trustees. If they sell without obtaining all consents they are breaking their trust.

11.6   Investigating the Equitable Interests

Usually, a purchaser has no need to investigate the equitable interests behind a trust for sale, as the conveyance by the trustees for sale will overreach the interests. If, however, the trustees dispose of the legal estate to the beneficiaries, then when the title is examined subsequently, the equitable interests do have to be brought into the title.

Suppose, for example, that Bill and Ben hold the legal estate on trust for sale for Xavier for life, remainder to Yvonne absolutely. On Xavier's death, Bill and Ben may convey the legal estate to Yvonne. A later purchaser from her will know that this conveyance had no overreaching effect, as it was not a *sale* by the trustees. The purchaser will have to investigate the equitable interests to check that Yvonne was entitled to have the legal estate conveyed to her. Otherwise he risks having constructive notice of outstanding equitable interests.

If the title is registered, it is the Registrar who will have to be satisfied that Yvonne should be registered as proprietor without any restriction appearing in the proprietorship register.

11.7   Co-ownership of the Equitable Interest

(a)   The Equitable Interest

If two people are, between them, buying a house, they must decide how they are to own the equitable interest. There are two possibilities. They could own it as beneficial *joint* tenants. If people own property jointly, it is as if they have been fused together to form a single unit. Between them there is what is called the right of survivorship. When one joint tenant dies the entire property belongs to the survivor(s). This is why a joint tenancy is considered apt for a married couple. If H and W own property jointly, say a joint bank account, then on the husband's death, the wife automatically owns the entire property. Her entitlement does not depend on her husband's will. For this reason, she does not need to get probate of her husband's will in order to prove her ownership of the property. She merely has to prove that he is dead, by producing his death certificate.

The other possibility is that the couple could own the equitable interest as tenants in common, i.e. they own shares in the property, although the property has not as yet been physically divided between them. There is no right of survivorship in a tenancy in common, so when one tenant in common dies, his share passes to his personal representative, and from him to the beneficiary named in the will, or the next-of-kin under the intestacy rules.

(b)   The Legal Estate

They must also decide as to who is to own the legal estate. If X and Y own the equitable interest, whether jointly or in common, and are both adult, it is common sense that they should both own the legal estate. This makes it impossible for either to sell the house without the consent of the other, as both signatures are needed on the conveyance. So the conveyance or transfer to X and Y:

 (i) will say that the legal estate is conveyed to them;
 (ii) will say how they own the equitable interest, i.e. either jointly or in shares, and if in shares the size of each share;
(iii) may declare an express trust for sale of the legal estate. We have already seen that if an express trust for sale is not created, a statutory trust for sale will be implied;
(iv) may increase the statutory powers of dealing with the legal estate.

So, as a tiresome recap, you must appreciate the following matters, otherwise you will always be in a muddle in this area:

1. If you read a conveyance that says the legal estate in Blackacre is conveyed to Ann and Bill, as beneficial joint tenants, the result is that Ann and Bill hold the *legal estate jointly*, on trust for sale, and they hold the proceeds of sale, or pending sale the income of the land, on trust for themselves as *beneficial joint tenants*. So that on Bill's death Ann owns the entire legal estate and, prima facie, the entire equitable interest. The provisions of Bill's will are irrelevant to the ownership of Blackacre.
2. If the conveyance says the legal estate is conveyed to Ann and Bill to hold in equal shares, the result is that they hold the legal estate *jointly* (remember that co-owners always hold the legal estate jointly) on trust for sale, but that they hold the *equitable interest as tenants in common*. The word 'equally' shows that they have *shares* and so cannot hold the

equitable interest jointly. On Bill's death, Ann will own the entire legal estate, but only half the beneficial interest. The other half is owned by Bill's personal representatives. The provisions of Bill's will are relevant to the ownership of his share of the equitable interest, but still irrelevant to the ownership of the legal estate.

3. If registered title is transferred to Ann and Bill, they will apply for registration of the transfer. The Registrar will read the transfer. The transfer will say how Ann and Bill own the beneficial interest. It may say expressly that the survivor of them can give a valid receipt for capital money (i.e. that they are joint tenants) or that the survivor cannot give a good receipt for capital money (i.e. that they are tenants in common). If the Registrar believes them to be joint tenants of the beneficial interest he will not put a restriction on the register. Otherwise, he will enter a restriction, preventing a sale by the survivor of Ann and Bill.

Bear this in mind when you read the following section.

11.8 A Conveyance or Transfer by the Sole Surviving Co-owner

The problem is this – Ann and Bill hold the legal estate on trust for sale for themselves. Do you accept a conveyance or transfer from Ann alone after Bill's death?

(a) Ann and Bill Hold on Trust for Themselves as Tenants in Common

You do *not* accept a conveyance from Ann alone. She now holds the legal estate on trust for herself and Bills's personal representative. Again, if the title is registered, there will be a restriction on the register. The solution is for Ann to appoint another trustee.

It may be, of course, that Bill left his share of the beneficial interest in the house to Ann by his will, so that in fact she does now own the entire beneficial interest. However, title should not be proved to a purchaser by tracing ownership of the equitable interest, and the purchaser should not agree to make the investigation. Never mind who now owns Bill's interest, the interest should be overreached. Bill's will is only of relevance to the trustees, when they divide the proceeds of sale. (Note that if the title is registered, and Ann has succeeded to the ownership of Bill's share, she could apply to the Registrar for the removal of Bill's name from the register, and for the removal of the restriction. She would have to provide the Registrar with a copy of Bill's death certificate, and a statutory declaration as to how she became solely and beneficially interested. Once the restriction is removed from the register, a purchaser would accept a conveyance from Ann alone.)

(b)   *Ann and Bill Hold on Trust for Themselves as Beneficial Joint Tenants*

This is the only occasion when the purchaser would consider taking a conveyance from Ann alone. *Prima facie*, on Bill's death, because the right of survivorship applied to both the legal estate and the beneficial interest, Ann became sole beneficial owner. Why only *prima facie*?

The difficulty is that the joint tenancy of the equitable interest can be severed and changed into a tenancy in common. This destroys the right of survivorship. There are various ways in which Bill could have severed the equitable joint tenancy before he died: for example, by selling his equitable interest, by serving written notice on Ann under s.36 of the Law of Property Act 1925, by going bankrupt, or by mutual agreement with Ann. Suppose, for instance, that Bill, before his death, served a notice on Ann, saying that henceforth they were to be tenants in common of the equitable interest. The result would be that Ann and Bill would remain joint tenants of the legal estate, as it is impossible to sever the legal joint tenancy, but they would become tenants in common of the equitable interest. Bill could make sure that the severance came to the notice of any prospective purchaser. In registered title, he could apply to the Registrar for the restriction to go on the register, ensuring that Ann could not transfer the house after his death without appointing another trustee. In unregistered title, he could write a memorandum on the conveyance to himself and Ann, saying that the severance had taken place. This again would prevent Ann from selling the property after his death without appointing a second trustee (see the later discussion of the Law of Property (Joint Tenants) Act 1964).

Bill, however, might do nothing at all, so that on his death Ann would look like a beneficial owner, but would in fact be a trustee for sale holding on trust for herself and for Bill's estate. Traditionally, the answer to the *possibility* of severance of the equitable interest was always to insist that Ann appoint a second trustee, so that if there were a half share of the equitable interest to be overreached, this would be done. It is now usually unnecessary to appoint a second trustee, for the following reason.

Registered Title   When Ann and Bill were first registered as proprietors, there would have been no restriction on the register, because of their *joint* ownership of the beneficial interest. So there is nothing on the register to forbid a transfer by Ann alone after Bill's death. A purchaser from Ann need only see Bill's death certificate, to check that he really is dead, and not just locked away somewhere in a cupboard.

Suppose Bill had severed the joint tenancy of the equitable interest before he died? Suppose when he was alive he sold his equitable interest to Xerxes? Or suppose he served notice of severance on Ann and then left his half-interest to Xerxes in his will. Xerxes could then have applied for the entry of a restriction on the register, or, if Ann would not cooperate in this, he could have lodged a caution. Either would alert the purchaser to the situation and lead to the appointment of a second trustee. Suppose Xerxes does not do this. He is then in the position of having an unprotected minor interest. Remember section 3.13. A transferee for value takes free of an unprotected minor interest. That is why a purchaser is safe in taking a transfer from Ann alone. The absence of a restriction or caution generally ensures that an interest belonging to someone other than Ann will fail to bind the purchaser. However, remember that a transferee for value *does* take subject to overriding interests. If Xerxes has moved in, his interest will be overriding under s.70(1)(g) of the Land Registration Act 1925. So it is the absence of an entry on the register *and* the absence of anyone else in occupation that enables the purchaser to buy from Ann alone in complete safety.

Unregistered Title   If a purchaser buys from Ann alone after Bill's death, he cannot claim that Bill's interest has been overreached. However, there remains the traditional defence of a purchase against an equitable interest, namely that of being a *bona fide* purchaser for value of the legal estate without notice of the equitable interest. However, no purchaser likes to rely on this defence, because of the difficulty of proving absence of notice, particularly of constructive notice. This is why, before 1965, a purchaser from Ann would have preferred her to appoint another trustee and rely on the defence of overreaching, rather than that of being without notice.

The Law of Property (Joint Tenants) Act 1964 aimed at making this precaution of having a second trustee unnecessary. This Act builds on the defence of being without notice, by providing that if the purchaser takes certain precautions he can assume that the sole survivor of the joint tenants does own all the beneficial interest. The actual wording of the Act is that in favour of the purchaser the sole survivor shall 'be deemed to be solely and beneficially interested if he conveys as beneficial owner or the conveyance includes a statement that he is so interested'.

It is not certain if the assumption that the purchaser can make it irrebuttable. In other words, can the purchaser rely on the Act even if he *knows* that Ann and Bill had become tenants in common before Bill's death? As the doubt exists, it would be unsafe for a purchaser who actually *knows* that Ann is not solely and beneficially entitled, to rely on the Act. Instead, Ann should be asked to appoint a second trustee, so that the equitable interests can be overreached. Indeed, should a purchaser rely on the Act if he merely *suspects* that someone other than Ann might be interested in the house? A purchaser might be suspicious because he finds that Xerxes occupies the house with Ann, although there could be other explanations for Xerxes's presence, apart from his owning an equitable interest. The Act is presumably designed to protect a purchaser against constructive notice of severance, even if not against actual notice. However, as there is doubt on this point, perhaps a purchaser who is merely suspicious should not rely on the Act either, but should insist on a second trustee.

The 1964 Act specifically says that it does not apply if there is a notice of severance endorsed on the conveyance to the joint tenants, nor if there is an entry in the Central Land Charges Registry as to the bankruptcy of Ann or Bill. On both these occasions a second trustee must be used. (The effect of Bill's bankruptcy would have been that the joint tenancy of the beneficial interest would have been severed, and half would belong to Bill's trustee in bankruptcy.)

So, to sum up, if you are buying from Ann after Bill's death, and wish to shelter behind the protection of the 1964 Act, you should take these precautions:

  (i) read the copy conveyance to Ann and Bill, sent to you as part of the abstract of title. Only rely on the Act if the conveyance says they are beneficial joint tenants. Do not use the Act if the conveyance says they are tenants in common, i.e. have shares. If the conveyance does not say whether they are joint tenants or tenants in common, then it is wiser not to rely on the Act;

 (ii) look at Bill's death certificate;

(iii) make a land charge search against the names of Bill and Ann, and check there is no registration as to bankruptcy;

(iv) raise a requisition asking for confirmation that there is no memorandum of severance on the conveyance to Ann and Bill, and check the original deed when you see it at completion;

 (v) be sure that the conveyance from Ann says that she conveys as beneficial owner.

You are then entitled to assume that Ann is the sole owner of the equitable interest, and can plead that you took free from Xerxes's claim because you had no notice of it. The Act also applies when it is not Ann who is conveying, but Ann's personal representative. If Bill dies, and then Ann dies, the Act entitles you to assume that Ann at her death owned the legal and all the equitable interest. In this case you must:

  (i) read the copy conveyance to Ann and Bill to check that it was to them as beneficial joint tenants;

 (ii) look at Bill's death certificate;

(iii) look at a copy of the grant of probate or letter of administration to Ann's estate. This is to confirm the identity of her personal representative;

(iv) make a land charge search as above;

 (v) check for a memorandum of severance as above;

(vi) be sure that the conveyance by Ann's personal representatives says that Ann was solely and beneficially interested in the land at her death;

(vii) as the sale is by a personal representative, you should also ensure that the conveyance says the personal representative has not made any previous assent or conveyance in respect of this property, that there is no memorandum on the grant of representation about a previous disposition by the personal representative, and that a memorandum about the conveyance to you *is* endorsed on the grant (see Chapter 10).

Do not forget that the Law of Property (Joint Tenants) Act 1964 Act does *not* apply to registered title. It does apply to a conveyance of unregistered title even before 1965, as the Act is retrospective to the beginning of 1926.

11.9 The Wolf in Sheep's Clothing, or the Problem of the Disguised Trustee for Sale

Suppose that X and Y both contribute towards the purchase price of the house. X contributes £30 000 and Y contributes £42 000. As a result, they share the equitable interest. The legal estate, in an ideal world, would have been conveyed or transferred to both of them. As we have seen, they would hold the legal estate on trust for sale. Any disposition would have to be by the two of them, be it a sale or a mortgage, and the purchaser or mortgagee would be safe from any claim that he took subject to X's and Y's beneficial interests, as these would have been overreached.

Suppose, however, that the legal estate is conveyed into the name of X alone. This could occur because, for example, Y is under 18 so cannot hold a legal estate, or because Y does not have his wits about him and does not realise that he is being put at a disadvantage, or perhaps because Y has not made a direct financial contribution, but a contribution, for example, in the form of considerable works of improvement. In a case such as that, Y may not consider the possibility of his owning part of the house beneficially until he has to defend that ownership against a third party.

X will hold the legal estate on trust for himself and Y, and the trust will be the statutory trust for sale, already considered in other cases of co-ownership (*Bull* v. *Bull* [1955]). (We are assuming that no express trust for sale is created.) X, of course, is a sole trustee for sale. The trouble is that he is a disguised trustee. There is no express trust for sale declared, and there is nothing in the conveyance or transfer to X that reveals the contribution made by Y and his co-ownership of the equitable interest. If X is registered as proprietor, no restriction will appear on the register. To the world at large, X looks like a beneficial owner.

Suppose now that X decides to sell the property or to mortgage it. The purchaser will want to move in. In the case of a mortgage, if X does not keep up the mortgage repayments, the lender will want to sell with vacant possession. Y might go quietly, but it is now that Y might decide to assert this equitable interest and to claim that it binds the purchaser or mortgagee, who as a result can only claim ownership or a mortgage of part of the property, and may not be able to get possession. As X is a sole trustee, the sale or mortgage could not have overreached Y's equitable interest. However, the purchaser or mortgagee may be able to raise the other defence, of having taken free of the interest because he 'had no notice of it'. We now meet 'the dangerous occupier'.

11.10   The Dangerous Occupier

(a)   Unregistered Title

If the title to the house is unregistered, the purchaser or mortgagee will be raising the classic defence that an equitable interest does not bind a *bona fide* purchaser for value of a legal estate without notice of the interest (re-read Chapter 4 and remember that Y's interest, being an interest of a beneficiary behind a trust, is not registrable under the Land Charges Act 1972). If Y is not living on the property and is not X's spouse, the purchaser may well be able to claim that his ignorance of Y's interest means that the purchaser takes free from it. This would leave Y with no claim against the land, but only with the right to pursue X for a share of the purchase price or mortgage loan.

If Y is living on the property, the purchaser will find it difficult to prove lack of notice, as the occupation would give the purchaser constructive notice of the occupier's rights (see section 4.4).

(b)   Registered Title

The doctrine of notice has no place in registered conveyancing. It is s.70(1)(g) of the Land Registration Act 1925 that presents the problem. As we have seen, if Y has an interest in the land, and is in actual occupation, Y's interest is overriding and will bind the purchaser, unless *Y* is asked if he has an equitable interest and he denies it.

(c)   Case Law

Litigation in this area shows a seesaw between the desire to protect Y and the desire to protect the innocent purchaser or lender. There is, at the moment, no way of reconciling their claims. The state of play at the moment seems to be this:

(a) it is now quite clear that the usual overreaching provisions apply, whether or not Y is in occupation. So X could overreach Y's interest by appointing a second trustee to join with X in selling or mortgaging (see *City of London Building Society* v. *Flegg* [1988].

(b) If X mortgages the house to the lender as part of the process of buying the house, i.e. the bank provides the purchase price, and Y *knows* of the intention of X to mortgage, the lender takes precedence over Y's interest and is not bound by it. One reason is that Y's equitable interest arises from a trust that is imputed to X and Y, i.e. the courts impute an agreement between them that as each has contributed towards the purchase price, then each will have a share of the beneficial interest. However, when imputing this agreement, the court will, when the balance of the purchase price is to be raised by a mortgage loan, also impute an intention by both X and Y that their interests are to be postponed to the mortgage (see *Bristol and West Building Society* v. *Henning* [1985]). Another way of putting the argument is to say that Y has authorised X to mortgage the house and to give the mortgage priority over Y's interest (see *Abbey National Building Society* v. *Cann* [1990]).*

This principle applies in both registered and unregistered title, and the fact that Y is living there at the time of the mortgage makes no difference. The lender cannot be affected by Y's interest, as the nature of the interest is one that is postponed to the mortgage. The principle seems to offer the lender an excellent defence against Y, because it is unlikely that Y will not know that the balance of the purchase price is being raised by a mortgage loan. However, this has happened, and it has been held (see *Lloyd's Bank plc* v. *Rosset* [1988] in the Court of Appeal) that the courts cannot impute to Y an intention that his interest should be postponed to the mortgage, when Y does not know that the mortgage will exist.

The lender may still not be affected by Y's interest, however, because of the principle stated in the next paragraph.

(c) In these circumstances (i.e. when the mortgage loan finances the purchase of the house) another reason why Y's interest will not bind the lender is that the conveyance or transfer of the property to X and X's immediate mortgage of it to the lender will be looked on as one indivisible transaction, so that the estate that vests in X is, from the outset, subject to the lender's mortgage, and it is only from that encumbered estate that Y can derive his equitable interest. It follows from this that the mortgage will have priority over Y's equitable interest, whether Y knew of the mortgage or not (*Abbey National Building Society* v. Cann [1990]).

(d) If X already owns the house, and then later mortgages it or sells it, then Y's interest might well bind the lender or purchaser, because of Y's occupation (as already shown).

(*d*) *What Do We Do about the Dangerous Occupier?*

From the Purchaser's Point of View Not surprisingly the property information form asks the seller if any other person is living on the property, and if that person has any claim of ownership.

If the answer is 'Yes, my Auntie Beryl, and she has an equitable interest', then at least the purchaser knows what to do about it. The seller is disclosed as a single trustee for sale, and must be asked to appoint another trustee for sale. This can be done before contract, so that the two trustees will be the sellers in the contract, or it can be done after the seller has entered into the contract, as the final step in his establishing the soundness of his title. Auntie Beryl would be a good choice as the second trustee, because if she is one of the sellers in the contract, she will be personally promising good title, and vacant possession.

If the seller answers 'No, there is no one in occupation but me', or 'Yes, Auntie Beryl is here, but she has no interest in the property', then this is not a satisfactory answer from the purchaser's point of view. If it is a lie, he will have an action against the seller for misrepresentation, but it will not clear Auntie Beryl's interest from the title. It is *Auntie Beryl's* statement that she has no interest that in unregistered conveyancing will save the purchaser from notice, or in registered title, will ensure that her interest is not overriding. So it is still advisable, once Auntie Beryl is discovered, to have her appearing in the contract. However, her role may be different. She is there to put *her* signature to the statement that she has no equitable interest.

From the Seller's Point of View   If the seller knows that there is an equitable interest to be overreached, the mechanism is simple enough. He must appoint another trustee to act with him. The cost of preparing the deed of appointment cannot be thrown onto the purchaser. Any condition in the contract saying that the purchaser must pay the cost is void (s.49 of the Law of Property Act 1925). Neither can the seller say that instead of overreaching the equitable interest, the owner of it will join in the conveyance or transfer to assign it. Any such condition in the contract would also be void (s.49 again). Anyway, a purchaser of the legal estate should never take the trouble and risk of investigating ownership of equitable interests if the equitable interests can be overreached.

The seller should remember that it is not enough to overreach the equitable interest. He is, in the contract, promising vacant possession. So, to revert to our two friends X and Y, X must be sure (if X is selling, rather than mortgaging) that Y actually leaves the house before completion. It is true that if Y remains, the purchaser could successfully sue him for possession, if Y's interest has been overreached, but there will be delay and expense, for which X will have to compensate the purchaser.

From the Point of View of the Seller's Legal Representative   Suppose that you are acting for the seller, and he tells you that his mother owns part of the property. If she is co-owner of the legal estate, it is impossible for your client to sell alone, and instructions to sell are also needed from the mother. You cannot approach the mother yourself; you must ask your client to discuss the matter with his mother, and explain that her cooperation is needed if the property is to be sold. If, as a result, she also instructs you to act in the sale, you would still be unable to act for her if you had any suspicion that the instructions were not given of her own free will. Otherwise, you can act for your original client and his mother, unless it transpires there is some conflict of interest between them. (These are rules of professional conduct. See *The Professional Conduct of Solicitors*, published by the Law Society.) You would expect any house bought from the proceeds of the sale also to be put in both their names, and the beneficial interest to be shared in the same way that it was shared in the house just sold.

If you discover that your client is the sole owner of the legal estate, but that his mother owns the entire equitable interest, your client is holding the legal estate on what is called a bare trust. In this case, no sale should take place without the mother's consent. It is her decision, not that of the estate owner as to whether or not the house is sold.

If you discover that your client is sole owner of the legal estate but that he and his mother share the equitable interest, her interest can be overreached, but as previously said, her consent is needed as your client is promising that the house will be unoccupied at completion. You can approach her to explain that her cooperation is necessary, either as the second trustee, or to join in the contract to promise vacant possession, but you cannot advise her to cooperate, and you should suggest she obtains legal advice. If, in fact, she is quite happy to move, she may instruct you. You can then act for her and her son provided that there is no conflict of interest.

11.11 The Dangerous Spouse

The problem of the concealed trustee for sale and the dangerous occupier is particularly likely to occur in the case of a married couple, and judging from the litigation on the subject, it usually takes the form of the husband holding the legal estate on a concealed trust for sale for himself and his wife, who co-own the equitable interest. That is why the facts in the next paragraph take that form, but of course everything said is equally applicable where the wife owns the legal estate on trust for herself and her husband.

Let us imagine the Henry and his wife, Winifred, are living together in the matrimonial home, 1 South Avenue. Henry is sole owner of the legal estate. It is true that Winifred may well own an equitable interest in the house. Her interest is overreachable, but as has been said earlier, her consent to any sale by her husband is in fact necessary, because Henry has to promise in the contract that the house will be empty on completion. However, this point about vacant possession would not apply if Henry were mortgaging the house, so that he could, by appointing a second trustee, create a mortgage that would override Winifred's interest.

However, an occupying *spouse*, whether or not she (or he) has an equitable interest, has another string to her (his) bow, namely the statutory right to occupy a house that is or has been the matrimonial home. The right is given to a spouse who does not own the legal interest in it. To put it at its simplest, as Henry owns the legal estate in the home, and Winifred does not, Winifred has this statutory right to remain in occupation until the right is destroyed by an order of the court (Matrimonial Homes Act 1983).

Winifred's right is capable of binding any purchaser from Henry, or any mortgagee. So you can see that Winifred has the power to prevent any disposition of the house without her consent. (You can see from this why the Matrimonial Homes Act 1983 does not apply when both spouses own the legal estate. No disposition is then possible anyway, without both spouses signing the deed.)

However, Winifred's right must be protected if it *is* to bind a purchaser or mortgagee. If the title to the home is registered she *must* put a notice on the register. (The 1983 Act specifically provides that the right of occupation is not overriding under s.70(1)(g) of the Land Registration Act 1925 even though the spouse is living in the home.) If the title to the home is unregistered, Winifred must register a class F land charge against Henry's name. So you can see that if Xerxes is buying from Henry, or lending money to him, Xerxes must be concerned about the possibilities:

(a) that Winifred owns part of the equitable interest;
(b) that Winifred will protect her statutory right of occupation by registering a notice or land charge before completion.

If Xerxes is buying, and is worried about the threat of the Matrimonial Homes Act, he can before contract check whether or not Winifred has already protected her right. If she has, and refuses to join in the contract for sale, it would be best for both Henry and Xerxes to abandon the idea of sale. Henry will be entering into a contract that he is probably doomed to break. He promises vacant possession and can only give it if Winifred cancels the registration, or if he obtains a court order for the ending of the right of occupation. (By virtue of s.4 of the 1983 Act, a seller who promises vacant possession is also deemed to promise the cancellation of any registration protecting the statutory right of occupation, or that he will on completion give the purchaser an application for its cancellation signed by the spouse.)

However, even if Henry and Xerxes satisfy themselves that Winifred has not registered her right before exchange of contract, there is nothing to prevent her from registering after contract. The last moment for registration would be the date of Xerxes's pre-completion search. The priority period given by the search would protect Xerxes from any registration after the date of the search. Therefore, both Henry and Xerxes must protect themselves against this registration: Henry, because he faces being liable for breach of contract; Xerxes, because he wants to acquire a house, rather than a right to damages for breach of contract.

The answer is to have Winifred as a party to the contract, in which she will promise not to register the right of occupation, or to cancel any registration that already exists.

To sum up, on the sale of a matrimonial home, you will expect to see both spouses appearing in the contract and signing it, either:

(a) because they both own the legal estate, and are, therefore, joint sellers. This will dispose of any equitable interests, as they will be overreached and no rights of occupation under the Matrimonial Homes Act will exist;

(b) because one spouse is sole beneficial owner, but the other spouse is joining in to confirm that he/she has no equitable interest, and will be releasing any rights under the Matrimonial Homes Act 1983.

(a) Protecting the Purchaser's Mortgagee

To recap, you can see that the purchaser's mortgagee faces *two* dangerous spouses, and may be bound by an equitable interest and/or right of occupation belonging to the seller's spouse, and by an equitable interest belonging to the purchaser's spouse.

Any claim by the seller's spouse should be cleared away by the drafting of the contract of sale between seller and purchaser (see above).

It now seems unlikely, following the House of Lord's decision in *Abbey National Building Society* v. *Cann* [1990] (see section 11.10 and case notes) that the mortgagee will be bound by an equitable interest belonging to the borrower's spouse, providing that the money is lent to finance the purchase. If the mortgage is created *after* the house has been acquired, the mortgagee will feel safe if:

1. both the purchase and the mortgage is by both spouses (overreaching); or
2. the purchase and the mortgage is by one spouse, but the other spouse, before completion, gives written confirmation to the lender that he/she knows of the mortgage and agrees that it takes precedence over his/her equitable interest (but see the next section).

11.12 Undue Influence

It has been previously suggested that if the home is in the name of, say, husband alone, the wife should nevertheless be made a party to any disposition of it, or at least give written confirmation that she does not claim any interest in it. Suppose you are the solicitor for someone lending money to the husband on the security of his existing house. You ask the husband to obtain the wife's signature to the mortgage papers. On the face of it, her signature should ensure that she would have no defence to a possession action by the lender, but this is not necessarily so. Her signature will be worthless if she can prove:

(a) that she was induced to sign by the undue influence of her husband, or by his fraudulent misrepresentation;
(b) that the transaction was manifestly disadvantageous to her; and
(c) that when he persuaded her to sign, her husband was acting as agent or representative of the lender, *or* that the lender had notice of the undue influence, or circumstances that might give rise to undue influence (see amongst others, *Kingsnorth Trust Ltd* v. *Bell** [1986]; *Midland Bank*

Ltd v. *Shephard* [1988] and *Bank of Credit and Commerce International SA* v. *Aboody & another*) [1989].

It is important, therefore, that neither the lender nor his solicitor impliedly constitute the husband as their agent to secure the wife's signature. The papers needing the wife's signature should be sent direct to the wife, and it should be suggested that she seek legal advice. There is no presumption that a husband has undue influence over his wife (see *Midland Bank* v. *Shephard* [1988] but if there is any suspicion that he does have, again the lender should advise the wife to seek independent advice.

This is not a problem that arises only in the context of spouses. It could arise in the context of a child having undue influence over his parents (*Coldunell* v *Gallon* [1986]). Nor is it a problem confined to the context of a mortgage. An occupier who is induced by the seller to sign a document that he does not claim any equitable interest in the property may be able to use the same defence, if the seller could be said to be acting as the purchaser's agent in obtaining the signature.

Case notes

Bristol and West Building Society v. *Henning and anor [1985] 2 A11 ER 606, [1985] 1 WLR 778, 50 P & CR 237*

Mr and Mrs Henning had lived together as man and wife for several years. They decided to buy a house. The title to the house was unregistered. It was bought with the aid of a mortgage loan. The legal estate was conveyed into the name of Mr Henning alone, and only he created the mortgage. Mrs Henning did not directly provide any of the purchase money, but it was agreed that she should run a self-sufficiency project using the large garden.

The relationship broke down, and Mr Henning left the house and ceased to make the mortgage payments. The Building Society claimed possession. Mrs Henning claimed that she had an equitable interest in the house, and that her interest bound the society, as she was living in the house when the mortgage was executed, and so the Society had notice of it.

It was held that any equitable interest she might have arose from a resulting trust, on the basis of an imputed agreement between herself and Mr Henning that she should have such an interest. If so, it must also be a term of that agreement that her equitable interest should be postponed to the mortgage. She knew and supported the proposal that the purchase price of the house should be raised on mortgage. It was their common intention that the man should have the power to create the mortgage, and it must also have been their intention that the mortgage should have priority over any equitable interests in the house. The mortgagee was, therefore, entitled to possession.

Abbey National Building Society v. *Cann and anor [1990] 1 All ER 1085 [1990] 2 WLR 832*

Mr Cann proposed buying a house. He told the Society that he intended to live there by himself, although in fact he was buying the house for his mother to live in. The Society made a formal offer of loan, which was accepted. Contracts for the purchase were then exchanged, and at 12.20 p.m. on 13 August 1984 the purchase and the mortgage were completed. Mrs Cann (the mother) was then abroad on holiday, but at 11.45 a.m. her son started to move the furniture into the house and carpets were laid.

On 13 September 1984 Mr Cann was registered at HM Land Registry as proprietor, and the mortgage was registered as a registered charge. By that date Mrs Cann was living in the house.Mr Cann failed to make the mortgage payments, and the Society sought possession of the house. Mrs Cann claimed an equitable interest in the house (for reasons based on a contribution towards the purchase price and proprietory estoppel) and that this interest was overriding by virtue of s.70(1)(g) of the Land Registration Act 1925 and therefore bound the Society. Her claim failed for the following reasons:

1. That although a purchaser or mortgagee took subject to overriding interests existing at the date of the registration of the dealing, nevertheless if it was claimed that the interest was overriding by virtue of s.70(1)(g), the claimant must prove that she was in occupation not at the date of registration but the earlier date of completion (i.e. in this case, at 12.20 p.m. on 13 August). Mrs Cann was not in occupation at that time (see section 3.17).
2. Alternatively, where the purchase of a property is financed by a mortgage loan, then although in theory there is a tiny gap in time between the completion of the transfer to the purchaser and his subsequent mortgage, so that it might be arguable that an equitable interest could arise after the transfer but before the mortgage and therefore potentially bind the mortgagee, realistically no such gap exists, or certainly not in the case where the loan has been made pursuant to an earlier agreement that it would be secured by a mortgage. It is all one transaction. The only thing ever available to Mr Cann to hold on trust for, or share with, his mother was a *mortgaged* property. For this reason, even if Mrs Cann *had* been in occupation on 13 August, her interest would still not have bound the mortgagee.

Kingsnorth Trust Ltd v. *Bell [1986] 1 All ER 423*

Mr Bell owned the legal estate in the matrimonial home, but his wife shared the equitable interest. Mr Bell wished to buy a new business, and to raise money to buy it by a mortgage on the home. The solicitors to the Kingsnorth Trust Ltd asked Mr Bell's solicitors to arrange for the execution of the mortgage deeds, and they asked Mr Bell to obtain his wife's signature. He lied to his wife, telling her he needed the money for his existing business. She did not instruct solicitors to act for her, and had no independent advice.

It was held that Kingsnorth Trust, through its solicitors, had instructed the husband to obtain his wife's signature. He had, in effect, been acting as Kingsnorth's agent, and the lenders were bound by his fraudulent misrepresentation.

Workshop

Attempt these problems yourself, then read the specimen solutions at the end of the book.

Problem 1

The legal freehold estate was conveyed in 1970 to three brothers, Albert Brick, Robert Brick and Sidney Brick. The conveyance declared that they were to hold the legal estate on trust for themselves as tenants in common as part of their partnership assets.

In August 1975 the legal estate was conveyed by Albert and Sidney Brick to Jennifer Cooper. A recital in the 1975 conveyance stated that Robert Brick had retired from the partnership.

You have a copy of a search certificate (the search having been made by Miss Cooper when she bought the land from the two Bricks) which reveals that a C(iv) land charge was registered against the name of Robert Brick and Albert Brick on 3 July 1975, but that there is nothing registered against the name of Sydney Brick.

If you are acting for a purchaser from Miss Cooper, is there anything on this title to cause you concern?

Problem 2

You have been instructed by Mrs Anne Mason to deal with a loan she is obtaining from the County Building Society for the purpose of installing central heating and double glazing in her house. The house was erected thirty years ago and is not in a mining area. She has handed you the land certificate which she explains she and her late husband were given because the title deeds were lost. You have also been instructed to act for the building society, and have obtained office copy entries. There are no entries on the charges register, and the proprietorship register looks like this:

B. *PROPRIETORSHIP REGISTER*
    Title: Possessory.
    First registered proprietors
    Alan Mason and Anne Mason
    both of 48 Queens Road, Loamster, Loamshire
    registered on 13 September 1974.

She has also handed you her late husband's will which has not been proved. It leaves all his property to her absolutely.

1. Does the will have to be proved in order to complete the mortgage? What steps do you need to take to have the title registered in her sole name?
2. What is the significance of registration with possessory title, and will this fact create any problems in dealing with the mortgage?
3. What searches will you make on behalf of the building society?

---

12 Easements and Restrictive Covenants

These two incumbrances have been mentioned in nearly all the previous chapters. This chapter discusses them in greater detail.

12.1 Sale of Land that Already Has the Benefit of an Easement Over a Neighbour's Land

Simple. Before you draft the particulars in the contract, re-read Chapter 5. Before you draft the conveyance, read Chapters 13 and 14.

12.2 Sale of Land that Is Already Burdened with an Easement

Simple. When drafting the contract, list the easement as a burden on the property (see the topic of disclosure in Chapter 5). When drafting the conveyance of unregistered title, mention the easement in the habendum (see Chapter 13).

12.3 Sale of Land, when the Seller will Continue to Own Land Nearby

Unfortunately, this is not simple. There are two dangers from the seller's point of view:

(a) that he may unintentionally give the purchaser rights over land that he is retaining;
(b) that he may not reserve a right to use the land he is selling, for example as a means of access, even though that use would add considerably to the enjoyment or value of the land he has retained.

Study Figure 12.1.

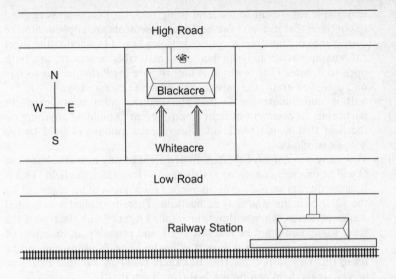

Figure 12.1

Blackacre is a house and surrounding garden. Whiteacre is a field. They are both owned and occupied by O. The house fronts on to the High Road, and if you look carefully you can see the front path, with a tub of flowers beside it. However, O often takes a short cut across Whiteacre to reach the railway station and surrounding shops.

The field is usually reached from Low Road, but O has often driven farm machinery along the edge of Blackacre as a short cut to and from Whiteacre, instead of going the long way round by road.

The arrows indicate light streaming across Whiteacre into the windows of the house on Blackacre.

At the moment there are no easements over either property, as a person cannot have an easement over land which he owns and occupies himself.

Suppose, however, that O now sells Blackacre to P. We will ignore the contract for sale for the moment, and concentrate on the conveyance or transfer. We will assume that it is a silent conveyance, i.e. it makes no express mention of easements. The result of the silent conveyance could be this:

(a) Blackacre may acquire an easement of light, and a right of way over Whiteacre.

There are various reasons why a sale of part of the seller's land may contain an implied grant of easements to the purchaser. The reason for the implied grant in these circumstances is what is known as the rule in *Wheeldon* v. *Burrows* [1879]. This says that if at the time O conveys, he is using the land he is retaining to the advantage of the land he is selling, and that use is continuous and apparent, and necessary for the reasonable enjoyment of the land being sold, the purchaser is entitled to continue that use, and the necessary easements are implied into the conveyance or transfer. Of course, between O and P, whether the short cut was apparent, and whether it is reasonably necessary, are both open to debate. That is why it is unfortunate for P that he has to rely on an *implied* grant, the existence of which O might deny.

It is unfortunate for O that the implied grant might exist. In particular, an easement of light could prevent O building anything on the field that would block off a substantial amount of light to the house's windows.

(b) Whiteacre will not have the benefit of a right of way over Blackacre, so O will be unable to continue to drive across it to reach the field. This is because there is scarcely ever an *implied* reservation of an easement by the seller over the land that he has sold. There is implied an essential means of access, when without the implied right of way the rest of the seller's land could not be reached at all, and probably an easement of support when an owner sells part of his building. Nothing else can be relied on. The short cut across Blackacre is *not* an essential means of access, as the field can be reached from Low Road.

From O's point of view, we can now see that he would have preferred the conveyance or transfer *not* to be silent. He would have liked to see in it:

(a) a clause saying that there was no implied grant of easements to P (*Wheeldon* v. *Burrows* can be ousted by agreements) or at least that there was not an easement of light.
(b) a clause saying that he did reserve a right of way over Blackacre.

From P's point of view, we can see that P would have preferred an express grant of, say, the right of way over Whiteacre. The existence of this right would then be beyond dispute, and could easily be proved when P re-sold. In other words, the conveyance should not have been silent. Instead, it should have spoken up.

Of course, neither party can insist on anything going into the conveyance, unless the preceding contract says that it can go in. It is the contract that governs the drafting and contents of the conveyance. So O and P, when agreeing the terms of the contract, should have decided on special conditions settling what easements were to be reserved expressly in the conveyance, what easements were to be granted expressly, and that the conveyance should state that no others were to be granted by implication.

The conditions in the contract are not creating the easements, but merely providing that the easements will be created by the conveyance or transfer. Therefore it is essential to have the necessary grant and reservation in the conveyance, together with the statement preventing any implied grant. If through carelessness, the conveyance was drafted without any reference to easements, the seller would have no easements over the part sold to the purchaser, and the purchaser could perhaps claim easements other than those that had been intended by the contract.

If O and P forget to put in special conditions to deal with the grant and reservation of easements but the contract incorporates the standard conditions, standard condition 3.4 will govern the drafting of the conveyance or transfer. Condition 3.4.1 defines 'retained land' as land which the seller owns and which is adjoining or near the land being sold. Condition 3.4.2 states first of all that the buyer will not have any right of light or air over the retained land. This prevents there being any implied grant by the contract to the purchaser of such rights, and also entitles the seller to put a clause in the conveyance similarly negativing the implication of any such grant.

Subject to this, condition 3.4.2 then provides that the seller as owner of the retained land and buyer as owner of the land being sold will each have the rights over the land of the other which they would have had if they were two separate buyers to whom the seller had made simultaneous transfers of the land being sold and the retained land, and that either party can request that the conveyance or transfer contain the necessary express grant or reservation.

At first sight this is incomprehensible, but it is based on this point of law; that if – in the case of Blackacre and Whiteacre – instead of selling Blackacre and retaining Whiteacre O had sold the two properties simultaneously, Blackacre to P and Whiteacre to Q, P would have had an implied grant of easements over Whiteacre and Q would have had an implied grant of easements over Blackacre. So P might well have had a right of light and way over Whiteacre and Q a right of way over Blackacre (not a right of light, as there were no windows on Whiteacre receiving light at the time of the conveyance). Condition 5 is, therefore, saying that you must imagine that O, instead of retaining Whiteacre, is buying it. What easements would have been impliedly granted to O? Answer – *Wheeldon* v. *Burrows* easements and possibly others. Then those are the easements that O can expressly reserve in the conveyance of Blackacre for the benefit of Whiteacre and himself. Similarly, P is entitled to have inserted in the conveyance as express easements those that would have been implied into the conveyance with the exception of easements of light and air. So the condition decreases P's right to easements, but does mean that P can ask for an *express* grant to be written on the face of the conveyance, instead of having to rely on an implied grant. O's right to easements is increased and put on a par with P's. Indeed O's rights are better than P's, because there is nothing in the condition to prevent O expressly reserving rights of light or air, providing that the facts justify it.

There are considerable drawbacks in relying on the standard condition: It may not represent the parties' intentions. The seller, for instance, might not want the purchaser to have any easements at all over his land. Another point is that if one party wants to insist on his rights under it, and have the express grant or reservation written into the conveyance, the other party can deny that the easement in question would have been the subject matter of an implied grant, e.g. because it is not continuous and apparent. If it would not have been the subject matter of an implied grant, it cannot, under condition 4.3 be the subject matter of an express grant. So the condition is a breeding ground for dispute.

(*Note*: A grant of easements is not only implied under *Wheeldon* v. *Burrows*. Easements of necessity are implied, and there may be a grant implied into the conveyance or transfer by s.62 of the Law of Property Act 1925. The rules are not dwelt on, as the purpose of this chapter is to urge you to replace an implied grant by an express grant, following a special condition in the contract.)

12.4   Particular Points about Easements and the Land Registration Act 1925

The Land Registration Act seems particularly obscure on the question of easements.

The principles *seem* to be as follows:

(a) If land has the benefit of a legal easement when the title to that land is first registered, then the easement remains legal. It will therefore bind a later purchaser of the servient tenement (the land over which the easement is exercised). If the title to the servient tenement is unregistered, the easement will bind the purchaser of it because the easement is legal. If the title to the servient tenement is registered, the purchaser of it will be bound by the easement, because the easement, being legal, is overriding under s.70(1)(a) of the Land Registration Act 1925;

(b) If *part* of a title that is already registered is sold, the transfer may well expressly grant and reserve easements. The creation of the easements by the transfer of part must be followed by registration. The principle involved here is one that has been met already in section 3.11. The creation of an easement out of registered title is a registrable dealing. The easement will not be legal until it is registered. Pending registration, the easement is only equitable, and possibly is only a minor interest (see section 3.15).

If an easement is granted out of registered title, and the servient tenement is also registered land, the registration of the easement has two aspects. The benefit of the easement must be registered on the title to the dominant tenement, and the burden must be registered on the title to the servient tenement.

The Registrar can only register the benefit if he is sure that the grant of the easement is valid. As the title to the servient tenement is registered, it should be quite clear that the servient owner has the power to grant the easement, providing that the servient owner is registered with absolute title. If there is doubt, the registrar may only be able to state in the register to the dominant tenement that the easement is *claimed.*

For the burden to be registered against the servient tenement, the servient owner should be asked to put his land certificate on deposit at the registry. If the land certificate is not put on deposit, a caution will have to be entered on the register to protect the easement.

If this situation – of an easement being granted out of, and for the benefit of, a registered title – occurs on the occasion of a sale of part of the land in the title, registration of the benefit and burden of the easements should present no difficulty. The title is known to the Registrar and the seller's land certificate will have been put on deposit to await the registration of the transfer of part. The Registrar can, therefore, check the validity of the grant, and can register the burden of the easements reserved by the seller on the purchaser's new title, and can register the burden of the easements given to the purchaser on the seller's title.

It is possible, however, that the easement could be granted by a deed of grant, quite independently of any transfer, e.g. by one neighbour to another. In this case it must be remembered that it is insufficient for the benefit to be registered. The burden must also be registered on the title to the servient tenement. If this is not done, there is the possibility that when the servient tenement is sold, the new owner may be able to claim that the easement does not bind him, as it is an unprotected minor interest.

Could this unregistered easement bind the purchaser because it is an overriding interest? There is no certain answer. Remember that the easement is only equitable, because it has not been registered. There is considerable controversy over whether an equitable easement can be overriding under s.70(1)(a) (see 3.15). Respected authors of leading textbooks differ on the point. In view of the uncertainty, it is clearly important that the easement be properly registered.

(c) If an easement is created by a deed of grant, and only the servient tenement is registered, the burden should be registered on that title. If only the dominant tenement is registered, the benefit will be entered on the register, provided that the registrar is satisfied that the grant is valid. He can only be satisfied if the title to the servient tenement is proved to him. Otherwise, at best he can only put a note to the effect that the easement is claimed.

(d) If part of the land in a registered title is sold, the purchaser may acquire easements over the seller's retained land by virtue of an implied grant, e.g. under *Wheeldon* v. *Burrows*, or by virtue of s.62 of the Law of Property Act 1925. These easements take effect as overriding interests, under rule 258 of Land Registration Rules 1925, and do not have to be noted on the servient tenement in order to bind a purchaser of it.

12.5   Covenants

When the seller will continue to own land near the property he is selling, he will also be considering whether it is desirable to insist that the purchaser, in the conveyance or transfer to him, give covenants back to the seller.

One purpose of the covenants will be that the seller can control the use of the land he has sold. If he has sold the end of his garden to a developer, he may be prepared to accept the building of a bungalow, but will want a covenant by the developer not to build anything else, for example, a block of flats.

Another purpose might be to force the purchaser to carry out work, for example, repairs or fencing. Of course, the covenant might equally well be given by seller to purchaser.

12.6   The Contract

Suppose that Sarah owns both Blackacre and Whiteacre. She contracts to sell Whiteacre to Patricia. The contract provides that in the conveyance or transfer Patricia will covenant:

(a) to use Whiteacre only as a single dwelling-house;
(b) to fence the boundary between Whiteacre and Blackacre.

Notice that the covenant is going to be given in the conveyance or transfer. The contract is merely giving Sarah the right to insist that the conveyance does contain the covenant. The contract can, and should, prescribe the exact wording to be used in the conveyance, because for example:

(a) The benefit of a covenant can be 'annexed' to the benefited land (in this case, Blackacre) by – amongst other possibilities – saying that it is given 'for the benefit of each and every part of Blackacre'. The result of the covenant being worded in such a way is that the benefit and the land become inseparable, so that a later purchaser of any part of Blackacre that does in fact benefit from the covenant, acquires not only the land but the power to enforce the covenant. There is then no need to show that the benefit of the covenant has been expressly assigned.

It is true that the benefit of a covenant may be annexed without any express wording, owing to the wording implied into the covenant by s.78 of the Law of Property Act 1925 (as interpreted in the case of *Federated Homes Ltd* v. *Mill Lodge Properties Ltd* [1980]) but as the benefited land should be identified in the conveyance, express words of annexation might as well be used.

(b) A covenant to repair or to fence should define the obligation exactly, so the wording should be settled in the contract.

12.7 The Conveyance or Transfer

In the conveyance, the covenant is actually given by purchaser to seller, or seller to purchaser, using the wording already settled by the preceding contract.

12.8 Protecting the Covenant

We must now distinguish between the two covenants in our imagined contract. The fencing covenant is positive, as it requires labour or the spending of money to perform it. The user covenant is negative. Nothing has to be *done* to observe it, it is rather the case of not doing anything to change the existing use.

The point of the distinction is, of course, that the negative covenant (or, as it is generally called in a conveyancing context, the *restrictive* covenant) is capable of becoming an incumbrance on the land and so may be enforceable not only against Patricia but against whoever claims the land through her (*Tulk* v. *Moxhay* [1848]). However, the incumbrance is an equitable one and so will not automatically bind a purchaser from Patricia. If Patricia's title to the land is unregistered, then any negative covenant created after 1925 is registrable as a D(ii) land charge. Sarah should be careful, therefore, to register the charge against Patricia's name. If she does not do this, the covenant will not bind a later purchaser of a legal estate in the land for money or money's worth. If Patricia is buying with the aid of a mortgage, Sarah should use the priority notice procedure (see section 4.5).

If Patricia's title to Whiteacre is registered under the Land Registration Act 1925, the negative covenant is a minor interest, and will only bind a transferee for value of the title if the covenant is protected by an entry on the register, either a notice or a caution. Usually, a covenant is given when part of the seller's land is sold (although this does not have to be so). For this reason a restrictive covenant is usually protected by a notice. Suppose that Sarah sells part of her registered title to Patricia, and Patricia covenants in the transfer to use the property only as a dwelling-house. Patricia will lodge the transfer in the Registry, to be registered as proprietor of the part she has bought. The Registrar, when registering the transfer, will also put a notice on the charges register of Patricia's title. If Sarah had given a negative covenant to Patricia, this covenant should be noted on the charges register of Sarah's title. This needs the deposit of Sarah's land certificate but in these circumstances it will already be on deposit to await registration of the transfer of part.

A positive covenant does not create an incumbrance on land, so that when Patricia conveys Whiteacre to Quentin, he will not have to perform the fencing covenant, at least not in the sense that it can be enforced against him directly by Sarah. Sarah could only enforce the user covenant against him.

However, Quentin may be affected by the enforcement against him of an indemnity covenant.

12.9 Indemnity Covenants

Return to Sarah and Patricia. When Patricia gave the two covenants she undertook a perpetual liability. She will have covenanted not only that *she* would perform the covenants but that *anyone* who later succeeded to the land would also perform them (s.79 of the Law of Property Act 1925). Therefore, when Patricia sells Whiteacre to Quentin, if he does not fence or does not observe the user covenant, Sarah can sue *Patricia* for breach of contract.

Sarah may not bother to sue Patricia if it is the negative covenant that is being broken. If the burden of that covenant has run with the land and Quentin has taken subject to it, Sarah's most effective remedy will be to proceed against *him* and obtain an injunction to prevent the breach being continued. However the possibility of being sued remains to haunt Patricia.

As regards the positive covenant, Patricia is the only person who can be sued by Sarah, as Sarah cannot take any action against Quentin.

As she is aware of this possibility of being sued at some time in the future, perhaps long after she has parted with the land, Patricia, when she sells to Quentin, will want a covenant from him to indemnify her against any consequences of a future breach of either covenant. Patricia can only insist on the conveyance or transfer to Quentin containing an indemnity covenant if the contract says that it will.

Condition 4.6.3 of the standard conditions provides for the insertion of an indemnity covenant into the conveyance or transfer, if despite the sale, the seller will remain liable on any obligation affecting the property. The condition requires the purchaser to give not only a covenant to indemnify the seller against the consequences of any breach, but also a covenant to perform the obligation. Under the condition, therefore, Patricia would not herself have to be sued, before insisting that Quentin fences in accordance with the covenant given by Patricia to Sarah.

A special condition in the contract is therefore not needed unless the standard condition is considered unsatisfactory. Again, remember that the contract does not create the indemnity covenant. It is the covenant that will be put in the conveyance or transfer as a result of the condition in the contract that will do so.

As Quentin has undertaken a perpetual responsibility to indemnify Patricia, when Quentin sells to Rosemary, he needs an indemnity covenant from Rosemary. He needs an indemnity against his promise to indemnify. The indemnity given by Rosemary should have the same wording as the indemnity given by Quentin. For example, if Quentin promised to *perform* and indemnify, Rosemary should be required to give the same promise to him. If Quentin only promised to indemnify, but not to perform, Rosemary should alter standard condition 4.6.3, so that in the conveyance *she* will only promise to indemnify.

A long chain of indemnity may eventually stretch from Patricia to the current owner of Whiteacre. The older the covenant and the longer the chain, the more ineffective the chain becomes. If Sarah, or Sarah's successor to Blackacre, decides to sue Patricia, Patricia may be untraceable. If Patricia is dead, while it is in theory possible to sue her estate, the expense and difficulty of finding her personal representatives and of tracing her assets into the hands of the beneficiaries will make the remedy impracticable. If Patricia is successfully sued, Patricia may not be able to find Quentin. Remember the only person who can sue Rosemary by virtue of the indemnity chain is Quentin, so if Patricia is unable to sue Quentin, Rosemary will not be called upon for an indemnity, so is unconcerned at the continuance of the breach either by her or her successor. However, if you are acting for a seller who gave an indemnity when he originally bought the land, you make certain that he is indemnified when he sells. You do this, even though it seems very unlikely that your client would ever be sued on the chain.

12.10 Particular Points about Covenants and Registered Title

The restrictive covenants will be set out in the charges register of the burdened land. They may be set out in full or if they are long the register may refer to the document that created them. This document or a copy will be filed at the Registry and a copy bound up in the land certificate.

If positive covenants are created in a transfer of registered title, they will also appear on the register. If in the transfer they were mixed in with negative covenants, the Registrar will not divide them, but will put both the negative and the positive covenants in the charges register. If the transfer contains only positive covenants, their existence will be noted on the proprietorship register. The positive covenants are not really part of the title to the land. They are only noted on the register as a matter of convenience. Without a note on the register their existence could be easily forgotten, as the transfer that created them is filed in the registry. If they were forgotten, the original covenantor or his successors might forget the necessity for an indemnity covenant when retransferring.

Notice that it is not the practice to enter on the register those positive covenants that already exist when the title is first registered. The registry considers this to be unnecessary. The original deeds are returned to the registered proprietor and *these* reveal the existence of the covenants. This is the one reason why the title deeds remain important, despite registration of the title.

Indemnity Covenants

An indemnity covenant given by the applicant for first registration will not be mentioned on the register of title. This is because when he resells, he can recall the fact that he gave, and therefore needs, an indemnity covenant by looking at the title deeds. If an indemnity covenant is given by a later registered proprietor, a note is put in to the proprietorship register, referring to the existence of the indemnity covenant.

Workshop

Attempt these problems yourself, then read the specimen solutions at the end of the book.

Problem 1

Your client is buying a freehold detached house, 21B Landsdown Crescent, from Alice Brown. Alice Brown also owns 21A. She used to own number 21, but this was sold by her to Catherine Douglas in 1986. Figure 12.2 is a plan of the three properties.

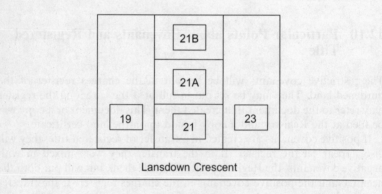

Lansdown Crescent

Figure 12.2

Additional enquiries of the district authority and the property information form reveal that Landsdown Crescent is a public road and that the pipes and wires serving 21A and 21B lead from Landsdown Crescent across number 21.

You are considering the draft contract prepared by Alice Brown's solicitor. You have to decide whether your client will obtain all the easements necessary for his enjoyment of 21B. Do you think he will? What documents should you read?

Problem 2

You are acting for Hebe, the seller of 1 Rosemary Avenue. You are investigating the unregistered title. You have the following title deeds.

- A conveyance dated 1 May 1940, made between the seller A and the purchaser B. This conveyance contains a covenant given by B to A that no buildings whatsoever would be put on the land other than one detached house.
- A conveyance dated 1 June 1980, made between the seller B and the purchaser C. This conveyance contains an indemnity given by C to B against breach of the 1940 covenant.

- A conveyance dated 1 July 1988 made between the seller C and Hebe the purchaser. The conveyance contains an indemnity given by Hebe to C against breach of the 1940 covenant. As soon as Hebe bought the property, she built a large garage.

1. Can the covenant be enforced against Hebe?
2. How do these facts affect your drafting of the contract of sale?

Problem 3

You are acting for Jacob Green, whose wife, Naomi Green, has just died. He has decided to sell 9 Havelock Street, where he has lived all his married life, and move in with his widowed sister. He has asked you to act for him in the sale.

He has handed you Naomi's will, which divides everything she owns equally between Jacob and their daughter, Dr Ruth Green.

The title to the house is registered. The land certificate is in the possession of the Equine Bank, but you have obtained an office copy of the entries on the register. The property register describes the property as '9 Havelock Street, Spa on Wells, together with the rights granted by but subject to the exceptions and reservations contained in the conveyance dated 1 April 1965, referred to in entry no.2 of the register.'

The proprietorship register names Jacob and Naomi as proprietors, and contains the restriction that no disposition by the sole survivor under which capital money arises will be registered.

Entry no.1 on the charges register states that a conveyance of 1922 contains restrictive covenants affecting the land, but that neither the original conveyance, nor a certified copy or an examined abstract of it was produced on first registration. Entry no 2 says that the conveyance of 1 April 1965 contains restrictive covenants affecting the land, and that a copy of the conveyance is in the certificate. Entries 3 and 4 relate to the registered charge in favour of the Equine Bank.

Jacob tells you that the sale is to include the fitted carpets and all curtains, but is to exclude the garden shed. You how have to draft the contract. How will the facts set out above affect the drafting of the contract.

13. Drafting a Conveyance of Unregistered Title

13.1 Introduction

When called upon to draft a conveyance, your first instinct might be to turn immediately to a precedent book. You must remember that a precedent is your servant, not your master. You must know what sort of clauses your conveyance needs before you turn to the precedent for an appropriate form of words. You should not rely on the precedent to alert you to the necessity for the clause in the first place.

This chapter will introduce you to a standard form of conveyance, discuss the effect and purpose of the various clauses, and then consider what changes should be made to suit particular circumstances. The clauses are not put forward as precedents, but serve only to illustrate the purposes that must be achieved by clauses in the conveyance.

It must be emphasised that it is the contract that governs the contents of the conveyance or transfer made in performance of the contract. Clauses affecting the rights of seller and purchaser against one another, e.g. easements, covenants, or the cutting down of an implied grant, can only be put in the conveyance if justified by a provision in the contract. The person drafting the conveyance on behalf of the purchaser must ensure that the conveyance gives the purchaser the rights which the contract promised would be given. The person checking the draft conveyance on behalf of the seller must check that it gives the purchaser nothing more.

Not only the *special* conditions in the contract must be considered. Some of the standard conditions affect the drafting of the purchase deed. These are:

Condition 3.4 possibly justifying the inclusion of an express reservation of easements by the seller, and an express grant to the purchaser. It also enables a seller to put in a declaration negating any implied grant of an easement of light or air to the purchaser. (These conditions are discussed in Chapter 12.)

Condition 4.6.3 justifying the inclusion of a covenant to perform and indemnify (see Chapter 12). This could be relevant not only when the property is sold subject to covenants, but also when the property is sold subject to, for example, a legal mortgage or rent charge.

Condition 8.1.5 this applies on the assignment of a lease, and justifies the seller who is conveying as a beneficial owner in amending the implied covenants for title so that they do not include a promise that the repairing obligations in the lease have been performed by him (see Chapter 15).

Condition 4.6.4 enabling a seller who is conveying as a trustee or a personal representative to refuse to give an undertaking for the safety of a deed retained by him (see later).

13.2 A Specimen Conveyance

This is a draft conveyance of a freehold. It takes a form that some would now criticise as being old-fashioned, but it is a form still frequently used.

This Conveyance is made the .... day of .... 19..... between Amy Baker of .... (hereinafter called the seller of the one part) and Catherine Douglas of .... (hereinafter called the purchaser) of the other part

Whereas the seller owns the freehold estate in the property hereinafter conveyed free from incumbrances, and has agreed to sell the same to the purchaser at a price of £76 000

Now this deed witnesses that in consideration of £76 000 now paid by the purchaser to the seller (receipt whereof the seller hereby acknowledges) the seller as beneficial owner hereby conveys all that property known as 39 Woodbrooke Avenue Nineoaks Kent to hold unto the purchaser in fee simple

In witness thereof the parties hereto have hereunto set their hands the day and year first above written

Signed as a deed and delivered)
by the said Amy Baker in)
the presence of ....)

Now look at the parts of the conveyance separately.

(a) The parties

The two essential parties to the deed will be the seller and the purchaser.

If four people were buying the property, they would still be one party as they are all performing the same role.

Sometimes, other parties will be introduced into the conveyance.

(i) If trustees for sale have to obtain a consent to the sale (see section 11.5) the person whose consent is needed can be made a party, so that the giving of the consent appears on the face of the conveyance.

(ii) If the seller is a tenant for life of a settlement under the Settled Land Act 1925, the trustees of the settlement will be joined as parties to give a receipt for the purchase price. (By virtue of s.18 of the Settled Land Act 1925, a conveyance by a tenant for life is void unless the purchase price is paid, not to the tenant for life, but to the trustees.)

Notice that the sale by the trustees for sale or by the tenant for life is capable of overreaching the interests of the beneficiaries. The beneficiaries would not, therefore, appear as parties to the conveyance.

(iii) Sale of a property subject to a mortgage.

    (aa) If the mortgage is to be redeemed on completion, the mortgage is treated as redeemed *before* completion, so the property is conveyed free from it. The conveyance does not, therefore, mention the mortgage, and the mortgagee is certainly not a party to the conveyance.

    (bb) If the mortgage is *not* to be redeemed on completion, so that the house is conveyed subject to it, the mortgagee does not *have* to be joined as a party (although it would be wise to obtain his prior consent to the conveyance, in case the conveyance prompts him to call in the mortgage).

        He is often joined in as a party since this has two advantages. He can confirm the exact amount now owing on the mortgage, and can take a personal covenant from the purchaser for the repayment of the mortgage loan. The conveyance will also contain a promise by the purchaser to indemnify the seller against any claim by the mortgagee.

(iv) A sale by a mortgagee under his power of sale If the sale is by a mortgagee under his statutory power of sale, he and the purchaser will be the parties to the conveyance. The mortgagee has the ability to convey the mortgagor's estate, and to give a good receipt for the purchase price. The mortgagor is not a party to the conveyance.

(v) Subsales If by the time completion arrives the purchaser (Paul) has already contracted to resell to someone else (Barnabas) the seller can be compelled to convey direct to Barnabas unless either this would prejudice the seller or the contract says otherwise.

    It will be necessary for Paul to be a party to the conveyance if he has resold to Barnabas at a higher price, as a receipt clause for the increase in price will be needed from him.

    The conveyance to Barnabas will be by the seller but will be expressed to be by the direction of Paul. The wording would be 'the seller as beneficial owner at the direction of the purchaser as beneficial owner hereby conveys unto' the sub-purchaser.

    The point is that if a person *directs* a conveyance as beneficial owner, that person will thereby give covenants for title. Barnabas therefore has the benefit of covenants for title given by both the seller and by Paul (see s.76(2) of the Law of Property Act 1925, and Chapter 19 of this book).

(b) *The words 'whereas . . .' introduce the part of the conveyance known as 'the recitals'. These are increasingly omitted in modern conveyances.*

The first recital in our form of conveyance explains that the seller is able to convey the property. It is usually pointless to recite how he came to be in this position as anyone later entitled to investigate the matter has only to read the earlier title deeds.

The second fact recited is the fact that the seller has contracted to sell the property to the purchaser. This explains the reason for the conveyance taking place, and what it is intended that the conveyance shall achieve. Recitals, although their purpose is largely explanatory, do have a legal effect.

(i) A recital of fact will create an estoppel against the person making it, and against that person's successors in title. This can be important. For instance, Amy Baker cannot now deny her ownership of the legal estate at the date of the conveyance. If she did not in fact have it then, but acquired it *after* the date of the conveyance, the legal estate would automatically vest in Catherine Douglas, without any need for a fresh conveyance by Amy. The estoppel is said to have been fed.

(ii) A recital of fact in a document 20 years old at the date of the contract must be taken to be sufficient evidence of the truth of that fact (s.45(6) of the Law of Property Act 1925). The assistance of this rule is not usually needed in modern conveyancing.

(iii) If the conveyance is by a personal representative, a recital that he has not made any previous assent or conveyance will give the purchaser the protection of s.36(6) Administration of Estates Act 1925 (see Chapter 10).

(iv) If the conveyance is by the personal representatives of a sole joint tenant, a recital that the deceased was at his death solely and beneficially interested in the property will give the purchaser the protection of the Law of Property (Joint Tenants) Act 1964 (see Chapter 11).

(c) *The words 'Now this deed witnesses' introduce what is known as the 'operative' part of the deed, that is, the part that actually does the job of transferring ownership from seller to purchaser*

(i) It traditionally starts with the statement of the consideration. Section 5 of the Stamp Act 1891 makes it essential for the consideration to be stated on the face of a conveyance. It is also convenient, as the statement will be accepted by the Stamp Office, and the calculation of stamp duty based on it.

(ii) This is followed by the seller's acknowledgement of the receipt of the purchase price. There are two reasons for inserting this:

(aa) Section 67 of the Law of Property Act 1925. If a receipt is contained in the body of the deed, the purchaser cannot ask for any other receipt.

(bb) Section 69 of the Law of Property Act 1925. Where a solicitor (or by virtue of s.34(1)(c) of the Administration of Justice Act 1985, a licensed conveyancer) produces a deed that has in it a receipt for the consideration money, and that deed is executed by the person entitled to give the receipt (i.e. usually the seller) the deed is sufficient authority to pay the money to the solicitor or licensed conveyancer, without the recipient having otherwise to prove that he has been authorised to receive it. In other words, if the solicitor then decamps with the money, the loss is the seller's, not the purchaser's.

It is sometimes argued in textbooks that s.69 authorises the purchaser to pay only the solicitor, and not the solicitor's employee. The argument has never impressed conveyancing practitioners, who happily hand over the purchase price to whatever representative of the seller's solicitor's firm materialises before them.

(iii) The conveyance will then state in what capacity the seller conveys (see Chapter 19).

(d)   *The parcels clause*

Introduced by the words 'all that . . .', a parcels clause falls into three sections, (i) the descriptive, (ii) the 'plus factor' and (iii) the 'minus factor'.

(i) *The Description of the Property being Conveyed*   Ideally, an accurate and adequate description was settled at the time of the contract, and this can now be reproduced in the conveyance. However, the purchaser, when drafting the conveyance, does not have to use the contract description. The drafting of a description of the property has been discussed in Chapter 5 in the context of the drafting of a contract.

Use of a plan   On the sale of part of the seller's land, a plan will usually be necessary in order to define the new boundary. A seller cannot refuse to convey by reference to a plan, unless one is unnecessary for the description of the property. (The reason why he might wish to refuse is that it involves him in checking the accuracy of the plan.)

It need scarcely be said that if a plan is to be used then that plan must be accurate and professionally prepared. It must also be on a sufficiently large scale. As well as the plan being physically attached to the conveyance, reference should be made to it in the conveyance (otherwise it is not strictly part of the deed at all).

There should, of course, be no conflict between the verbal description in the conveyance and the plan. The main role of the plan will be to supplement the verbal description, particularly in the role of defining boundaries, where it is difficult to frame a sufficiently clear verbal description. In such a case, where the plan is to prevail as it gives the more precise description, the plan should be referred to as 'more particularly' describing the property.

The verbal description will prevail if the plan is inadequate, or unclear, or is referred to as only being for the purpose of identifying the property. (You might ask yourself before using such a plan of what use it is if it does not make the position clearer than the verbal description does.)

Fixtures Fixtures are part of the land, and pass automatically with a conveyance of it. There is, therefore, no need to mention such things as garages, as they will pass to the purchaser anyway. The same could be said of the house, but it is usual to include the house in the description of the land being conveyed. Indeed the description of the house often stands as the description of the land, for example, 'all that house and garden known as 1 Roseberry Crescent . . .'.

(ii) *The 'Plus Factor'* The second part of a parcels clause may be called 'the plus factor', and is introduced by the words 'together with . . .'. There are then listed:

(aa) existing easements that the property already enjoys over neighbouring land;
(bb) new easements, being granted in this conveyance by the seller over land that he is retaining nearby.

The existing easements would pass to the purchaser anyway, as they are part of the land being conveyed. The benefit of listing them is that they are not later forgotten.

(iii) *The 'Minus Factor'* The final part of the parcels clause may be called 'the minus factor' and is introduced by the words 'except' and 'reserving'. There are then listed any *new* easements that the seller is reserving for the benefit of his land over the property he is conveying.

A reservation takes effect as a grant by the purchaser. Thus, if the conveyance says 'reserving to the seller a right of way on foot over the property hereby conveyed along the route marked green on the said plan . . .' this is, in fact a right of way granted by the purchaser over the property which he is acquiring. This has the result that as an ambiguous grant is always construed against the grantor, any ambiguity in the reservation of the easement will be construed against the purchaser and in favour of the seller.

The reservation takes effect even if conveyance is not executed by the purchaser (s.65(1) of the Law of Property Act 1925).

Any exception, for example, of mineral rights, also appears in this part of the parcels clause. (Strictly, an exception is where the seller retains something from the land that is already in existence, for example, mineral rights. A reservation is where the seller acquires a right not previously existing, such as an easement or a profit. In practice, the distinction is unlikely to be of importance, as the two are always put together.)

(e)   The Habendum

The words 'to hold . . .' introduce what is known as the *habendum*. This describes the title that is to be conveyed, that is, the estate, and the incumbrances to which the estate is subject.

Further points about the habendum are made in sections 13.4(a) and 13.4(d).

(f)   The Testimonium and Execution

The testimonium (in witness, etc.) introduces the signatures of the parties. In many cases, there is no need for the purchaser to execute the conveyance (for exceptions, see section 13.5).

13.3   Formalities of Execution

(a)   By an Individual

What is written here applies to deeds executed after the coming into effect of s.1 of the Law of Property (Miscellaneous Provisions) Act 1989 on 31 July 1990. (The formalities for execution of deeds before that date are set out in section 9(2)(f).

A conveyance of a legal estate must be by deed. A document will only be a deed if:

- it is signed by its maker;
- if that signature is witnessed and attested;
- if it is clear that the document is intended to be a deed. That intention can be made clear either by describing the document as a deed (e.g. 'This Deed of Conveyance is made 1 September 1990 _____) or because the document is expressed to be executed or signed as a deed (e.g. the attestation clause might say 'signed by the seller as his deed in the presence of _____ ');
- if the deed is delivered as a deed.

The delivery of a deed may be a matter of intention only. A deed is delivered by a seller when it is signed by him with the intention that he shall be bound by it.

Signature by Another   The Act makes it possible for an individual to direct another person to sign a deed on his behalf, provided that the signature is made in his presence and there are *two* attesting witnesses.

Delivery by Another   A deed may be delivered absolutely, and is then of immediate effect. Alternatively, it may be delivered conditionally, and is then known as an *escrow*.

A deed may be delivered by its maker, or it may be delivered by someone on his behalf.

Until the coming into effect of s.1 of the 1989 Act, conveyancing practice has been that the conveyance has been signed and *delivered* by the seller some days before completion. This has ensured that every conveyance has been delivered conditionally. Had the delivery been absolute, the legal estate would there and then have vested in the purchaser, although he had not yet paid the purchase price. Delivery has been conditional upon completion taking place and the purchase price being paid. The conveyance has come into full effect when the condition has been fulfilled.

So every sale has produced an escrow but escrows create difficulties. One is the so-called doctrine of 'relation back', which has the effect that the true date of the conveyance (whatever date it might bear on its face) is the date of the conditional delivery (i.e. some days before completion) rather than the date the condition is fulfilled (i.e. the actual date of completion). Another is that delivery in escrow is binding. It commits the seller; he cannot withdraw from the deed while the time limit for fulfilment of the condition is still running. Only if completion does not take place in due course can he renounce the escrow (see *Glessing* v. *Green* [1975]). One suggested solution to the problem of an escrow is that the seller should sign the conveyance only, and authorise his solicitor to deliver the deed at completion. Up until the time of writing [1990] the idea has not been put into practice as the authority would have had to be given by a power of attorney. This difficulty is now swept aside by s.1 of the 1989 Act, for the section abolishes the rule that the authority to deliver can only be given by deed. It will, therefore, be possible for the deed to be delivered at completion by the seller's solicitor. The purchaser need not check the solicitor's authority to deliver the deed, as the Act provides that where a solicitor or licensed conveyancer (or his agent or employee) delivers an instrument on behalf of a person for whom he is acting, it shall be conclusively presumed in favour of the purchaser that such a person *is* authorised to deliver the instrument. The aim is, therefore, to make it unnecessary for a deed to be delivered by the seller in escrow. What may happen instead is that before completion the seller will sign the deed, without any intention of being then bound by it. He will then send it to his solicitor. At completion, the solicitor will hand or send it to the purchaser's solicitor, and thereby manifest the seller's intention to be bound. The deed will be physically and legally delivered at the same time.

(b) By a Company

What is written here applies to a deed executed by a company after the coming into effect of s.130 of the Companies Act 1989, i.e. again 31 July 1990. (The formalities for the execution of a deed before that date are set out in section 9.4.) For a document to be executed as a deed by a company, it is necessary that the document be executed (i.e. signed or sealed) and delivered as a deed.

Execution   Section 36A Companies Act 1985 (inserted by s.130 of the 1989 Act) provides that the document can be executed *either*

- by the affixing of the company seal, *or*
- by being signed by a director and the secretary, or by two directors of the company, provided that the document is expressed to be executed by the company. In other words, it must be made clear that the signatures amount to execution by the *company*, rather than execution by the directors *personally*.

Delivery   If the executed document makes it clear on its face that it is intended to be a deed, it will be a deed when delivered as a deed. It is presumed, unless the contrary appears, to be delivered at the time it is executed.

Protection of Third Parties   Section 36A(6) provides that a purchaser for value can presume (a) that the document has been properly executed as a deed by the company if it bears two signatures purporting to be those of a director and the secretary, or those of two directors, and (b) that it has been delivered as a deed, providing it is clear on its face that it is intended by the signatories to be a deed.

The purchaser will be content, therefore, if he sees a statement in the document that it is signed *as a deed by the company*, and sees accompanying this statement two signatures purporting to be those of directors or director and secretary.

13.4   Variations to our Standard Form of Conveyance

(a)   *Where the sale is of an incumbered freehold*

Suppose that the contract states that the sale is subject to restrictive covenants contained in a conveyance dated 1 July 1950.

First, the recital as to the seller's ownership should be changed. It should not say that he owns an unincumbered estate. It will instead say something like 'the seller owns the freehold estate in the property hereby conveyed subject as hereafter mentioned, but otherwise free from incumbrances . . .'.

Second, the habendum must be changed. It will now read 'to hold unto the purchaser in fee simple, subject to the restrictive covenants contained in a conveyance dated 1 July 1950, made between Mark Old of the one part and Ian Stone of the other part'. In the case of covenants, there are also often added the words 'so far as the same are valid and subsisting and can be enforced against the land hereby conveyed'.

There are two reasons for listing incumbrances in the habendum. One is that it keeps remembrance of them alive. The other is that it modifies the covenants for title given by a seller who conveys as beneficial owner (see Chapter 19).

It must be pointed out that whether or not the incumbrance is mentioned in the conveyance has no effect on whether or not the incumbrance will bind the purchaser. In the case of the 1950 covenant, its enforceability depends on whether or not it is registered as a D(ii) land charge. If it is not registered it will not bind a purchaser, even though the conveyance is said to be subject to it (but see *Lyus* v. *Prowsa* [1982]). Similarly, if the land were subject to a legal easement, the easement would bind a purchaser because it is legal, and whether or not the conveyance mentions it is irrelevant to the issue.

We have seen that new easements are reserved by the seller in the parcels clause, but note that existing easements burdening the land are mentioned in the habendum. The same point can be made in respect of restrictive covenants. A covenant is not, of course, created by a reservation. It takes the form of a promise, and will be created by a separate clause following the operative part of the conveyance.

Example

1 April 1970   Conveyance from Alice to Beryl. Parcels – except and reserving to Alice a right of light. Covenant clause – Beryl promises Alice to use only as a dwelling-house.

1 April 1990   Conveyance from Beryl to Carol. Parcels – no reservation (unless Beryl *is* reserving a *new* easement). Habendum – subject to easement of light and 1970 covenant. No covenant clause, unless Carol is giving Beryl a *new* covenant.

As soon as you find yourself writing that the property is conveyed subject to covenants, you should also think about the inclusion of an indemnity covenant, whereby the purchaser promises to indemnify the seller against breach of the covenants. The standard conditions will justify the inclusion of an indemnity covenant, and also govern its wording (see Chapter 12).

(b)   Sale of Part of the Seller's Land

The fact that it is a sale of part will cause the following alterations:

(i) The parcels clause:

- particular care must be taken in describing the land conveyed. If a new boundary is to be defined, a plan is probably essential. Great care must be taken if a building is being divided (see *Scarfe* v. *Adams* [1981].
- the contract may justify the inclusion of a reservation or grant of an easement. These new easements will be created in the parcels clause. (This point has already been discussed.)

(ii) The contract may provide for the inclusion of positive and restrictive covenants. The wording of restrictive covenants is discussed in Chapter 12.

(iii) The inclusion of an acknowledgement and undertaking. The seller, if selling only part of the land covered by the title deeds, is entitled to, and will, retain the title deeds in his possession. (The normal rule is, of course, that the seller must hand over the title deeds to the purchaser on completion. However, s.49(9) of the Law of Property Act 1925 enables the seller to retain title deeds if they relate to land he is retaining, or to a subsisting trust.) The purchaser will need access to the title deeds when he resells, as the person to whom he resells will wish to read them.

When the seller retains deeds, the purchaser is entitled to a written acknowledgement of his rights to have the retained deeds produced and to an undertaking that the seller will keep them safe. This does not depend on any stipulation in the contract. It is a matter of general law.

The seller's acknowledgement, by virtue of s.49 of the Law of Property Act 1925, gives the purchaser the right to ask for the production of the documents covered by the acknowledgement, at the purchaser's expense. This right can be enforced by a decree for specific performance.

The undertaking for safe custody gives the purchaser a right to damages if the documents are lost, destroyed or injured, unless, to quote s.49, this is due to 'fire or other inevitable accident'.

The burden of these obligations runs with the deeds, so it can be enforced against whoever at the time has control or possession of them. The benefit of the obligations runs with the land, so can be enforced by the purchaser's successors (but not by a tenant of the land at a rent).

A person selling as personal representative or as a trustee, or a mortgagee selling under his power of sale, will be prepared to give the acknowledgement, but would prefer not to give the undertaking, because of the possible liability to damages. The refusal is probably pointless, as the seller has the burden of undertakings given by his predecessors. Furthermore, he has no right to refuse the undertaking, although the traditional refusal has been traditionally accepted. Standard Condition 4.6.4, however, *entitles* a fiduciary seller to refuse to give the undertaking.

Section 49 demands that the acknowledgement and undertaking be in writing. They are invariably put in the conveyance itself. The usual wording is 'the seller hereby acknowledges the right of the purchaser to the production of the documents specified in the schedule hereto (the possession of which documents is retained by the seller) and to delivery of copies thereof and undertakes with the purchaser for the safe custody of the said documents'.

This wording actually extends the statutory rights, which do not include the right to take copies. The documents will be described in the schedule by their nature, date and parties, for example:

1 April 1980	Conveyance	Ian Williams (1)
		Percy Bishop (2)
3 March 1989	Mortgage (with	Percy Bishop (1)
	receipt endorsed	Norward Bank (2)

Section 49 refers to documents. This clearly gives the purchaser the right to an acknowledgement and undertaking in respect of the title deeds. It probably does not cover such things as search certificates, marriage or death certificates, nor is there any reason why a purchaser should want it to do so.

In the absence of an acknowledgement, it seems that there is an equitable right for a person the proof of whose title depends on deeds, to require production of these deeds. Section 45(7) of the Law of Property Act 1925 says that if the purchaser has an equitable right to production of the title deeds, he cannot object to the seller's title on the ground that the seller cannot give him the benefit of a statutory acknowledgement. So suppose, for example, that when Alan sells part of his land to Bill and retains the title deeds, Bill carelessly fails to obtain an acknowledgement from Alan. When Bill contracts to sell to Charles, Charles can demand production of the deed from Alan by virtue of the equitable right, so he cannot say that Bill's failure to get the statutory acknowledgement is a flaw in Bill's title. Bill however, should, have altered standard condition 4.6.4 in the contract or he would otherwise have promised that Charles would have the benefit of a written acknowledgement.

(c) Sale of Part of the Seller's Land when the Title is Mortgaged

Suppose that Alec owns the whole of Blackacre and it is mortgaged to the Elephant Building Society. He is thinking of selling the north-east corner to Benjie, but Benjie will only buy if he can get the property free from the mortgage. That is no difficulty if Alec has the funds to pay off the entire mortgage debt. If he has not, he must approach the Society and ask if it will release the corner from its security, leaving the rest of Blackacre still subject to the mortgage. If the rest of Blackacre offers good security for the loan, the Building Society may agree, or it may agree in return for receiving part of the proceeds of sale towards reduction of the debt. (If the Society does not agree, there is nothing Alec can do, if he cannot pay off the entire loan. That is why Alec must ensure that the Society will cooperate *before* he enters into the contract.)

In order to release the land from its mortgage, the Society will usually be joined into the conveyance, so the following differences will be made to our conveyance:

(i) the parties will be the seller of the first part, the Building Society of the second part and the purchaser of the third part;
(ii) the recitals will include the statements that the property is mortgaged to the Society, and that the Society has agreed to join in the conveyance for the purpose of releasing the land from its mortgage;

(iii) the operative part of the conveyance will say something like 'the seller as beneficial owner hereby conveys, and the Society *hereby releases* all that property known as . . .';

(iv) the acknowledgement and undertaking clause will read something like:

'The Society hereby acknowledges the right of the purchaser to production of the documents specified in the schedule hereto and to delivery of copies thereof
The seller covenants with the purchaser as to the said documents that as and when any of them come into his possession, he will when requested at the cost of the purchaser or his successor in title execute a statutory undertaking for their safe custody'

What lies behind this clause is the fact that an acknowledgement is only effective if given by the person who then has custody of the deeds, in other words, the Building Society. That is why the Society and not the seller, gives the acknowledgement. The Society will refuse to give the undertaking. This again cannot be given at the moment by the seller, because he does not possess the deeds. Hence the covenant that he will give the undertaking when the deeds return to him, that is, on redemption of the mortgage.

(d)   A Purchase by Co-Owners

If the property is to be owned by more than one person, the conveyance (or perhaps a separate trust deed) must declare how the equitable interest is to be held by them. This may be done, in simple cases, in the habendum. For example, if two people are buying the property, the habendum might read 'to hold unto the purchasers in fee simple as beneficial joint tenants'. If they wish to be tenants in common, the habendum might read 'to hold unto the purchasers in equal shares'. (The creation of shares means that there is a tenancy in common.)

It is clearly important to the purchasers that the conveyance declares how they own the equitable interests. This declaration will be binding on them, and in any later dispute will be decisive as to their ownership. The declaration is also important from the point of view of making title. If one co-owner dies, the declaration of ownership will decide whether the surviving owner can convey the property by himself, or must appoint a second trustee for sale to act with him. Unless there is a declaration that the co-owners held as beneficial joint tenants, no purchaser will be prepared to accept a conveyance from the survivor alone (see Chapter 11).

The purchaser's solicitor needs instructions from his clients as to how they intend to own the equitable interest. A married couple may well choose to own it as joint tenants, as the right of survivorship will ensure that the whole house belongs automatically to the surviving spouse. However, some married couples choose otherwise. Two people joining together to buy a house for the simple reason that neither could afford to buy a house alone, will wish to be tenants in common, so that there will be no right of survivorship. They will not necessarily wish to be tenants in common in equal shares, as the size of the shares should reflect the size of the contributions towards the total purchase price. The size of the shares should always be stated. It is insufficient merely to say that the purchasers are tenants in common.

The co-ownership of the equitable interests will automatically mean that a statutory trust for sale is imposed on the legal estate (see Chapter 11). There is often little point in creating an express trust for sale to replace the statutory trust for sale, although this is frequently done.

A clause is also often inserted increasing the powers of the purchasers (who will be the trustees for sale) to deal with the legal estate. This is because the power of trustees for sale are limited, and in particular they can only mortgage the property if it is to raise money for authorised purposes, e.g. for the improvement of the property. In a simple case, where the trustees and the beneficiaries are the same people, there is no real need for such a clause, as what the owners cannot do as trustees they can do by virtue of their beneficial ownership. A bank or building society does not hesitate to lend money to, for example, a husband and wife on the security of their house, no matter for what purpose they need the money, as the bank looks through their ownership of the legal estate, to find that they are the only owners of the beneficial interest. However, this does involve investigation of the equitable interests, so many draftsmen would feel it desirable expressly to extend the powers. Such a clause should always be considered if the equitable interests are complicated.

(e)   *A Sale by a Personal Representative*

If the sale is by a personal representative, the following changes will be made to our form of conveyance:

(i)   the recitals will generally explain the seller's ability to convey the legal estate. The facts that will be noted are:

    (aa)   that Digby (the deceased) died, the date of his death, and the fact that probate (or letters of administration) was granted to the seller;

    (bb)   that Digby at the date of his death, owned the freehold estate free from incumbrances (or as appropriate);

    (cc)   that the seller has contracted to sell the property to the purchaser;

    (dd)   there must then be added the recital that the seller has not made any assent or conveyance in respect of this property. This recital gives the purchaser the protection of s.36(6) of the Administration of Estates Act 1925 (see Chapter 10).

(ii) The seller will be retaining the grant, so the conveyance will contain an acknowledgement for production of the grant. The acknowledgement is needed, because it is insufficient for a later purchaser to see an office copy of the grant. He will wish to see the original to check for the presence or absence of memoranda of previous assents.

13.5   A Specimen Conveyance of Part

There are now outlined the clauses that might appear in a conveyance of part of the seller's land:

(a) The date of conveyance
(b) The parties. Let us suppose there is one seller and two purchasers.
(c) The standard recitals as to the seller's ownership of the freehold estate, and the contract to convey it to the purchasers.
(d) The operative part:

   (i)   consideration and receipt clause;
   (ii) the fact that the seller conveys, and his capacity;
   (iii) the parcels clause;
   (aa) the description of the land being conveyed, possibly 'as more particularly delineated and outlined in red on the plan annexed hereto'
   (bb) 'together with' existing easements and new easements justified by the terms of the contract.
   (cc) 'except and reserving' to the seller any new easements justified by the terms of the contract.
   (iv) the habendum, that is, the fact that the freehold is being conveyed, and details of all existing incumbrances. Let us suppose it is said that the land is subject to restrictive covenants created in 1950.

(e) A clause declaring that the purchasers are not by virtue of the conveyance to become entitled to any right to light or air over the land retained by the seller, and any enjoyment of light or air by the purchasers from the retained land is deemed to be had by the consent of the seller.
(f) New covenants given by the purchasers to the seller, or vice versa.
(g) A covenant for indemnity and performance given by the purchasers to the seller in respect of the 1950 covenants.
(h) A declaration by the purchasers that the land has been conveyed to them on trust for sale for themselves as beneficial joint tenants.
(i) A declaration that the purchasers have the same powers of dealing with the land as if they were a sole beneficial owner.
(j) The seller's acknowledgement and undertaking in respect of the deeds retained by him.

(k) A certificate that the consideration does not exceed £30 000.
(l) Execution of the deed by the seller and both purchasers. The signatures will be witnessed.

The provisions of this conveyance should now be clear, but the following points should be noted:

1. Clause e - the purpose of the first part of this clause is to negative any grant of an easement of light or air to the purchasers that might otherwise have been implied into the conveyance, for example by *Wheeldon* v. *Burrows* or by s.62 of the Law of Property Act 1925 (see Chapter 12). It can be included in the conveyance by virtue of a special condition in the contract, or by virtue of standard condition 3.4.2.

   The second part of the clause prevents any future acquisition of an easement of light or air by prescription, because it provides evidence that the receipt of light or air from over the seller's land is by virtue of his written consent, and not as of right.

   This part of the clause could be included by virtue of a special condition in the contract, but it is doubtful if its inclusion is justified by the standard condition.

2. Clauses h and i create an express trust for sale, declare the equitable ownership, and extend the powers of the purchasers to those of a sole beneficial owner – that is, without restriction. They will not, therefore, have to prove their equitable ownership before borrowing money on the security of the land.

3. In this case, the conveyance has been executed by the purchasers as well as the seller. Although it was said earlier that the execution of the conveyance by the purchaser is not generally necessary, execution of *this* conveyance by the purchasers is important. There are two separate reasons:

   (i) a purchaser should execute a conveyance if he is giving covenants to the seller. If the purchaser does not execute the conveyance, the seller could not bring an action in law for damages for the breach, although the covenant might be enforceable in equity;

   (ii) if there are two or more purchasers, and the conveyance declares how they own the equitable interests, the purchasers should execute the conveyance. If the conveyance is executed, the declaration binds the parties, and will be treated by the courts as being decisive of their ownership. It has been said that if the conveyance is not executed, then a party can give evidence that the declaration is incorrect (see, for example, *Robinson* v. *Robinson* (1976) – but for the opposite view see *In re Gorman (a bankrupt)* [1990].

4. Notice the traditional order of the clauses. Matters affecting the relationship between seller and purchaser are dealt with first (clauses a

to g). Then come the clauses affecting the purchasers *inter se* (clauses h and i).

The acknowledgement and undertaking clause is traditionally the last before the attestation, yielding this place of honour only to the certificate of value. The certificate is of course only included if the purchase price is £30 000 or less.

Workshop

Attempt to solve this problem yourself, then read the specimen solution at the end of the book.

Problem 1

The contract is for the sale of the northern half of Blackacre.

The sellers are Vera Brown and William Brown (her husband). The purchasers are Phyllis and Pauline White, two sisters, who have contributed to the purchase in equal shares, and wish to own as tenants in common. The purchase price is £30 500 of which £500 is being paid for carpets, curtains, and a refrigerator.

The contract incorporates the standard conditions. The special conditions provide that:

1. the sale is subject to restrictive covenants contained in a conveyance dated 19 September 1960 made between Ann Rogers of the one part and Buck Thompson of the other part;
2. the sellers and their successors in title will have the right to walk along the eastern boundary of the plot being sold as a means of access to the southern half of Blackacre, which they are retaining; but they are not entitled to any other right.
3. standard condition 3.4 is excluded;
4. the purchasers will covenant not to build or allow to be built on the land conveyed to them more than one bungalow, and that to be built in accordance with plans approved by the sellers.

List the provisions that should be contained in the conveyance.

---

14 Drafting a Transfer of a Registered Title

14.1 A Transfer of Whole

The form of a land registry transfer is prescribed by the Land Registration Rules 1925. A completed land registry form 19 (transfer of title) would look like this:

HM LAND REGISTRY
Transfer of Whole

County and District or London Borough	Kent, Nineoaks
Title No.	KT 00007
Property	39 Woodbrooke Avenue
Date	19 —

In consideration of SEVENTY SIX THOUSAND POUNDS (£76 000) the receipt of which is acknowledged I AMY BAKER of 39 Woodbrooke Avenue Nineoaks Kent civil engineer as beneficial owner hereby transfer to CATHERINE DOUGLAS of 39 Woodbrooke Avenue Nineoaks Kent market gardener the land comprised in the title above mentioned

Signed as a deed and delivered)
by the said Amy Baker in   )   (signed) Amy Baker
the presence of:)
Norma Hopeless
40 Woodbrooke Avenue
Nineoaks Kent

Compare this with the conveyance in section 13.2:

(a) There are no recitals.
(b) The address of the purchaser should be the address at which he will be living after the registration of the transfer (often the address of the property that is being transferred). This is because the address on the transfer is the address that will be entered on the proprietorship register, and that will be the address to which the Registrar writes, e.g. giving warning of the application for entry of a caution.
(c) There is a statement of consideration, receipt clause and statement of capacity. They appear in a transfer for the same reasons as they appear in a conveyance.

(d) There is no parcels clause, nor habendum. These are unnecessary because of the phrase 'comprised in the title above mentioned'. The description of the land being conveyed and the title comes from the register, not from the transfer.

14.2   Variations

(a)   A Transfer to Co-Purchasers

Land Registry form 19(JP) can be used for a transfer to co-owners. It varies from the standard form 19 by adding a clause which says either that the sole survivor of the transferees *can* give a good receipt for capital money arising on a disposition of the land, or alternatively, that he *cannot*. This clause amounts to a declaration as to whether or not the transferees are beneficial joint tenants and will govern whether or not a restriction is put on the proprietorship register (see Chapter 11).

However, while the declaration that the survivor cannot give a good receipt shows that the transferees are tenants in common, it does not establish the *size* of their shares. It is quite possible to declare the size of the share in the transfer, so that the transfer will state, for example that the registered proprietor transfers to Catherine Douglas and Charles Deering 'as tenants in common in equal shares the land comprised in the title above mentioned'. It is then unnecessary to state that the survivor cannot give a valid receipt, as that is clearly evident from the statement that they are tenants in common. However, remember that the transfer is sent to the Registry for registration, and is retained there. It is, therefore, a sound idea not to depend on the transfer for a declaration of the shares, or at least not if they are in any way complicated. A separate document should be signed by the transferees setting out their equitable ownership. This is not sent to the Registry as the Registrar is not concerned with the ownership of the equitable interests. He will merely see the statement in the transfer that the sole survivor cannot give a good receipt for capital money.

(b)   Transfer of Part of the Land in the Title

(i) It is essential for the transfer to describe which part of the land within the registered title is being transferred.

The transfer will read something like 'the land shown and edged red on the annexed plan and known as ... being part of the land comprised in the title above mentioned'. The Land Registration Rules 1925 require that a plan be used, unless the part being transferred can be clearly defined by means of a verbal reference to the filed plan. If a plan is used in the transfer, it must be signed by the transferor and by or on behalf of the transferee (see rule 98 and Land Registry form 20).

(ii) No acknowledgement or undertaking are required. On completion the seller will hand the purchaser the transfer of part, but not the land certificate, as the seller is retaining some of the land in the title. The seller should, before completion, send his land certificate to the registry. He will be given a deposit number, which he passes on to the purchaser. The purchaser, on applying for registration of his transfer, will quote this number. The transfer and the land certificate will meet at the registry. The seller's register and land certificate will be noted with the fact that the land has left the title, the filed plan will be amended and the land certificate returned to the seller. The part transferred to the purchaser will be registered under a new title number, and the new land certificate relating to that title will be sent to the purchaser.

(iii) A transfer of part may create new easements in favour of seller or purchaser, or new restrictive and positive covenants (see Chapter 12 for the question of their registration).

(c) Indemnity Covenant

A transfer may contain an indemnity covenant, either because the seller gave positive or restrictive covenants when he bought or because he gave an indemnity covenant. (For disclosure by the register of personal covenants, see Chapter 12.)

14.3 A Transfer of Part

To illustrate the points made, there now follows a form of a transfer of part (based on Land Registry Form 20). It is usually easier when drafting a transfer of part to abandon the first-person approach used in a transfer of whole.

HM LAND REGISTRY
Land Registration Act 1925 and 1971
Transfer of Part of Freehold Land

County	Kent
Title No.	K000007
Property	2 River View
	Hoo St Werburgh
Date	4 June 1990

1. In consideration of TWENTY EIGHT THOUSAND POUNDS (£28 000) the receipt of which is acknowledged ALEC HERBERT and ANN HERBERT (his wife) both of 2 River View Hoo St Werburgh Kent (hereinafter called the sellers) as trustees hereby transfer to Ian Bigge and Belinda Bigge (his wife) both of 1 Marshy Close Cliffe Kent (hereinafter called the purchasers) the land shown and edged with red on the annexed plan being part of the land comprised in the title above mentioned

2. The sellers reserve the right set out in the first schedule to this transfer for the benefit of the remainder of the land comprised in the above mentioned title (hereinafter called the retained land)
3. This transfer does not include any right to light or air over the retained land
4. The purchasers jointly and severally covenant with the sellers that the purchasers will at all times observe and perform the covenants contained in the conveyance dated 1 February 1980 referred to in entry number 1 of the charges register of the above mentioned title so far as they are still enforceable against the land transferred hereby and will to the same extent indemnify the sellers against all claims in respect of any future breach of the said covenants
5. The purchasers jointly and severally covenant with the sellers so as to benefit each and every part of the retained land and so as to bind the land hereby transferred and every part thereof into whosesoever hands the same might come to observe and perform the covenants contained in the second schedule hereto
6. The purchasers declare that the survivor of them is entitled to give a valid receipt for capital moneys arising on a disposition of the land
7. It is hereby certified that the transaction hereby effected does not form part of a larger transaction or of a series of transactions in respect of which the amount or value or aggregate amount or value of the consideration exceeds THIRTY THOUSAND POUNDS (£30 000)

The First Schedule
(details of reserved easements)
The Second Schedule
(covenants)

Signed and delivered as a deed by all parties, with each signature attested.

14.4   Rule 72 of the Land Registration Act 1925

This rule provides that a person who has the right to apply to be registered as first proprietor of the land can deal with the land before he is in fact registered as proprietor in the same manner as he could do if he were registered. So, for example, imagine that Pauline buys an unregistered title in an area of compulsory registration of title. She intends to re-sell to Queenie. She may do so, without herself applying for first registration. However, the document that she uses to convey to Queenie should be in the same form as it would have been had Pauline been a registered proprietor, i.e. it should be drawn up as a land registry transfer, rather than as a conveyance of unregistered land. Of course, it will not be quite the same as a land registry transfer, as no title number can be quoted and the transfer must describe the property rather than referring to it as that comprised in the registered title.

Queenie will then apply for first registration of title, proving by the title deeds that Pauline had the right to be registered as proprietor and also proving by the transfer drawn up under rule 72, her own right to be registered as first proprietor instead.

15 Buying a Leasehold

15.1 Introduction

The procedure for buying or selling a leasehold house differs little from the procedure for buying a freehold house. This chapter, therefore, serves only to point out those parts of a conveyancing transaction which are peculiar to leaseholds, and which have not yet been mentioned. [Note that this chapter is dealing with the purchase of an *existing* lease. The grant of a *new* lease will be dealt with in Chapter 16]

Three topics will be discussed generally first, and then set in the context of the transaction.

15.2 Title to be Shown

(a)   What the Purchaser May See

Unless the contract says otherwise, s.44 of the Law of Property Act 1925 provides that a person who has agreed to buy an existing leasehold is entitled to two things:

1.   He is entitled to see the document (i.e. the lease) which granted the estate he is buying. The reasons for this are obvious. The lease must be seen to check that the estate was ever granted in the first place. It must also be seen to discover the terms of the grant, e.g. the covenants, forfeiture clause, etc. Although an open contract allows the purchaser to call for production of the lease, it is a point rarely considered in practice, as a copy of the lease will be provided with the draft contract. No purchaser will contract to buy a leasehold estate without seeing the lease.
2.   He is also entitled to evidence that the seller owns the leasehold estate. This is the same as in freehold conveyancing, and the nature of the evidence is the same.

So how will the seller prove his ownership of a lease registered under the Land Registration Act 1925? By providing a copy of the entries on the register, a filed plan, etc., to comply with s.110 of the Act. The fact that the seller is registered as proprietor of the leasehold estate, whether with absolute or with good leasehold title, means that he owns the legal estate. The register may warn us of third-party interests by disclosing a notice, caution, restriction or registered charge. (Remember that the register is not conclusive as to the contents of the lease, so the lease must be seen, as well as the entries on the register.)

Suppose the title is unregistered. Title to an unregistered freehold is proved by producing past conveyances of it. Equally, title to an unregistered leasehold is proved by the production of past conveyances, although for some reason a conveyance of a leasehold estate is usually called an assignment. To take some examples:

(i) Peter is buying a leasehold from Tom. Tom is the person to whom the estate was granted by landlord Len. Peter will see the lease. Tom establishes his ownership of the leasehold simply by the fact that he is the tenant named in the lease.

(ii) Some years later, Quentin is buying the leasehold from Peter. As Peter is not the original tenant he must produce the assignment of the lease into his name. As the assignment was by the original tenant, that is the only document that can be produced.

(iii) Robert is buying from Quentin. Quentin must produce the assignment into his name. If this assignment between Peter and Quentin took place more than fifteen years ago, Quentin need *only* produce this assignment. This is because he has traced title to the lease from a good root at least fifteen years old. So once Robert has seen an assignment that is fifteen years old, he cannot demand to see any earlier ones, as these would be pre-root (s.44 of the Law of Property Act 1925). This will mean that Robert may not know how the leasehold ever came to be vested in Peter.

If the assignment between Peter and Quentin took place less than fifteen years ago, Robert would be entitled to see the preceding assignment, between Tom and Peter. As this is an assignment by the original tenant, investigation would end there.

(b)   *What the Purchaser May Not See*

Section 44 does not permit the purchaser of a leasehold to demand evidence of any reversionary title. This means that Robert cannot investigate Len's title to grant the lease. This carries considerable risks.

(i) Robert does not know if Len owned the freehold estate, or a leasehold estate, or indeed any estate at all.

(ii) Robert does not know in what capacity Len held the estate. Fiduciary owners such as trustees for sale or a tenant for life under the Settled Land Act 1925 may have only limited statutory powers of leasing.

(iii) Robert does not know if Len's estate was mortgaged when he granted the lease. Section 99 of the Law of Property Act 1925 empowers a mortgagor who is in possession of the mortgaged property to grant a lease which will bind the mortgagee. In other words, the mortgagee will not be able to obtain possession against the tenant, and will only be able to sell subject to his lease. This statutory power is naturally unpopular with mortgagees, and it can usually be, and usually is, excluded by a clause in the mortgage deed. It may either exclude the power altogether, or make it exercisable only with the mortgagee's consent. Either provision ensures that any lease granted by the mortgagor after the date of the mortgage will not bind the mortgagee, unless the mortgagee consents to its grant. A tenant can, therefore, find himself with no security at all should his landlord fail to keep up with the mortgage payments. If the mortgagee wishes to exercise his power of sale he will evict the tenant if a better price could be obtained by selling the property with vacant possession.

So Robert would like to know if Len's estate was mortgaged when he granted the lease to Tom, and if it was, if the mortgagee consented to the grant. Yet s.44 prevents this enquiry.

(iv) As Robert does not know if Len owned the freehold or a leasehold estate when he granted the lease to Tom, Robert does not know if he is buying a headlease or an underlease. If he is buying an underlease, he would like to see copies of the superior leases. This is because Robert does not want inadvertently to break a covenant – for example, a user covenant – in a superior lease. This is explained in Problem 1 in the Workshop section.

(v) Robert does not know if there are third-party rights affecting the superior titles – for example, any restrictive covenant on the freehold, if it is protected by being registered as a land charge D(ii), or by the entry of a notice or caution on the register of title, will bind the tenant or undertenant, as the registration amounts to actual notice (see s.198 of the Law of Property Act 1925, s.50(2) of the Land Registration Act 1925, and *White* v. *Bijou Mansions* [1938]). Yet the registration cannot be discovered, as s.44 prevents investigation of the freehold title.

The risks that s.44 presents do not exist only on the purchase of an unregistered lease. They are the same when buying a registered lease *if* it is registered only with good leasehold title. The title does not guarantee that the landlord had power to grant the lease, nor will it contain details of incumbrances on the superior titles, which may nevertheless bind the purchaser of the lease.

Section 44 has never presented the same risks to a purchaser of a lease registered with absolute title. This class of title follows investigation of all the superior titles by the Registrar. It guarantees that the lease is valid, and incumbrances affecting the superior titles will be noted on the register of title.

N.B. If the landlord's title is registered under the Land Registration Act 1925, the fact that s.44 Law of Property Act 1925 does not compel the seller to give details of the landlord's title to the purchaser will, from 3 December 1990, be mitigated by the fact that the landlord's register of title will be open to public inspection. (Land Registration Act 1988). The purchaser will be able to obtain office copies of the register for himself. The only effect of s.44 will be that the purchaser, rather than the seller, will have to pay for these copies.

Section 44 remains a difficulty if the landlord's title, or, if relevant, any superior title, is not registered.

A public index map search will disclose whether or not the titles are registered, and the title numbers. (See section 6.2).

(c)　*A Special Condition in the Contract*

A purchaser can oust s.44 by a special condition in the contract which compels the seller to give details of the freehold title and of any superior leasehold titles. The seller, of course, will not accept the inclusion of such a condition if he has no evidence of the superior titles to supply.

(d)　*Standard Condition 8.1.3*

This provides that the seller is to deduce a title which will enable the buyer to register the lease at HM Land Registry with an absolute title, (or would enable him to do so if the lease were in fact registrable. So the condition also applies on the assignment of an unregistered lease with less than twenty-one years to run.)

What does this mean?

 (i) If the lease being assigned is already registered with absolute title, no details of superior titles will have to be provided.
 (ii) If the lease is registered with good leasehold titles, details of superior leasehold titles and of the freehold will have to be provided, so that on registration of the transfer to the purchaser, the class of title can be upgraded to absolute.
(iii) If the title of the lease is unregistered, the seller must provide details of all superior titles so that on application for first registration of the title to the lease, the purchaser will be registered as proprietor with absolute title.

As regards (ii) and (iii) the problem remains, what *sort* of evidence of the superior titles, and how much? In Ruoff and Roper's *Registered Conveyancing* (5th edition) it is said that an application for first registration of an absolute leasehold title should be accompanied by, amongst other things, strict proof, in accordance with normal conveyancing practice, of the titles to the freehold reversion and any leasehold reversion. As the original title deeds will not be available to the applicant, the applicant must lodge examined copies or abstracts. He must also lodge evidence of any consent to the grant of the lease needed from a mortgagee of a superior title, or from the landlord or any superior landlord.

Applying this to a simple example, suppose that Ann in 1960 granted a lease of ninety-nine years to Beryl. Ann's freehold title was unregistered, and the area was not then one of compulsory registration of title. Beryl therefore did not apply for registration of the title to the lease. In 1990, Beryl contracts to sell the leasehold estate to Catherine. The area is now an area of compulsory registration. Catherine must apply for first registration. Under standard condition 8.1.3 Beryl must supply evidence to Catherine of the freehold title sufficient to ensure that Catherine will be registered with absolute title. The Registrar will want evidence of Ann's ability to grant the lease in 1960 and of the incumbrances on the freehold at that date. This could be done by tracing the title of the freehold from a good root that in 1960 was at least fifteen years old, down to 1960.

Suppose that the history of the freehold title was

- 1930 conveyance on sale from X to Y
- 1958 conveyance on sale from Y to Ann
- 1958 mortgage by Ann to the Z Bank
- 1960 grant of lease by Ann to Beryl.

Beryl must supply Catherine with examined copies of the 1930 and 1958 conveyance, and of the 1958 mortgage and the Bank's consent to the grant of the lease. (She must also, of course, supply a copy of the lease.) Should Beryl's solicitor alter the standard condition?

(i) Definitely, if Beryl does not possess these examined copies. If she did not investigate Ann's title in 1960 she can give no evidence of it at all. The condition must be excluded. She must not promise what she cannot perform. The exclusion of the condition may discourage a purchaser from entering into the contract. Beryl suffers now from her carelessness in 1960.

  If she did investigate Ann's title, but forgot to mark the abstract or copy deeds that she retained as having been examined against the originals, she must alter the standard condition, so that she promises only unexamined copies.

(ii) Even if she feels she does have the necessary evidence of title, she might still be unwilling to offer what is in effect a guarantee that if that evidence is sent to the Registry, an absolute title will result. Why should she rather than the purchaser have to evaluate the sufficiency of the evidence? If she feels any doubt on the matter, she could replace the standard condition by a special condition which promises deduction of the freehold title from the 1930 conveyance, but does not promise registration with absolute title.

To end with a more difficult example, suppose the sale were of a sublease. The seller would have to provide:

- a copy of the sublease;
- evidence of her ownership of the sublease;
- the headlease;

- if the sublease were granted not by the original head tenant, but by a successor, evidence of the successor's ownership of the head lease at the time the sublease was granted;
- details of the freehold title, establishing the freeholder's power to grant the headlease.

Again the seller must alter the standard condition if she cannot provide the necessary evidence of the superior titles, or is reluctant to guarantee that the sublease will be registered with absolute title.

15.3   Consent to Assignment

A lease may contain a prohibition against assignment or subletting. If this prohibition is absolute, i.e. it says simply 'no assignment', then assignment cannot take place unless the landlord agrees to waive the covenant, and permit the particular assignment. An assignment without his consent would be valid, in the sense that ownership of the lease would pass, but the proud new owner would probably face a forfeiture action, as it is most unusual for a fixed-term lease not to contain a clause allowing the landlord to forfeit the leasehold estate for breach of covenant.

A lease usually contains a qualified covenant against assignment. It says that the tenant covenants not to assign or sublet *without the landlord's consent*. As soon as the covenant is qualified in this way, a statutory proviso is automatically added, whether the landlord likes it or not, to the effect that the landlord cannot unreasonably withhold his consent (s.19(1) of the Landlord and Tenant Act 1927).

The proviso still makes it necessary for a tenant proposing to assign or sublet to seek his landlord's consent. An assignment made without asking for the consent is a breach of covenant even if the landlord had no grounds for withholding it. If the landlord refuses his consent when asked for it, the tenant must consider the reasons for the refusal. If the landlord has reasonable grounds for refusing, the tenant can do nothing. Any assignment without the consent would be a breach. If the grounds are unreasonable, the tenant:

(a)   is now free to assign or sublet without the landlord's consent, and there will be no breach of covenant. The risk is that if the landlord then threatens forfeiture of the lease, the court may disagree with the tenant, and consider that the landlord *was* acting reasonably. In order to persuade a purchaser to buy the lease, the tenant may have to go to court, and obtain a declaration that the landlord's grounds for refusal of consent are unreasonable.

It is outside the scope of this book to consider what may or may not be considered reasonable. An instructive case is *International Drilling Fluids Ltd* v. *Louisville Investments (Uxbridge) Ltd* [1986].

(b) may be able to obtain damages from the landlord. The Landlord and Tenant Act 1988 places a statutory duty on a landlord who is asked for consent to an assignment or subletting to give a decision within a reasonable time, and to give his consent, unless there are reasonable grounds for withholding it.

If the tenant can prove a breach of this duty, he will be able to obtain damages, and an injunction that consent be given. This on the face of it still involves a disappointed tenant in litigation but the hope is that the threat of damages will dissuade a reluctant landlord from acting unreasonably in the first place.

Purchaser's Position

A purchaser of a lease (or a prospective subtenant) will not complete the purchase without the consent of the landlord to the assignment. Ideally, the consent should be obtained before exchange of contracts. However the purchaser and the seller may safely enter into the contract *before* the consent is obtained. Under standard condition 8.3, if the consent is not given by the landlord at least three working days before the contractual completion date, either party can rescind the contract. This means that the contract will be wiped out, no damages will be recoverable by either party against the other, and the deposit will be returned to the purchaser. Of course, this is cold comfort to a purchaser who has already contracted to sell his present house, and such a purchaser would have been better advised to have ensured before contract that the landlord's consent would be given.

The condition places an obligation on the seller to use his best efforts to obtain the landlord's consent and he cannot rescind the contract if he fails in this duty. He would face a claim for damages by the purchaser.

15.4 Breach of Covenants

If the seller of the lease has broken a covenant in it, the purchaser can object to the seller's *title* to the lease. A breach of covenant is a matter of title, because the breach will usually give the landlord the right to forfeit the lease. A title liable to forfeiture is not a good title.

Therefore, strictly, on completion a purchaser is entitled to ask for evidence that the covenants in the lease that he is buying and in any superior lease, have been performed and observed (forfeiture of a headlease leading to forfeiture of underleases). However, s.45(2) of the Law of Property Act 1925 provides a rule of great convenience for the seller. It states that if on completion he produces a receipt for the last rent due before completion under the lease that the purchaser is buying, the purchaser must assume, unless the contrary appears, that the rent has been paid, and all the covenants have been performed, both in the lease that he is buying and all superior leases. Therefore, the purchaser *cannot* ask for evidence that the covenants have been performed and observed, unless there are grounds for suspecting that they have not. One reason for suspecting a breach of covenant by the seller would be the disrepair of the property. However, the purchaser will probably find himself barred from complaining about the seller's breach of the repairing covenants in the lease by the terms of the contract. Standard condition 3.1.5 provides that the purchaser accepts the property in its present physical state. The effect of this when a leasehold is being sold is that the purchaser has no right to complain of the breach of a repairing covenant in the lease. This leads to a consideration of standard condition 8.1.5 and consequent care in drafting the assignment or transfer of the lease (this will be considered later).

15.5   Changes in Procedure

(a)   The Property Information Form

The seller will supply the purchaser with the usual property information form used in freehold transactions, and will also supply the additional information form (part of the protocol documentation) which contains questions peculiar to leasehold sales. They cover areas such as:

(i) Service charges On the purchase of a flat (or indeed a suite of rooms in an office block) the lease may provide for each tenant to contribute towards the cost of the maintenance and repair of the common parts of the building, e.g. the entrance hall, stairs, lift, roof, etc.

The payment of the service charges can be as burdensome as payment of the rent, and the amount to be paid is unpredictable, as it will depend from year to year on the amount of repairs to be done and their cost. A service charge is often expressed to be payable as additional rent, so that non-payment may lead to forfeiture of the lease.

A tenant of a residential flat or dwelling is protected against unjustified and excessive claims for such charges by ss.18 – 30 of the Landlord and Tenant Act 1985 as amended by the Landlord and Tenant Act 1987. For the purposes of these sections, a service charge is defined as an amount payable by the tenant of a dwelling for services, repairs, maintenance, insurance, or the landlord's costs of management. The landlord can only recover his costs to the extent that they are reasonably incurred, and if the costs relate to the provision of services or to works, only if the services and works are of a reasonable standard. If the cost of the proposed works will exceed an amount prescribed from time to time by statutory regulations, the landlord must obtain at least two estimates of the cost (one of the estimates must be from a person unconnected with the landlord) and copies of the estimates accompanied by a notice, must be given to the tenants for their comments.

A tenant may require information as to the costs incurred by the landlord. When the information is given, it must be certified by a qualified accountant unconnected with the landlord.

A landlord may ask for service charges to be paid in advance. This enables a fund to be built up in expectation of future repairs. However, a sum can only be requested in advance if there is provision to that effect in the lease, and only to the extent that the sum is reasonable.

The information form will therefore:

(aa) give details of past service charge payments over the previous three years, and for copies of all accounts invoices or certificates relating to these payments.

(bb) say if past service charges have been challenged by the seller or his predecessors.

(cc) give details of any substantial expenditure incurred or contemplated by the landlord likely substantially to increase the contribution by the tenants.

On completion, consideration will have to be given to the apportionment of the service charges. Apportionment will be difficult, as the amount to be charged by the landlord may not be known on completion. An apportionment may be made on the basis of the figures for the previous period, with an agreement to readjust when the figures for the current period are known. Otherwise, one party may agree to pay the whole amount for the current period, with the other party promising an appropriate reimbursement.

Standard condition 6.5.3 provides for apportionment on the best estimate available, with a later adjustment.

(ii) complaints by the landlord of a breach of any of the covenants contained in the lease, or complaints by the seller of a breach of covenant by the landlord or management company.

(iii) details of insurance The lease may provide for insurance by the landlord, with the right for him to recover premiums from the tenant, or may require the tenant to insure, possibly with a particular company specified by the landlord. The purchaser's mortgagee will want details of the insurance arrangements to check that they are sufficient to protect his security. If it is a sale of a flat, the landlord will often have arranged a block policy, on which the interest of each tenant will be noted. The purchaser will ask for a copy of this policy, any current schedule to it, and a copy of the receipt for the last premium.

(b) Drafting the Contract

(i) the seller's solicitor must consider the question of deducing title to the freehold and to any superior leases (see section 15.2).

(ii) the seller's solicitor must consider the need for the landlord's consent to assignment. The landlord will ask for references, and the necessary details of referees should be obtained from the purchaser.

(iii) the particulars of sale will refer to the description of the property in the lease, and a copy of this lease will be supplied with the contract. Standard condition 8.1.2 provides that before the contract is made, the seller must provide the purchaser with full details of the lease. The purchaser is then treated as entering into the contract knowing and accepting the terms of the lease.

(c) *Approval of the Draft Contract by the Purchaser's solicitor*

As well as approving the contract, he will also be considering the provisions of the lease, such as the repairing obligations and the outgoings, to check that they will not be too heavy a burden on the purchaser.

The solicitor must consider his client's future plans. If it is a lease of business premises, the solicitor must know what use his client intends to make of the premises. If this will be a change from the existing use, the lease must be checked for any covenant to the effect that the use cannot be changed, or can be changed only with the landlord's consent. In the latter case, there is *no* statutory provision that the consent cannot be unreasonably withheld, so the purchaser must ensure that the landlord's consent is obtained before exchange of contracts.

The lease may also contain a covenant against alterations and additions. If the consent is qualified by the words 'with the landlord's consent' the landlord cannot unreasonably withhold his consent to an alteration that would, from the tenant's point of view, be an improvement, but can require that the property be reinstated before the end of the lease. (s.19(2) of the Landlord and Tenant Act 1927.)

(d) *The Drafting of the Assignment or Transfer*

This is a form of assignment of an unregistered lease.

This Assignment is made the __ day of ___ Between AB (hereinafter called the seller) of the one part and CD (hereinafter called the purchaser) of the other part.

Whereas
(1) By a lease dated 1 September 1986 and made between Mary Short of the one part and the seller of the other part the property known as 1 Shortlands Grove in the City of York was demised to the seller for a term of 50 years from 1 September 1986 at a yearly rent of £104 subject to the performance and observance of the covenants on the part of the tenant therein contained.
(2) The seller has contracted to sell the said property for all the residue now unexpired of the said term at the price of £75 000.

Now this deed witnesseth

(1) that in consideration of £75 000 now paid by the purchaser to the seller, (the receipt whereof the seller hereby acknowledges) the seller as beneficial owner hereby assigns to the purchaser all the property comprised in the said lease to hold unto the purchaser for all the residue now unexpired of the term granted by the said lease subject to payment of the rent reserved by the said lease, and to performance and observance of the covenants on the part of the tenant contained in it.

(2) The covenants implied by the seller assigning as beneficial owner are hereby modified so that it shall not be hereby implied that the covenants contained in the lease and on the part of the tenant to be performed and observed which relate to the repair of the above mentioned leasehold property have been observed and performed up to the date hereof.

In Witness whereof etc.

You can see that is very similar to a conveyance of an unregistered freehold, except, of course, that the recitals and the habendum change. However, clause 2 needs explaining.

As we have seen, a purchaser is not by virtue of the standard conditions in the contract entitled to object to the fact that the seller has broken the repairing covenants in the lease. However, when a seller conveys for value as beneficial owner, there is implied into the conveyance a covenant by him that all the covenants in the lease have been performed (see Chapter 19). Hence the purchaser would be able to sue under the terms of the conveyance when he could not have sued under the terms of the contract. This is why standard condition 8.1.5 provides that the assignment shall include a provision that the implied covenants for title shall not extend to any breach of the terms of the lease as to the condition of the property.

A transfer of a registered leasehold title differs little from a transfer of a registered freehold title. A transfer of a registered lease, by virtue of s.24 of the Land Registration Act 1925 has in it an implied covenant that the transferor has performed the covenants in the lease. This implication is made whatever the capacity in which he conveys. The transfer will therefore contain a clause negativing the effect of s.24 and if necessary the effect of the beneficial-owner covenants, so that no promise is given as to the performance of the repairing obligations.

Covenants for indemnity On assignment of a lease, the seller will wish to be indemnified by the purchaser against the consequences of any future breach of the obligations of the lease. Such an indemnity will be implied into a conveyance for value by virtue of s.77 of the Law of Property Act 1925, and in the case of a transfer of registered title, additionally by s.24 of the Land Registration Act 1925. The covenant is not, therefore put in expressly, unless an unregistered lease is disposed of by way of a gift.

(e)   The Pre-Completion Searches

If the lease being transferred is registered with absolute title, the pre-completion search will be made at the District Land Registry, in the same way, and with the same results, as if it were a transfer of a freehold with absolute title.

If the lease being transferred is registered with good leasehold title, then again a land registry search will be made. If the superior titles are unregistered and have not been deduced the purchaser will know the name of at least one superior owner, i.e. the landlord. It is worth making a land-charges search against that name. If the landlord is a freeholder, it might reveal a registration of restrictive covenants. It might also reveal a second mortgage, leading to the query as to whether the lease binds that mortgagee. (It will not reveal a first mortgage, as this will be protected by deposit of title deeds, and not registrable as a land charge). Of course, if the superior titles are unregistered and have been deduced, the land charges search will be made against the names of all the estate owners revealed by the copy documents.

If the lease is unregistered, a land-charges search will be made against the name of the landlord, original tenant, seller and any other estate-owners revealed by the abstract of title to the lease. A search will also be made against the names of superior owners if the superior titles are deduced.

(f)   Completion

At completion, the purchaser of an unregistered lease will pick up the lease, past assignments of it, and the assignment executed by the seller. He may also, if appropriate, pick up the landlord's written consent to the assignment and a marked abstract of the title to the freehold and superior leases. The purchaser of a registered lease will pick up the lease, the land certificate and the transfer executed by the seller. He may also pick up the landlord's consent to the assignment, and if the title is good leasehold, a marked abstract of the freehold title and superior leases.

If the leasehold estate is mortgaged, the purchaser will want a receipt on the mortgage deed or Land Registry form 53 as appropriate, or undertakings in respect of them.

The purchaser will also want to see a receipt for the last rent due (see section 15.4).

(g)   Post Completion

The purchaser must consider:

(i) Whether the transfer of the assignment needs stamping with *ad valorem* stamps, and a PD stamp (see section 2.17).

(ii) If it is an assignment of an unregistered lease, whether the purchase must be followed by an application for first registration (see section 3.2).

(iii) If it is a transfer of a registered lease, the need to apply for registration of the transfer, before the priority period given by the Land Registry search expires (see section 3.11).

(iv) The assignment of a share in a management company. Where the landlord has let flats, the upkeep of the common parts and enforcement of the covenants of the leases are often managed through a management company, in which each tenant has a share. The share will be transferred on completion and the transfer must then be registered with the company.

(v) Notice of assignment The lease may provide that any assignment of the lease, or mortgage of it be notified to the landlord's solicitors, and a fee paid. A failure to do this will be a breach of covenant.

Workshop

Attempt these two problems yourself, then read specimen solutions at the end of the book.

Problem 1

You act for Pamela who is considering buying a lease from Vera. The lease was made between Len as landlord and Vera as tenant for a term of eight years. It contains

1. a covenant against assignment without the landlord's consent;
2. a covenant against change of use without the landlord's consent;
3. an option for the tenant to renew the lease for a further term of eight years.

The premises are currently being used as an office, but Pamela would like to use it as a shop for selling her designer knitwear.

Consider:

(a) What consents should be obtained before Pamela contracts to buy the premises?
(b) Whether Pamela will be able to exercise the option for renewal?

Problem 2

A leasehold estate of ninety-nine years was granted in 1965 by Lena to Alice. The title to the lease remains unregistered. In 1969 Alice assigned the lease to Beatrice. In 1971 Beatrice assigned the lease to Carol. In 1973, she assigned it to Deirdre. In 1988 Deirdre assigned it to Enid, Enid has just contracted to sell the leasehold to Pamela. What assignments is Pamela entitled to see?

---

16 The Grant of a Lease

16.1 Procedure

The grant of a lease is often not preceded by a contract that it will be granted. There is then no legal tie between the parties until the leasehold term itself comes into existence. The lease is usually prepared in duplicate, one part being executed by the landlord (the lease), the other part being executed by the tenant (the counterpart lease). The leasehold term comes into existence on the exchange of the two parts.

If there is a contract, standard condition 8.1.2 provides for the seller to engross both lease and counterpart, and to send the counterpart to the purchaser for signature at least five working days before completion.

16.2 Title

(a) A Lease to be Granted Out of the Freehold Estate

If the title to the freehold is unregistered s.44 of the Law of Property Act 1925 provides that the prospective tenant is not entitled to any evidence of the freehold title. This is really buying a pig in a poke. The same problems arise as have been discussed in 15.2(b). The purchaser may be sinking a large premium into the purchase of a void lease, an encumbered lease or a lease that does not bind the landlord's mortgagee. However, remember that s.44 implies a term into the *contract*. So if the proposed tenant has not entered into a contract to accept the grant of the lease, he is free to break off negotiations for the lease if the landlord refuses details of his title. If there is to be a contract, the tenant must beware of s.44, and must have a condition in the contract promising deduction of the freehold title (see later).

Section 110(1) Land Registration Act 1925 does not apply to the grant of a lease, so if the title to the freehold is registered, the prospective tenant cannot insist that the landlord supply a copy of the entries on his register of title.

However, on 3 December 1990 the register of title becomes public, and a prospective tenant will be able to obtain office copy entries for himself from the Registry.

(b) The grant of an underlease

1. *Out of an Unregistered Lease*   If there is a contract for the grant of an underlease s.44 Law of Property Act 1925 provides that the prospective undertenant is entitled to see

(i) the document creating the leasehold term out of which the underlease is to be granted;

(ii) evidence of the prospective landlord's ownership of the leasehold term (in other words his power to grant the underlease).

He is not entitled to see any evidence of superior titles.

So imagine that Len is the freeholder and Tom is the head tenant. Susan is to be granted an underlease by Tom. Susan is entitled to see the headlease and evidence of Tom's ownership of the leasehold estate granted by it. If Susan later contracts to subunderlet to Ursula, and the contract does not alter the effect of s.44, Ursula may see a copy of Susan's underlease and require Susan to prove her ownership of it (in other words, exactly the same evidence as if Ursula were buying Susan's underlease rather than taking a term granted out of it). Ursula could not ask for a copy of the headlease, nor for proof that Tom had power to grant the underlease; nor can she ask for evidence of the freehold title.

2. *Out of a Registered Lease* A sensible person would think that the position of a prospective undertenant would be the same, whether his lease was to be granted from an unregistered or a registered lease. A sensible person would be wrong. We have seen that s.110(1) of the Land Registration Act 1925 does not apply on the grant of a lease. It seems that this covers not just the grant of a headlease, but also that of an underlease. So a prospective tenant whose underlease is to be granted from a registered leasehold estate cannot insist on being supplied with either a copy of his landlord's register of title or a copy of his lease. If we look at the previous example, we can see that if Tom's lease were registered and he contracted to grant an underlease to Susan, she could not ask for a copy of the lease Len granted to Tom, nor require Tom to prove his ownership of the leasehold estate. As has been said, she could acquire a copy of the register of Tom's title from the Registry, but not a copy of his lease. The Registry does not always keep a copy of a lease when registering a leasehold title. Even if the Registry does, the lease, unlike the register of title, is not a public document, and the Registry will not supply a copy. A condition in the contract should require Tom to provide an office copy of the entries on his register and a copy of his lease, and possibly to provide evidence of Len's freehold title.

3. *The Effect of Standard Condition 8.2.3* This alters the statutory rules, as it provides that the prospective landlord must deduce a title that will enable the proposed tenant to register the lease at HM Land Registry with absolute title. What evidence is necessary to do this has already been discussed in section 15.2. It would mean that Tom would have to provide evidence of the freehold title to establish that the headlease was validly granted, a copy of the headlease and evidence of his ownership of it. If Tom cannot provide this evidence, or does not wish to guarantee that the evidence he supplies will lead to registration with absolute title, he should alter the standard condition.

Of course, if Tom's title to his headlease is a registered absolute title, this in itself should ensure that the underlease will be registered with absolute title. All Susan needs as proof of title is an office copy of the entries on Tom's register, filed plan, and a copy of Tom's lease.

16.3 Stamping a New Lease

The lease must be stamped with *ad valorem* stamp duty. This is calculated on the amount of the premium and the rent payable. There will be no duty payable if the lease contains a certificate that the premium does not exceed £30 000 and the rent does not exceed £300 per annum.

If the lease is granted for seven years or more, the lease must be impressed with a 'particulars delivered' stamp.

The counterpart lease must be stamped with 50p duty.

16.4 Registration

After the lease has been granted, you must decide if the title to the leasehold should be registered under the Land Registration Act 1925. Do you remember the contents of Chapter 3? If not, the points are made again here.

(a) If the landlord's title is unregistered, a tenant who is granted a lease of over twenty-one years should, within 2 months of the grant apply for first registration of the title to the leasehold estate (s.123 of the Land Registration Act 1925). If he can give details of all the superior titles to the Registrar he will be registered with absolute title. Otherwise, he will be registered with good leasehold title. If the landlord then sells his reversion any purchaser of it will be bound by the lease as a purchaser of an unregistered title is bound by all legal estates.

   If the lease is for twenty-one years or less, the title to it cannot be registered.

(b) If the landlord's title is registered, a tenant who is granted a lease of over twenty-one years must apply for registration of his title. This is because it is a registrable dealing with a registered title. If the tenant made a pre-completion search, he should apply for registration before the priority period expires. It is not sufficient that the title to the lease is registered. A notice of the lease should also be entered on the landlord's register, to ensure that if the reversion is sold, the purchaser of it will be subject to the lease. There is no need for the tenant to apply for this entry. It is done automatically by the registry staff, as part of the process of registering the title to the lease.

   There is some dispute as to whether the landlord's land certificate must be put on deposit to perfect the tenant's application. It is clear that if the lease is granted at a rent but without a premium, the application does not have to be accompanied by the landlord's land certificate. This is under the authority of s.64(1)(c) of the Land Registration Act 1925. If the land certificate is not deposited, the Registry will put a notice on the landlord's register. This is an example of how there can be a discrepancy between the register of title and the land certificate. If the lease is granted at a premium, the Land Registry takes the view that the tenant's application for registration is incomplete unless the landlord's land certificate is deposited in the Land Registry, despite the criticism of this viewpoint in the judgements in *Strand Securities Ltd* v. *Caswell* [1965]. It should therefore be agreed between the parties before completion that the landlord will put his certificate on deposit.

(c) If there is no entry on the landlord's title as to the existence of the lease, a purchaser will still be bound by the lease if it is an overriding interest. It may be overriding either under s.70(i)(k) or s.70(i)(g) of the Land Registration Act 1925 (see Chapter 3).

16.5 The Contents of the Lease

If there is a contract that a lease will be granted, standard condition 8.2.3 provides that the lease is to be in the form of the draft attached to the contract. The solicitor for the prospective tenant must, therefore, check that the terms of both the contract and the lease are acceptable before contracts are exchanged. After that date, the tenant will be unable to ask that the terms of the draft lease be altered.

It is outside the scope of this book to consider the drafting of the lease in any detail, but the following is an outline of some of the major matters you should consider when acting on behalf of a prospective tenant of a house or flat.

(a) The Parcels Clause

If the lease is of a flat or part of a house, the exact boundaries of the flat should be stated in the lease, even to the joists below the floor and above the ceiling. The vertical division of the flat's walls should be clear. This is important as it may determine where the tenant's repairing responsibilities end, and the landlord's (or another tenant's) begin.

You should check that the tenant is given any necessary rights of access, car parking, use of communal garden, etc.

(b) Repairing Obligations

You must check that the repairing and decorating obligations to be imposed on the tenant are not too onerous. If the lease of a house will contain a covenant by the tenant to do internal and external repairs (or if the tenant of a flat will have to contribute towards the cost of external or structural repairs via a maintenance charge) the tenant should consider having a survey done before he agrees to take a lease on those terms.

If the property is a flat, you must check that the landlord does covenant to repair the exterior and the common parts of the building such as the entrance hall, stairways, lifts, etc. It is true that the cost of doing this will probably be channelled back to the tenant through a service charge, but it is better for a tenant to contribute towards the cost of repairs than face the dilapidation, danger and devaluing of the property if the repairs are not done at all. Check also that the landlord covenants to provide the services for which any service charge will be levied, e.g. central heating.

(c) User

There are likely to be clauses restricting the tenant to residential use, and preventing immoral use. In the case of a flat, it is important that the landlord promises to put the same covenants in all the leases, and to *enforce* them. Then, indirectly, your client will be able to control the use of the neighbouring flats by suing the landlord if the landlord does not insist on residential use. A lease of a flat may also contain rules about the keeping of pets, playing of musical instruments, etc. These may seem restrictive to your client, but on the other hand they will protect him from the thoughtlessness of his neighbours, provided the landlord promises to enforce the rules. Alternatively, the lease may say that the rules (in so far as they are negative – i.e. what *not* to do) can be enforced directly by tenant against tenant, creating a leasehold equivalent of a development scheme.

(d) Restrictions on Assignment and Subletting

In a long lease of a house (e.g. ninety-nine years) you may consider it unreasonable for the landlord to restrict in any way the assignment or subletting of the entire house. Even so, the landlord could justifiably:

- restrict the assignment or subletting of *part* of the house, either by totally forbidding it, or by making it subject to his consent;
- say that any assignment, even of the whole, in the last, say, seven years of the term must be with his consent. It is important for the landlord that the person who is tenant at the end of the lease be solvent, as it is against him that the landlord will be enforcing the tenant's covenant to leave the premises in repair.

In the case of a flat, the landlord may wish to make a disposal even of the whole of the flat subject to his consent. The character of any proposed assignee and his intended use of the property is important not only to the landlord, but also to the tenants of the other flats in the building.

(e)   Insurance

If the landlord covenants to insure, he should also covenant to use any insurance monies to reinstate the damaged premises.

If the lease is of a flat, the landlord will probably arrange the insurance of the entire building, each tenant promising to reimburse part of the premium. The tenant should check that his interest in the building is noted on the policy.

(f)   Forfeiture

In a fixed-term lease the tenant will have to accept the inclusion of a clause permitting the landlord to forfeit the lease for non-payment of rent or breach of covenant. You should not permit the inclusion of a right for the landlord to forfeit should the tenant become bankrupt, as lenders will not lend on the security of a lease containing such a clause.

17 Chain Transactions

In domestic conveyancing, the seller and purchaser are likely to be part of a chain. X's purchase depends on his sale as it is the proceeds from the sale of his present house that will be helping to finance the purchase of his new house. The chain presents problems to the conveyancer.

17.1 Drafting the Contract

The following points arise.

(a) The Deposit

We have already seen in section 5.9 that standard condition 2.2.2 allows the deposit paid to the seller to be used by him as a deposit on his own purchase. The seller should resist any attempt by the purchaser to change that condition.

(b) The Rate of Interest

As we have seen (in Chapter 5) the contract will provide a rate of interest to be paid in the event of late completion. The interest is paid on the balance of the purchase price by the person responsible for the delay. (See Chapter 18 for further detail). It is desirable, if *possible*, for the interest rate to be the same in all the contracts in the chain. For example, suppose Q is selling Blackacre to R (Contract 1) and at the same time R is selling Whiteacre to S (Contract 2). Both contracts contain the same completion date. Suppose Q fails to complete on the agreed date, but completes ten days later. As a result R completes the sale to S ten days late as well. R is going to have to pay interest to S under contract 2 but is entitled to interest from Q under contract 1. There is no problem for R if the amount he has to pay is roughly the same as the amount he will receive. If the amount that R has to pay to S is more than the interest he will receive from Q, R suffers a loss, which he will have to recover from Q by way of damages for delayed completion.

The problem is that having the same rates of interest in contracts 1 and 2 will not necessarily safeguard R if the purchase prices are substantially different.

On the assumption that it is Q who causes the delay, R is all right if he is 'trading up', i.e. buying a property that is more expensive than the one he is selling. He will be receiving interest on the higher sum, and paying interest on the lower sum.

If he is trading down, and selling his large house to replace it with a smaller one, he will be receiving interest on a lower sum, and paying it on a higher sum.

If it is S who causes the delay, R faces a problem if he is trading up. S will pay him interest on the smaller price, and R will have to pay Q interest on the higher price. The loss would have to be recovered by R claiming damages for delay from S.

Ideally, the contract with the lower price should contain a higher rate of interest to remove this sort of imbalance, but this may not be possible. Assuming that R is trading up, we would want a higher rate of interest in contract 2 than in contract 1. However, if we raise the interest in contract 2 this may produce a rate too high for S to accept. If we decrease the interest in contract 1, this may produce a rate too low for Q to accept. It will certainly become impossible to juggle the rates of interest in this way if there are other links in the chain, at different prices.

(c) The Time for Completion

The time for completion should also be considered. A special condition can be put in contract 1 that completion takes place before, for example, 11.30 a.m. so that funds can be transferred to finance the purchase in the afternoon. (Remember that standard condition 6.1.2 permits completion at any time up to 2.00 p.m.)

17.2 Synchronisation of Exchange of Contracts

There should be no time-lag between the exchange of the contracts to sell, and the exchange of the contracts to buy, or as little time-lag as is practically possible. Otherwise, the purchaser faces two unpleasant possibilities:

(a) He might exchange contracts on his sale but find that the exchange of contracts on his purchase falls through at the last moment. He then has a choice of temporary homelessness, or delaying completion of his sale beyond the agreed completion date, and so becoming liable for financial penalties (see Chapter 18).

(b) Alternatively, he might exchange contracts on his purchase, and then find that the exchange of the contracts on the sale falls through. This is a worse problem. He might find temporary finance to complete his purchase on time, but bridging loans are expensive. He might attempt to delay completion of the purchase until he has found a new buyer for his own house, but any attempt at delay can be thwarted by the seller serving a completion notice. If completion does not take place by the date specified in the notice the seller can withdraw from the contract, and keep the 10 per cent deposit. So it is probably better for your client to run the risk of having no house than of having two houses, *if* there has to be a risk at all.

A straightforward method of synchronising exchange of contracts is set out in the answer to problem 1 at the end of this chapter, which would be adequate when only two transactions are involved. Undertakings are given in accordance with Law Society Formula A (see section 1.6). If the chain had been longer, this method would not have been satisfactory. For chain transactions the Law Society has recently devised a formula C. Like formulae A and B it rests on undertakings given by solicitors or licensed conveyancers which, as a matter of professional conduct, they have to fulfil.

Formula C works in two stages, cunningly named by the Law Society as Part 1 and Part 2. Imagine a chain of sales. W is selling his home to X. X is selling his present home to Y. Y is selling *his* present home to Z, a first-time buyer. It is Monday. The order of events is as follows:

1. Z's solicitor telephones Y's solicitor. They agree a latest time that contracts can be exchanged that day, say 5.00 p.m. They agree that formula C Part 1 shall apply. This means that each confirms that he holds a part of the contract signed by his client, and Z's solicitor confirms that if Y's solicitor wishes to exchange contracts by 5.00 p.m., Z's solicitor will exchange. Notice the effect of this. Z's solicitor has undertaken that he will exchange contracts today if Y's solicitor wishes it. Obviously Z's solicitor needs his client's authority to give that undertaking.
2. Y's solicitor now telephones X's solicitor. Again they agree that formula C Part 1 shall apply but that the latest time for exchange shall be, say, 4.30 p.m. So now Y's solicitor must exchange contracts on the purchase if X's solicitor asks him to do so, before 4.30 p.m. Y's solicitor can give his undertaking, because he knows that if a contract for the purchase is forced on him, he can force the sale contract on Z.
3. X's solicitor now phones W's solicitor. W is at the top of the chain, as he has no related purchase. So exchange between W and X can take place, using formula B.
4. X's solicitor phones Y's solicitor. Part 2 of formula C now applies. It is agreed that each solicitor holds the part of the contract in his possession to the order of the other (so exchange has taken place) and each promises to despatch it to the other today.

    What if Y's solicitor has gone out when X's solicitor tries to phone him? Within Part 1 of the formula is an undertaking by the purchaser's solicitor that he or a colleague will be available until the agreed time, in this case 4.30 p.m. in order to exchange. So Y's solicitor cannot go out, unless his colleague remains in.
5. Y's solicitor now phones Z's solicitor. Part 2 of the formula applies, and contracts are exchanged.

What about the deposit? Formula C envisages a deposit travelling up the chain, so that any deposit paid by Z helps to fund the deposit to be paid by X to W. This is the way it works.

Each contract will contain the standard condition stating that the deposit shall be paid to the seller's solicitor (or licensed conveyancer) as stakeholder, but that the seller may use it to pay a deposit on his own purchase.

Suppose W is selling to X for £80 000, X is selling to Y for £75 000. Y is selling to Z for £60 000. To go through the events again:

1. When Z's solicitor and Y's solicitor speak to one another on the telephone, Y's solicitor will ask Z's solicitor to pay the deposit of £6000 to X's solicitor (Y's solicitor knowing nothing yet of W). The Part 2 undertakings that will be given on exchange of contracts include an undertaking by the purchaser's solicitor to despatch the deposit to the seller's solicitor, or some other solicitor specified by the seller's solicitor to be held in formula C terms (i.e. according to the standard condition that should be in the contract, discussed above.)
2. X's solicitor will ask Y's solicitor, in the course of their conversation, to pay the deposit of £7500 to W's solicitor on the same terms, or to *procure its payment*. An undertaking to that effect will be given on exchange of contracts, in accordance with Part 2 of the formula.
3. On the exchange of contracts between W and X, X's solicitor will undertake that he will send £500 to W's solicitor and ensure that £7500 is sent by Y's solicitor.
4. Y's solicitor will undertake that he will send £1500 to W's solicitor, and procure payment of the remaining £6000.
5. When contracts are exchanged with Z's solicitor, Y's solicitor will now ask him to send the £6000 not to X's solicitor but to W's solicitor.

All these payments should be despatched on the day of exchange. W's solicitor will receive £500 from X's solicitor, £1500 from Y's and £6000 from X's. If the money is not forthcoming from Y's or Z's solicitors X has broken his undertaking to W's solicitor, which is a serious matter. But then Y and Z's solicitors are in breach of their undertakings to X's solicitors.

If the full 10 per cent deposits are not being paid, or if the deposit guarantee scheme is to be used, the undertakings in respect of the deposits will have to be changed.

The deposit held by W's solicitor will be held by him as stakeholder, as there is no related purchase. (If Z had been paying more for Y's house than Y was paying for his, so that Y was receiving a deposit larger than he needed for his related purchase, the excess would be held by Y's solicitor as stakeholder.) You must realise that if Y delays in completion of the sale, perhaps because there is something wrong with his title, so that Z discharges the contract by a completion notice, Z has no claim against the deposit held by W's solicitor. Z's deposit was paid to Y (no matter how Y may have utilised it) and must be recovered from him.

17.3   The Transfer of Funds

Funds can be transferred from the sale to the purchase by split banker's drafts. (A banker's draft is an order by a bank to itself to pay the stated sum to the payee named in the draft. It is inconceivable that a bank would dishonour its draft.)

Suppose that the solicitors for Q, R and S all have offices in the same town.

Q is selling his house to R for £40 000. It is mortgaged to B Building Society, and the redemption money needed is £15 000.

R is selling his present house to S for £34 000. R's house is mortgaged to C Building Society for £14 000. S's solicitor can arrive at R's solicitor's office with banker's drafts, one for £20 000 and one for £14 000.

R's solicitor sets the £14 000 draft aside for C Building Society, and hastens off to the offices of Q's solicitor. He takes with him the draft for £20 000 which he will endorse over to Q's solicitor, plus a second draft for £20 000.

Exciting manoeuvres such as these are becoming increasingly rare, as completions by post become the normal thing (see section 2.15). Funds are telegraphed from one solicitor's bank account to another solicitor's bank account, through the Clearing House Automated Payments System.

17.4   The Client's Finances Generally

Your client's finances should be checked at an early stage before he is committed to any contract. The object is to contrast what he will have coming in to finance the purchase, with the total cost of the purchase. If the former is less than the latter, the result, as foreseen by Mr Micawber, will be misery. So do this sum.

Coming in

A   *Net* proceeds of sale i.e. contract price *less*:

>   (i) money needed to redeem first mortgage. Obtain an approximate redemption figure now from the lender.
>   (ii) money needed to redeem a second or later mortgage. The possibility of a second mortgage should be checked. Your client may forget to tell you about it, or may not have realised the significance of the piece of paper he signed some time ago. A search of HM Land Registry or the Land Charges Registry should be made if there is any doubt.
> (iii) solicitor's fees and disbursements.
>   (iv) estate agent's fees.

B   *Net* loan to be secured by mortgage. Check the amount offered, and deduct

- any arrangement fee.
- in the case of an endowment mortgage, the first premium on the life policy, if this is payable on completion.
- any retention money. If the lender wants substantial work done to the property, the practice is for part of the loan to be withheld until the work is done. The borrower cannot usually do the work before completion, for the simple reason that he has not got possession of the house, so he will have to budget without that part of the loan. He should also consider whether he will have the money to do the work after completion. If the work to be done is minor, the lender will not make a retention, but the borrower may have to undertake to do the work fairly soon after completion, and again he should consider whether he will have the money to do it.
- any legal fees.
- any other payment indicated by the lender. Some lenders deduct the first month's payment of interest.

C   Other sources – e.g. client's savings.

Going out

Purchase price, plus:

- solicitors fees and disbursements, including Land Registry fees and search fees;
- stamp duty if the consideration is over £30 000;
- money for all the general expenses like removal costs.

Workshop

Attempt these problems yourself, then read the specimen solutions at the end of the book.

Problem 1

(This is based on the Law Society 1983 Exam)

You have been instructed by Mr John and Mrs Arabella Archer to act for them in connection with their sale for £40 000 of 5 King Street, Ledsham. You have also been instructed to act for them in the purchase for £60 000 of 'Greenbank', Juniper Close, Ledsham, and you have been instructed by the West Kirby Building Society to act for them in connection with the mortgage advance on 'Greenbank' and the discharge of the mortgage on 5 King Street. The offer of advance from the Building Society states that it is willing to lend £32 000, but subject to a retention of £2000 until the house has been rewired, and a new damp course put in.

The draft contract for the sale of 5 King Street has been approved by the purchaser's solicitors who have just informed you that their client is now ready to exchange contracts. You have obtained the title deeds to 5 King Street from the Building Society, and they include the first mortgage to the Society, and a notice of a second mortgage to Grasping Bank plc. Your clients inform you that approximately £10 000 is owing on the first mortgage and that the second mortgage to the Bank is security for various loans made to Mr Archer's business. You have established that the second mortgage to the Bank has been registered as a Class C(i) land charge.

What advice would you give your clients regarding the financial arrangements? Is it necessary for you or your clients to make any further enquiries or arrangements regarding the financial aspects of either transaction before exchange of contracts?

It is necessary that exchange of contracts on both sale and purchase be as simultaneous as possible. Explain how this can be achieved in view of the fact that all the firms of solicitors involved are some distance from each other.

Problem 2

You are acting for Mr Fawkes who is selling his house called The Plot, and buying a house called The Tower. He has arranged a loan from the Parliamentary Building Society (for which you will also be acting), and that and the net proceeds of sale of The Plot will ultimately finance the purchase of The Tower. However, although the purchaser of The Plot is prepared to exchange contracts now, he will not agree to a completion date earlier than three months away. As Mr Fawkes wishes to buy The Tower immediately, he has arranged a bridging loan from his bank. The bank will require an undertaking from you to pay the proceeds of the sale of The Plot into Mr Fawkes's account to discharge the loan.

You have received the deeds of The Plot, and you have noticed that the house is owned jointly by Mr Fawkes and his wife.

Mr Fawkes tells you that nearly all the proceeds of sale will be needed to pay off the bridging loan, but says that his wife accepts this and wishes you to act for her as well as himself in connection with the sale.

Will you accept the instructions to act for Mrs Fawkes? What advice will you give, either to her or to Mr Fawkes, and to the Building Society concerning the arrangements? How will you word the undertaking to the bank?

Problem 3

(This is based on the 1984 Law Society Examination question)

Samuel Savage and his wife Sara instructed you some days ago that they wished you to act in the sale of their present property, 22 Mount Road, Mixford. Your clients have come to see you again, and on this occasion they are accompanied by Mr and Mrs Coward who are Sara's elderly parents. Mr and Mrs Savage inform you that they have received two firm offers of £25 000 for Mount Road, and Mr and Mrs Savage and Mr and Mrs Coward inform you that they also wish you to act for them in connection with the purchase by them all of 'The Knoll', 2 Little Acre, Southmaster, Loamshire for £72 000.

Mr and Mrs Coward are retired, and have no property to sell. They live mainly on the income from £50 000, their life savings. They had intended to move to a private nursing home and use their savings to pay the fees, but their daughter has offered to look after them if a suitable house can be found to accommodate both families. The Knoll is a large detached house and the two couples intend to convert the property into two separate flats. Mr Coward tells you that he thinks the cost of conversion will be about £5000 and that he and his wife will bear all this cost, and in addition they have agreed to contribute £40 000 towards the purchase price. Both Mr and Mrs Coward have made Sara a beneficiary under their wills. After the purchase of The Knoll they wish Sara to remain the only person who will benefit from their death. Mr and Mrs Savage are to raise the balance of the purchase price of £32 000 and to pay all the legal costs and disbursements, and have agreed to make all payments due under any mortgage which may be required to raise this sum. Mr and Mrs Savage expect to receive approximately £7000 as the net proceeds of their sale after repayment of the outstanding mortgage and all the expenses of these transactions. Mr and Mrs Savage and Mr and Mrs Coward have received an offer of advance of £25 000 from the Omega Building Society, and the Society have instructed you to act in connection with the mortgage advance.

(a) Explain to Mr and Mrs Savage and Mr and Mrs Coward whether or not you can act for all four of them.
(b) Explain whether the intended financial arrangements are satisfactory and whether any further information is necessary.
(c) Explain whether the interests and wishes of either couple need protection or explanation, and if so, what steps are recommended by you.

18 Remedies for Breach of Contract

18.1 Introduction

Either seller or purchaser may fail to meet his obligations under the contract. The seller may fail to show the good title he has promised; may be found to have wrongly described the land in the contract; may not be ready to complete on the agreed date. The purchaser may fail to find the money in time for completion.

We are assuming, therefore, in this chapter, that completion has not taken place, and that one party has established that the other party has broken a term of the contract. What remedies has the injured party?

As in any contract, the remedies for the breach will depend on the gravity of the breach.

(a) A breach may be so serious that it gives the right to the innocent party to treat the contract as discharged by the breach. The choice is the innocent party's. He may decide to continue with the contract and confine his claim to damages. If he does decide to treat the breach as discharging the contract, and tells the other party of his decision the contract is terminated as regards future obligation of both parties. So the purchaser is released from his obligation to buy, and the seller can now sell the house to someone else. It is not discharged as regards responsibilities that have already arisen. This is why a seller who elects to treat a contract as discharged can sue to recover any part of the deposit not paid on exchange of contracts (see *Dewar* v. *Mintoft* [1912] approved in *Damon Cia Naviera SA* v. *Hapag-Lloyd International SA* [1985]). The discharge of the contract can also be accompanied by a claim for damages.

(b) If the breach is not considered by the court to be sufficiently serious to enable the innocent party to treat the contract as discharged, he can only claim damages.

18.2 Assessment of Damages

Damages for breach of contract are designed to put the innocent party in the same position as if the contract had been performed. However some loss suffered may be irrecoverable, as being considered too remote from the breach. The rule governing remoteness of damage for breach of contract is *Hadley* v. *Baxendale* (1854). The innocent party can recover loss that arises naturally from the breach (i.e. that anyone could reasonably have contemplated arising), and loss that was actually in the contemplation of the parties at the time the contract was made.

Let us look at this from the seller's point of view. He may be able to claim loss of bargain. This would arise if the contract price was £80 000, but the property was worth only £76 000. He would have lost £4000. Remember, however, that he will be entitled to treat the deposit as forfeited. The deposit of £8000 will be set against any loss he suffers. (Note that s.49(2) of the Law of Property Act 1925 empowers the court to order a seller to repay the deposit to the purchaser and will apparently do so if that would be the fairest course – see *Universal Corp* v. *Five Ways Properties Ltd* [1979].)

If the property were worth only £70 000 the loss of bargain would be £10 000, so he could claim £2000 actual loss, having taken into account the forfeited deposit.

Common-law damages are usually assessed at the date of the breach, so the value of the property at that date will be used in the calculation. However, in *Johnson* v. *Agnew* [1980] this was said not to be an invariable rule, and circumstances may lead the court to consider that a different date would be fairer. In the case, the purchaser obtained a decree of specific performance, which proved to be unenforceable, as the seller's mortgagees sold the property to someone else. The purchaser returned to the court, and asked for an award of common-law damages. Damages were awarded, assessed on the value of the property at the date the decree proved to be unworkable.

It may not be possible for a seller to prove loss of bargain, because the property has been steadily appreciating in value. He can then claim wasted conveyancing expenses, e.g. legal fees incurred both before and after contract. He cannot claim both loss of bargain and wasted conveyancing costs, as the costs would have been necessary to secure the bargain.

Looking at it from the purchaser's point of view, we can see that the purchaser will be entitled to the return of his deposit, and can claim either loss of bargain, or wasted costs. Suppose that the purchaser was a developer, buying the land with a view to building on it, and then reselling land and house at a large profit. Can the developer recover this profit? The profit will not be treated as loss flowing naturally from the breach *(Diamond* v. *Campbell-Jones* [1961]) and so can only be recovered if the seller knew when the contract was made of the purchaser's intention to develop. Damages will be given to compensate the purchaser for the profits that both parties contemplated he would make (*Cottrill* v. *Steyning and Littlehampton Building Society* [1966]).

18.3   The Seller Breaking his Promise as to Title

(a)   Damages

Damages for this particular breach used to be limited by the rule in *Bain* v. *Fothergill* (1874). This rule was abolished by the Law of Property

(Miscellaneous Provisions) Act 1989, and damages are now assessed as they are for any other breach, under the rule in *Hadley* v. *Baxendale* (1854).

(b)   A Contractual Right of Rescission

Standard condition 4.5.2 gives the seller a right to rescind the contract if the purchaser persists in a requisition on title which the seller cannot, or is unwilling to, satisfy. The point of the condition is that if the seller can take advantage of it, he can wipe out the contract as if it had never existed. He has only to return the deposit. He escapes any claim for damages or for specific performance. Because the power is so drastic, any contractual right to rescind is interpreted restrictively by the court, and no matter what the condition might say, the court will only allow the seller to rescind if he is using the power reasonably, and not as a capricious method of escaping his contractual responsibilities.

In *Selkirk* v. *Romar Investments* [1963] the seller was allowed to rescind under a contractual condition when he was faced with a defect of which he had known nothing, and which would have been difficult and expensive to put right. He would not have been able to rescind if faced with a defect which he could fairly easily, have remedied, or if he had acted unreasonably or recklessly in committing himself to the contract. In *Baines* v. *Tweddle* [1959] the seller failed to check before contract that his mortgagee would release the land to be conveyed from the mortgage. When, after contract, the mortgagee refused to release the land, the seller could not use the contractual right to escape the consequences of his own foolishness.

18.4   Misdescription

A misdescription occurs when the property is not as described on the face of the contract. There is clearly a breach of contract as the seller will not be able to convey what he has promised to convey. Usually, the misdescription will be as to the physical characteristics of the property, e.g. a misstatement of the area, or land that is not suitable for development because of an underground culvert being described as valuable building land (re *Puckett and Smith's Contract* [1962]). It can, however, also be of title, as when a sublease is wrongly disclosed as a headlease (re *Beyfus and Master's Contract* (1888)).

In an open contract, the purchaser's remedies depend on whether or not the misdescription is considered to be 'substantial'. The classic definition of a substantial misdescription comes from *Flight* v. *Booth* (1834) which defines it as one that so far affects the subject matter of the contract that 'it may reasonably be supposed that, but for such misdescription, the purchaser might never have entered into the contract at all'. (In the case, a lease was described in the contract as prohibiting offensive trades. In fact it prohibited many inoffensive trades as well, including that of vegetable-

and fruit-selling, a serious matter, as the shop was in London's main vegetable market. The misdescription was substantial.)

If the misdescription is substantial, the purchaser can escape the contract. He can claim his deposit back, and specific performance will not be awarded against him. If the purchaser wishes to continue with the contract, he can ask for specific performance at a reduced price. If the misdescription is insubstantial and not fraudulent, the purchaser can only claim a reduction in the purchase price by way of damages. He is not released from the contract.

Standard condition 7 restricts the remedies available for misdescription. It has been held (see, for example, *Flight* v. *Booth* (1834)) that no exclusion clause can prevent a purchaser escaping from the contract if the misdescription is substantial. The standard condition does not attempt to do this, as it permits the purchaser to rescind the contract if the error is due to fraud or recklessness, or if the property differs substantially from what the misdescription led the purchaser to expect and the difference prejudices him. The condition also permits the seller to rescind the contract if there is a substantial difference prejudicial to him, but favouring the purchaser. The seller can thus escape a decree of specific performance, but will not escape liability for damages.

Whether or not the contract is or could be, rescinded, a 'material' difference between the property as described and as it is will entitle the affected party to compensation. The condition differentiates between 'substantial' differences, and 'material' ones, so that some errors will lead to a claim for compensation, because material, but will not justify rescission, because not substantial. 'Material' is not defined. The provision for compensation means that just as the purchaser is entitled to a reduction in the price if the property is worse than as described, the seller is entitled to an increase if the property is better than its description. So a purchaser who finds he is getting more than he expected must either pay compensation, or refuse to accept a conveyance on the ground that the difference is substantial.

· 18.5   Delayed Completion

(a)   Specific Performance

(i) *The nature of the remedy* A party who wishes to force completion through, despite the reluctance of the other party, can apply to the court for a decree of specific performance. This decree, if obtained, will order a reluctant seller to execute a conveyance to the purchaser, or will order the reluctant purchaser to pay the agreed purchase price. It is particularly a purchaser's remedy. If the seller refuses to complete as agreed, the purchaser may be able to treat the contract as discharged, and recover damages for breach of contract, but this is cold comfort for a purchaser who wanted the house rather than compensation for failure to get it. A decree of specific performance will secure the house itself. If the seller refuses to comply with the order to convey, the court can order someone to execute the necessary conveyance on his behalf, or can make an order automatically vesting the property in the purchaser.

A seller who is faced with a reluctant purchaser may not want a decree of specific performance. He can, instead, after service of a completion notice treat the contract as discharged, and treat the deposit as forfeited. He may then be able to resell at the same or a higher price, or if forced to sell at a lower price, recover compensation from the purchaser. The occasion when a seller would consider specific performance is when he has succeeded in selling a white elephant which he sees little chance of selling to anyone else.

(ii) *A discretionary remedy* Specific performance is an equitable remedy, and the court has therefore, a discretion as to whether or not to award it. However, in the case of a contract for the sale of land, the decree will be awarded as a matter of course, unless there are special circumstances. Factors which might lead a court to refuse the decree include:

(aa) impossibility of performance. The court will not order the seller to convey the property if he has already conveyed it to someone else.

(bb) The badness of the seller's title. If the seller is in breach of contract because his title is bad, he cannot obtain specific performance, because he cannot fulfil his own part of the contract. However, it may be that the purchaser agreed in the contract not to raise requisitions on the title. As we have seen, such a condition is valid provided the seller fully disclosed any defect known to him, so the purchaser should complete, notwithstanding the fact that the title is defective. If the title is totally bad, however, equity will not force the purchaser to accept a conveyance. The purchaser does not thereby escape common-law damages. If the title, although defective, seems to offer the right to undisturbed possession the seller will be granted the decree (see Re *Scott and Alvarez's Contract, Scott* v. *Alvarez* [1895]).

(cc) Delay. A plaintiff who is tardy in applying for the decree may be refused it, certainly if the delay has prejudiced the defendant.

(dd) Hardship. The decree may be refused if to grant it would cause undue hardship to the defendant. Usually, the court will only consider hardship that arises from circumstances at the time the contract was made, or from its terms. In *Wroth* v. *Tyler* [1974] for example, the purchaser failed to get the decree, because the seller could only comply with the contractual promise of vacant possession by litigating against his own wife for the discharge of her rights of occupation under Matrimonial Homes Act 1983. The outcome of the litigation would be uncertain and unlikely to have an improving effect on the marriage.

Hardship arising from a change in circumstances after the contract was made is not usually considered – for example, the fact that the purchaser has lost his money. This is not an absolute rule, and was not applied in *Patel* v. *Ali* [1984] where the grave illness of one of the sellers arising after the date of the contract would have had meant great hardship had she been compelled to move from her home, and specific performance was not, therefore, awarded against her.

(iii) *Failure to obtain a decree* A plaintiff who is refused the decree may still be able to pursue the common-law remedies e.g. common-law damages for breach of contract. Alternatively, if the plaintiff had a proper case to apply for the decree, but the court refuses it – for example, because of hardship to the defendant – the court can order what are often known as 'equitable damages' which are in substitution for the decree (s.50 of the Supreme Court Act 1981.) These damages were awarded in the case of *Wroth* v. *Tyler* [1974]. In that case, the damages were assessed on the value of the house at the date the decree was refused, rather than the date on which the contract was broken; a logical choice as the damages were to compensate for not obtaining the decree. It resulted in a substantial increase in the size of the award, as the value of the house had been increasing throughout the litigation.

(iv) As has been said, enforcement by the purchaser is comparatively easy, as the court can order transfer of ownership to him. It is not so easy for the seller to enforce the decree. He has in some way to obtain the purchase price. The methods available to any judgement creditor are available to him. He may proceed against other property of the purchaser, or may present a petition for the purchaser's bankruptcy.

When the seller realises that the purchaser is not prepared to comply with the decree he may regret his choice of remedy. If so, he can return to court, and ask it to terminate the contract as having been discharged by the purchaser's breach, and to award common-law damages for breach of contract (see *Johnson* v. *Agnew* [1980].)

(b) Completion Notice

(i) Any delay in completion, even a single day, is a breach of contract. However, delay in itself is not necessarily a breach that is sufficiently grave for the non-delaying party to claim that the contract has been discharged.

Time of the essence If time is 'of the essence of the contract' any delay is a sufficiently serious breach to lead to termination of the contract. Time will only be of the essence if a special condition in the contract makes it so, or if it is made so by implication. The fact that the sale is of a wasting asset, so that delay affects its value, would lead to such an implication.

Time not of the essence In such a case, the delay must be unreasonably long if it is to lead to the right to treat the contract as discharged.

The difficulty is in establishing whether or not the delay is unreasonable. The unreasonableness of the delay is traditionally established by the service of a completion notice by the innocent party on the guilty party. Under an open contract, the rule appears to be that the innocent party must wait a reasonable time after the agreed completion date has passed before serving a notice demanding completion on a date that is itself a reasonable time from service of the notice. The new date is 'of the essence' in the sense that if completion does not take place then, delay has been established as unreasonable, and sufficient to discharge the contract.

In view of the uncertainty as to the calculation of two reasonable periods, it is not surprising that the conditions in a contract provide for the service of a contractual completion notice.

Standard condition 6.6 provides that if the sale is not completed on the agreed date, then either party, provided he is himself ready able and willing to complete, can at any time on or after that date give the other party notice to complete. It then becomes a term of the contract that completion will take place within ten working days of the giving of the notice, and that time shall be of the essence in respect of that period.

(ii) *Its validity*

    (aa) The notice is only valid if the person serving it is himself ready to complete the transaction. A person is ready to complete if there are only administrative matters to finish, such as the preparation of a completion statement or the execution of a conveyance. He is not able and ready to complete if there are matters of substance still to be dealt with, so a seller who has not shown good title cannot serve a valid notice. (These examples are taken from the case of *Cole* v. *Rose* [1978].)

    (bb) A notice to complete must be clear and unambiguous and leave no reasonable doubt as to how and when it is to operate. (*Delta Vale Properties Ltd* v. *Mills and ors* [1990]). It need not, however, specify an exact date for completion. A letter requiring the recipient to 'treat this letter as notice to complete the contract in accordance with its terms' has been held to be sufficient (*Babacomp Ltd* v. *Rightside Properties Ltd*) [1974]. It is probably better not to specify the date on which the period for completion expires, in case the wrong date is specified. If this misleads the recipient of the notice, the notice may be declared void.

(iii) the completion notice makes time 'of the essence' for both parties, not just for the party who served the notice. In *Finkielkraut* v. *Monahan*

[1949] the completion notice was served by the seller, but it was the seller who failed to complete on expiry of the notice. It was held that the purchaser could treat the contract as discharged, and recover his deposit.

The recipient of the notice need not wait to complete until the last day of the specified period. He can complete on any day before the period expires, so can choose whatever date is convenient to himself. However, it seems that any date chosen within this period is not of the essence for either party. It is only the final expiry date of the period that is of the essence (*Oakdown Ltd* v. *Bernstein & Co.* (1984)). For example, if the ten-day period under the standard condition expires on 1 April and the notice is served by the seller, the purchaser can say that he intends to complete on 27 March. If completion does not take place on that day, neither party could treat the contract as discharged, as the obligation of both parties remains that of completing on or before 1 April.

(iv) *Remedies for non-compliance with completion notice*
- (aa) Non-compliance by purchaser The seller can forfeit the deposit, and is free to sell the property to someone else. Any loss incurred on the resale can be recovered as damages, a point repeated by standard condition 7.5.2.
- (bb) Non-compliance by the seller The purchaser can recover his deposit, (and, under standard condition 7.6.2, interest on it) and can also recover any loss caused by the seller's breach of contract.

(v) *Use of the completion notice* The true function of the completion notice is to establish a ground on which the contract can be treated as discharged by breach. It is not designed to force an unwilling party to complete, although it is often used as such, in the sense that, say, a purchaser serves a completion notice in the hope that the seller will be forced to complete for fear of losing the contract. If the seller is undismayed, and still refuses to complete, the notice has achieved nothing if in fact the purchaser still wants to buy the property.

The remedy to be used against a seller who is unwilling to complete at all is specific performance. Application for a decree may be made as soon as the agreed completion date has passed, whether or not time is of the essence. Indeed, application for a decree can be made before the completion date has arrived, if the seller has already indicated that he does not intend to complete the sale (see *Hasham* v. *Zenab* [1960]).

(c) *Compensation for the Fact that Completion has Taken Place Later Than Agreed*

Damages To repeat, any delay is a breach of contract. So if completion takes place, but later than agreed, the innocent party can claim damages from the guilty party, even though time is not of the essence. This was established in the case of *Raineri* v. *Miles* [1981]. Suppose that Alan has contracted to sell Blackacre to Bill, and that Bill has contracted to sell his existing house, Whiteacre, to Charles. If Alan delays completion, Bill will either have to live in a hotel, or delay in completing the sale to Charles, so becoming liable to Charles for damages (or possible interest, see later). The expense to which Bill is put can be recovered by him from Alan. If it is Charles who delays completion, Bill will either have to obtain a bridging loan, or delay the purchase from Alan, becoming liable to Alan for damages or possibly interest. Bill can recover this expense from Charles.

Interest   Standard condition 7.3.1 obliges the party responsible for the delay in completion to pay interest at the contract rate on the purchase price (or, if it is the purchaser paying interest, on the price less the deposit). The condition does not remove the right to claim damages for the delay, but any claim must be reduced by the amount of interest paid under this condition.

If the purchaser has been allowed to go into occupation of the property before completion, he will already be paying interest under condition 5.2.2, so if he then delays completion he will be paying double interest.

Workshop

Attempt this problem yourself, then read the specimen solution at the end of the book.

Problem

(This question is based on a question in Law Society Summer 1980 paper)

You are acting for Green who has contracted to purchase a dwelling-house number 27 Leafy Lane from Black. The contract includes the standard conditions of sale. He has also contracted to sell his present house with completion on the same date, and this contract also incorporates the standard conditions. Black has gone abroad and will not return for another three months. The contract has been signed by his attorney White who is appointed by a power of attorney dated 31 March 1990 in the form set out in the Powers of Attorney Act 1971.

(a) Can White execute the conveyance? What special documents would you require White to hand over on completion?

(b) A few days before completion, your client tells you that he has heard from White that Black has been killed in an accident. He is concerned that there should not be any delay in completing the purchase and asks what will happen now. Advise Green whether White can complete the sale, and if not, what steps will have to be taken to enable completion˜to take place.

(c) Assuming there is a delay in the completion of either transaction:

   (i) explain the rights which Green's purchaser will have;
   (ii) what will Green's own rights be under his contract to buy number 27 Leafy Lane?

19 Remedies Available to the Parties after Completion

19.1 For Breach of Contract

The principle is that on completion of the sale, the contract ceases to exist. It is said to 'merge into the conveyance'. It has been discharged through its performance.

If the sale is of registered title, it is not clear whether the merger takes place on completion (at which point the seller has fulfilled his contractual obligations) or when the transfer is later registered, (which is the point at which the legal estate vests in the purchaser).

If the contract has ceased to exist, there cannot be an action brought on it. So, after completion, it is generally speaking impossible for a disappointed purchaser to sue for breach of contract. However, some terms of a contract do survive completion, and do, therefore, continue to offer a purchaser a remedy. The principle is that a condition will survive if that is what the parties intended. Examples are:

(a) *The promise for vacant possession* This promise must survive completion, as it is only after completion that a purchaser will discover that it has been broken. In *Beard* v. *Porter* [1948] the seller was unable to give vacant possession on completion, because of his inability to evict a tenant. The purchaser nevertheless completed the purchase. He was awarded damages which consisted of:

(aa) the difference between the purchase price, and the value of the house subject to the tenancy;
(bb) payment for somewhere to live until a second house was bought;
(cc) legal fees and stamp duty connected with the purchase of the second house.

(b) *An express condition* giving the right to compensation for misdescription (*Palmer* v. *Johnson* (1884)).

(c) *A promise by the seller* to build a house on the land (*Hancock* v. *B.W. Brazier* (Anerley) Ltd [1966]).

(d) *Possibly, damages for late completion* This was stated to be the case in *Raineri* v. *Miles* [1981] although in that case the plaintiff had issued his writ for damages before completion took place. Standard condition 7.4.1 expressly states that interest on the purchase price payable under condition 7.3 is recoverable after completion.

19.2   On the Covenants for Title

(a)   *The Right to Sue on the Covenants*

The right to sue on the contract, lost through merger, is said to be replaced by a right to sue on the conveyance, i.e. on the covenants for title implied into it. Much can be written about these covenants, but little is going to be written here, as the main point of the following paragraphs is to show how rarely these covenants will provide an effective remedy for a disappointed purchaser.

(i) *The beneficial owner covenants*   By virtue of s.76 of the Law of Property Act 1925, when a seller 'conveys and is expressed to convey' a freehold estate as beneficial owner, there will be implied into the conveyance covenants by him as to his title. He does not categorically covenant that he has a good title. He promises that he has the power to convey the property, that the purchaser will be able quietly to enjoy the property, for freedom from incumbrances, and to do anything further that is necessary for vesting the property in the purchaser.

   If the conveyance is of a leasehold property, there are also implied covenants that the lease is valid and subsisting, and that the seller has not broken any of the covenants in the lease.

   So why do these covenants only rarely offer a remedy? It is because they are qualified in two ways:

(aa) the covenants 'relate to the subject matter of the conveyance as it is expressed to be conveyed'. The basis of an action on the covenants, therefore, is a discrepancy between what the conveyance promises by way of title, and what the purchaser actually gets. If the conveyance is expressly said to be subject to a defect or incumbrance there can be no action under the covenants in respect of that matter. Hence the importance in unregistered conveyancing of setting out incumbrances in the habendum, e.g. 'To hold unto the purchaser in fee simple subject to the restrictive covenants continued in a conveyance of 2 February 1954 made between Alice Baynes of the one part and Christine Davis of the other part' (see Chapter 13).

(bb) the seller is not giving absolute covenants as to the soundness of his title. He is covenanting only in respect of defects or incumbrances arising from the acts or omissions of persons for whom he is responsible.

   He is responsible for himself; for his predecessors in title, but not if he claims through those predecessors through a conveyance for money or money's worth; for people who derive a title through him, e.g. his tenants and mortgagees; and for people claiming in trust for him.

An example may make this qualification clear. Suppose that Alex owns Blackacre, and incumbers the land by granting a right of way over it. Alex conveys Blackacre for £75 000 to Vera, and the conveyance says he conveys it as beneficial owner. Vera later conveys Blackacre for £80 000 as beneficial owner to Paul. Neither conveyance says the land is conveyed subject to the easement.

After completion, Paul is irritated to discover a stranger strolling across his backyard.

The first thing for Paul is to consider is whether or not he did take subject to the easement. If the title is unregistered, and the easement is legal, Paul is bound by it.

If the title is registered, Paul is bound by the easement if it is overriding under s.70(1)(a) of the Land Registration Act 1925, or if it registered on the title (a fact which surely would not have escaped Paul's attention until now).

If Paul is bound by the easement he will naturally feel a sense of grievance towards Vera. He cannot sue her for breach of contract even if she is guilty of non-disclosure because the contract no longer exists. He must therefore, sue her for breach of her covenants for title. The covenants have been implied because Vera conveyed as beneficial owner and for value. However, Vera did not create the right of way herself and she is not liable for the acts of Alex, because she claims ownership from him through a conveyance for money.

This is why the covenants given by Vera turn out to be worth so little. As she bought the property from Alex, she is not liable for any defect in title at all, unless she created it. (She is liable for her own omissions, as well as acts, so it seems she would be breaking her own covenants for title if she failed to pay off a mortgage created by a predecessor, but only, it seems if she knew of the mortgage when she conveyed (*David* v. *Sabin* [1893]. She is not liable for a failure to get rid of the easement as this is not something she has power to do.)

Although Paul could not sue Vera, he could sue Alex.

Covenants for title were implied into the conveyance between Alex and Vera; the benefit of the covenants has passed to Paul as the benefit of the covenants runs with the covenantee's estate in the land; and Alex has broken the covenant because he is liable for his *own* acts. Of what use, though, is a right of action against a seller's predecessor in title, when the predecessor is probably untraceable?

If Alex had given the property to Vera, Vera would have broken her covenants, as she would have been responsible for anything done by Alex, as no conveyance for money separates her from Alex. This does not necessarily mean that she is also liable for things done by Alex's predecessors. If Alex bought the property for money, she derives title from *them* through that conveyance, and so is not responsible for their acts.

If a borrower mortgages his property to the lender, and the mortgage deed says he does this as beneficial owner, the covenants for title are absolute, not qualified, so the borrower cannot escape liability to the mortgagee by proving that the incumbrance or default was created by another person.

(ii) If the seller conveys and is expressed to convey as *trustee, personal representative* or as *mortgagee*, he impliedly covenants only that he has not himself incumbered the property. A purchaser who wants the benefit of the beneficial owner covenants, but who is in fact buying from a personal representative or a trustee, might ask the seller to state in the conveyance that he conveys as beneficial owner. It is doubtful if that is sufficient to imply the covenants into the conveyance, as s.76 uses the phrase 'conveys and is expressed to convey as beneficial owner'. It seems it is not sufficient for the seller to *say* he is conveying in that capacity, he must actually be doing it. If the purchaser in these circumstances wants the benefit of the beneficial-owner covenants, it would be better expressly to incorporate them.

If co-owners convey as beneficial owners, the covenants may be implied. Although the capacity in which they hold the legal estate is that of trustees for sale, they could also fairly be described as beneficial owners as they do between them own the entire beneficial interest. A purchaser who greatly desires the benefit of the beneficial-owner covenants, and who feels doubtful about this point, should again expressly incorporate the covenants.

(b)   Covenants for Title and Registered Title

The covenants for title would also seem to be implied into a transfer of registered title. Rule 76 of the Land Registration Rules 1925 recognises this:

> For the purposes of introducing the covenants implied under ss.76 and 77 of the Law of Property Act 1925, a person may in a registered disposition, be expressed to execute, transfer or charge as beneficial owner....

Rule 77 states that the covenants take effect subject to all charges and other interests appearing on the register when the transfer is executed and to all overriding interests of which the purchaser has notice. So no action can be bought on the covenants for title in respect of these matters. Rule 77 therefore seems to envisage a purchaser being able to bring an action in respect of an overriding interest of which he did not know.

Although that seems clear to the average person it has been the subject of considerable academic controversy. The argument, put briefly, is this. A transfer of registered title transfers 'all the property comprised in the above title' (see Chapter 14). The transfer promises the title as registered. That is what the purchaser obtains, so there is never any discrepancy between what the transfer promises and what the purchaser gets, and there can be no action on the covenants for title.

There has been a recent successful case on the covenants for title. In *Dunning (AJ) & Sons (Shopfitters) Ltd* v. *Sykes and Son (Poole) Ltd* the defendants had previously sold part of the land comprised in their registered title. This land was described in the case as the 'yellow land'. The defendants then sold another part of the land to the plaintiffs. The transfer contained two descriptions of the land being transferred. One verbal description said it was part of the land comprised in the defendants' title. This description did not include the yellow land, as it was no longer part of that title. The other description was by reference to the plan annexed to the transfer, and the plan clearly purported to include the yellow land. The transfer also said that the defendants conveyed as beneficial owners.

When the plaintiffs realised that they had not acquired the yellow land they sued the defendants for breach of the covenants for title and were successful.

It is held that the description in the plan prevailed over the description by title number. The transfer did, therefore, promise a title to the 'yellow' land, and the defendants could not give that title by virtue of their own act in conveying it elsewhere. If no plan had been used the plaintiffs would have failed. The transfer would have promised the land in the title, and that is what they would have got, albeit less than they expected. Nor does the case destroy the above argument so far as it relates to overriding interests. The transfer is silent as to incumbrances on the property. It promises the title as registered and registration is subject to all overriding interests. Nevertheless, any decision that there is no right of action in respect of undisclosed overriding interest makes nonsense of rules 76 and 77.

19.3 Under s.25 of the Law of Property Act 1969

This remedy is only available to a purchaser of unregistered title. We saw in Chapter 4 that it is possible for a purchaser to take subject to a registered land charge without having an opportunity to discover the fact of registration, as it is against a pre-root name. If the purchaser had discovered the land charge before completion he would have had remedies for breach of contract. When he discovers it after completion he may have no remedy against the seller under the covenants for title, because of the qualified nature of the covenants.

In recognition of the fact that it is the system of registration that is at fault, a purchaser who is affected by a pre-root land charge can claim compensation from the Chief Land Registrar under s.25 of the Law of Property Act 1969. The conditions are (a) that the purchaser must have completed in ignorance of the existence of the charge and (b) that the charge is not registered against the name of an estate-owner appearing as such in the title which the seller was entitled to investigate under an open contract. If a document in the title that the purchaser is entitled to investigate refers to an incumbrance, the document creating that incumbrance is treated as part of the title open to investigation by the purchaser.

Consider this example: The title deeds are:

- A 1940 conveyance made from A to B. B gave restrictive covenants to A which were duly registered against B's name.
- A 1950 conveyance from B to C. C later gave an option over the property to D, which D registered against C's name.
- A 1952 conveyance from C to E.
- A 1979 conveyance from E to F.

Under a contract made in 1990, F contracts to sell to G, and G agrees to accept a title traced from the 1979 conveyance. The contract does not disclose the covenants or the option. G completes, and then discovers their existence. G cannot claim compensation for the fact that he has bought subject to the option. Had he not accepted the contractual condition cutting short his investigation of title he could have traced title back to a root at least fifteen years old, so back to the 1952 conveyance, and would have been able to search against C's name.

F can claim compensation for the covenants. Even had he traced title back to 1952, he would still not have discovered B's name. However, he cannot claim compensation if either the 1952 or 1979 conveyance says that the property is conveyed subject to the covenants.

No compensation can be claimed in respect of a land charge registered against a name appearing on a superior title which the purchaser or grantee of a lease cannot investigate because of s.44 of the Law of Property Act 1925. The purchaser's loss is caused by s.44, not by the system of registration under the Land Charges Act 1972.

19.4   For Misrepresentation

A representation is a statement of fact made by the seller or his agent before the contract comes into existence, which helps to induce the contract and on which the purchaser relies. (It is possible for a misrepresentation to be made by a purchaser, but this is likely to be rare.)

If the statement is incorrect, the purchaser will have remedies, both before and after completion. He may be able to rescind the contract or claim damages. A question on misrepresentation appears in the workshop section of this chapter.

Workshop

Attempt this problem yourself, then read the specimen solution at the end of the book.

Problem 1

Pauline has contracted to buy Roger's house. The contract incorporates the standard conditions. She is told by Roger's estate agent before contract that the house has the benefit of a planning permission for the ground floor to be used as a shop but in fact the permission had expired the previous year. Pauline has just discovered this, and she asks if she has any remedies against Roger.

Appendix A

Standard Forms

AGREEMENT

(Incorporating the Standard Conditions of Sale (1st Edition))

Agreement date: _____

Seller: _____

Buyer: _____

Property: (freehold/leasehold) _____

_____

Burdens on the Property: _____

_____

Capacity in which the
Seller sells: _____

Completion date: _____

Contract rate: _____

Root of title/Title Number: _____

Purchase Price: _____

Deposit: _____

Amount payable for chattels: _____

Balance: _____

The Seller will sell and the Buyer will buy the Property for the Purchase Price.

The Agreement continues on the back page.

WARNING This is a formal document, designed to create legal rights and legal obligations. Take advice before using it.	SIGNED _____ SELLER/BUYER

(*The following text is the back page of the Agreement.*)

1. (a)   This Agreement incorporates the Standard Conditions of Sale (1st Edition). Where there is a conflict between those Conditions and this Agreement, this Agreement prevails.

   (b)   Where the context so admits terms used or defined in this Agreement have the same meaning when used in the Conditions.

2.   The Property is sold subject to the Burdens on the Property and the Buyer will raise no requisitions on them.

3.   The chattels on the Property and set out on any attached list are included in the sale.

4.   All sums payable under this Agreement are exclusive of Value Added Tax.

SELLER'S SOLICITORS

BUYER'S SOLICITORS

Appendix B

Standard Conditions of Sale

STANDARD CONDITIONS OF SALE (1ST EDITION)

(National Conditions of Sale 21st Edition, Law Society's Conditions of Sale 1990)

1 General

1.1 **Definitions**

1.1.1 In these conditions:

    (a) "accrued interest" means:

        (i) if money has been placed on deposit or in a building society share account, the interest actually earned;

        (ii) otherwise, the interest which might reasonably have been earned by depositing the money at interest on seven days' notice of withdrawal with a clearing bank;

        less, in either case, any proper charges for handling the money;

    (b) "adverse interest" has the meaning given in condition 3.1.2;

    (c) "clearing bank" means a bank which is a member of CHAPS and Town Clearing Company Limited;

    (d) "completion date", unless defined in the agreement, has the meaning given in condition 6.1.1;

    (e) "contract rate", unless defined in the agreement, is the Law Society's interest rate from time to time in force;

    (f) "lease" includes sublease;

    (g) "notice to complete" has the meaning given in condition 6.6.1;

    (h) "public requirement" has the meaning given in condition 3.2.1;

    (i) "requisition" includes objection;

    (j) "retained land" has the meaning given in condition 3.4.1;

    (k) "solicitor" includes barrister, duly certificated notary public and licensed conveyancer;

    (l) "tenancy" has the meaning given in condition 3.3.1;

    (m) "transfer" includes conveyance and assignment;

    (n) "working day" means any day from Monday to Friday (inclusive) which is not Christmas Day, Good Friday or a statutory bank holiday.

1.1.2 The following terms which have a special meaning in the Land Registration Act 1925 are used in the same sense in these conditions: "absolute title", "office copies", "overriding interest".

1.2   Joint parties

If there is more than one seller or more than one buyer, the obligations which they undertake can be enforced against them all jointly or against each individually.

1.3   Notices and Documents

1.3.1   A notice required or authorised by the contract must be in writing.

1.3.2   Transmission by fax is a valid means of giving a notice or delivering a document where delivery of the original document is not essential.

1.3.3   Notices or documents sent by the following means are to be considered as given or delivered:

(a)	by first class post:	two working days after posting;
(b)	by second class post:	three working days after posting;
(c)	through a document exchange:	on the first working day after the day on which it would normally be available for collection by the addressee;
(d)	by fax:	on the day of the transmission if sent before 4pm, or otherwise on the next working day.

2   Formation

2.1   Date

2.1.1   If the parties intend to make a contract by exchanging duplicate copies by post or through a document exchange, the contract is made when the last copy is posted or deposited at the document exchange.

2.1.2   If the parties' solicitors agree to treat exchange as taking place before duplicate copies are actually exchanged, the contract is made in accordance with that agreement.

2.2   Deposit

2.2.1   The buyer is to pay a deposit of 10 per cent of the purchase price no later than the date of the contract. Except on a sale by auction, payment is to be made by banker's draft or by cheque drawn on a solicitor's bank account.

2.2.2   If the seller is buying another property in a related transaction, he may use all or part of the deposit as a deposit in that transaction to be held on terms to the same effect as this condition and condition 2.2.3.

2.2.3   Any deposit or part of a deposit not used in accordance with condition 2.2.2 is to be held by the seller's solicitor as stakeholder on terms that on completion it is paid to the seller with accrued interest.

2.2.4   If a cheque tendered in payment of all or part of the deposit is dishonoured when first presented, the seller may, within seven working days of being notified that the cheque has been dishonoured, give notice to the buyer that the contract is discharged by the buyer's breach.

2.3   Auctions

2.3.1   On a sale by auction the following conditions apply to the property and, if it is sold in lots, to each lot.

2.3.2   The sale is subject to a reserve price.

2.3.3   The seller, or a person on his behalf, may bid up to the reserve price.

2.3.4   The auctioneer may refuse any bid.

2.3.5   If there is a dispute about a bid, the auctioneer may determine the dispute or restart the auction at the last undisputed bid.

3   Rights which affect the property

3.1   **Adverse interests**

3.1.1   The seller is selling the property free from incumbrances, other than:

    (a)   any adverse interest existing when the contract is made; and

    (b)   any matter mentioned in the agreement.

3.1.2   "Adverse interests" are:

    (a)   public requirements

    (b)   legal easements benefiting the owners or occupiers of other property

    (c)   entries on public registers not maintained by H.M Land Registry or its Land Charges Department

    (d)   if the title to the property is registered, overriding interests.

3.1.3   The seller is to disclose to the buyer, before the contract is made

    (a)   all adverse interests of which he knew

    (b)   anything in writing which he knew about concerning an adverse interest.

3.1.4   It is for the buyer, before the contract is made, to make all the searches, enquiries and inspections which a prudent buyer would make; he buys the property subject to anything which they did reveal, or would have revealed, to him.

3.1.5   The buyer accepts the property in the physical state it is in when the contract is made, unless the seller is building or converting it.

3.1.6   After the contract is made, the seller is to give the buyer details without delay of any new public requirement and of anything in writing which he learns about concerning any adverse interest, whether or not it existed before the contract was made.

3.2   **Public requirements**

3.2.1   A "public requirement" is something validly ordered by a body acting on statutory authority.

3.2.2   The buyer is to bear the cost of complying with any outstanding public requirement, whenever it was made, and is to indemnify the seller against any liabilitiy resulting from a public requirement.

3.3   **Tenancies**

3.3.1   The buyer is to be given vacant possession of all the property on completion; this does not apply to any part of it included in a lease or tenancy ("tenancy") subject to which the agreement states the property is sold.

3.3.2   Before the contract is made, the seller is to provide the buyer with full details of each tenancy or copies of the documents creating it. The buyer is treated as entering into the contract knowing and fully accepting the tenancy terms.

3.3.3   The seller is to inform the buyer without delay if any tenancy ends; the seller is then to act as the buyer directs, provided that the buyer agrees to indemnify him against all loss and expense.

3.3.4   The following terms apply even if the details in the agreement about any tenancy are incomplete or inaccurate.

3.3.5   After the contract is made, the seller is to inform the buyer without delay of any change in the tenancy terms.

3.3.6   The buyer is to indemnify the seller against all future claims arising under any tenancy, even if void against a purchaser for want of registration.

3.3.7   It is for the buyer to satisfy himself whether and how any legislation affects any tenancy and what rent is legally recoverable; the seller takes no responsibility for this.

3.4 **Land retained by seller**

3.4.1 "Retained land" is land which the seller owns and which is adjoining or near the property.

3.4.2 Where there will be retained land after the property has been sold:

    (a) the buyer will not have any right of light or air over the retained land;

    (b) the seller as owner of the retained land and the buyer as owner of the property will each have the rights over the land of the other which they would have had if they were two separate buyers to whom the seller had made simultaneous transfers of the property and the retained land.

Either party may require that the transfer contains appropriate express terms.

3.4.3 If any tenancy includes all or part of the property and includes retained land and the rent has not been apportioned under statutory authority, the seller may apportion the rent.

4 Title and transfer

4.1 **Timetable**

4.1.1 Subject to the provisions of condition 4.5, the following are the steps for deducing and investigating the title to the property to be taken within the following time limits:

Step	Time Limit
1. The seller is to send the buyer evidence of title in accordance with condition 4.2.	Immediately after making the contract.
2. The buyer may raise written requisitions.	Six working days after either the date of the contract or the day of delivery of the seller's evidence of title on which the requisitions are raised whichever is the later.
3. The seller is to reply in writing to any requisitions raised.	Four working days after receiving the requisitions.
4. The buyer may make written observations on the seller's replies.	Three working days after receiving the replies.

The buyer's right to raise requisitions or make observations is lost after the expiration of the relevant time limit.

4.1.2 The parties are to take the following steps to prepare and agree the transfer of the property within the following time limits:

Step	Time Limit
A. The buyer is to send the seller a draft transfer.	At least twelve working days before completion date.

B. The seller is to approve or revise that draft and either return it or retain it for use as the actual transfer.	Four working days after delivery of the draft transfer.
C. If the draft is returned the buyer is to send an engrossment to the seller.	At least five working days before completion date.

4.1.3 Periods of time under conditions 4.1.1 and 4.1.2 may run concurrently.

4.1.4 If the period between the date of the contract and completion date is less than 15 working days, the time limits in conditions 4.1.1 and 4.1.2 are to be reduced by the same proportion as that period bears to the period of 15 working days. Fractions of a working day are to be rounded down except that the time limit to perform any step is not to be less than one working day.

4.2 Proof of title

4.2.1 The evidence of registered title is office copies of the items required to be furnished by section 110(1) of the Land Registration Act 1925 and the copies, abstracts and evidence referred to in section 110(2).

4.2.2 The seller authorises the buyer's solicitor and the buyer's mortgagee's solicitor to inspect the register.

4.2.3 The evidence of unregistered title is an abstract of the title, or an epitome of title with photocopies of the relevant documents.

4.2.4 Where the title to the property is unregistered, the seller is to produce to the buyer (without cost to the buyer):

(a) the original of every relevant document, or

(b) an abstract, epitome or copy with an original marking by a solicitor of examination either against the original or against an examined abstract or against an examined copy.

4.3 Defining the property

4.3.1 The seller need not:

(a) prove the exact boundaries of the property

(b) prove who owns fences, ditches, hedges or walls

(c) separately identify parts of the property with different titles further than he may be able to do from information in his possession.

4.3.2 The buyer may, if it is reasonable, require the seller to make or obtain, pay for and hand over a statutory declaration about facts relevant to the matters mentioned in condition 4.3.1. The form of the declaration is to be agreed by the buyer, who must not unreasonably withhold his agreement.

4.4 Rents and rentcharges

The fact that a rent or rentcharge, whether payable or receivable by the owner of the property, has been or will on completion be, informally apportioned is not to be regarded as a defect in title.

4.5 Requisitions

4.5.1 The time limit on the buyer's right to raise requisitions contained in condition 4.1.1 applies even where the seller supplies incomplete evidence of his title but the buyer may within six working days from the delivery of any further evidence raise supplementary requisitions resulting from that evidence.

4.5.2 Where the seller is unable or, on reasonable grounds, unwilling to satisfy any requisition, he may give the buyer notice of that fact and of his reasons and require the buyer within seven working days to withdraw the requisition. Unless the buyer withdraws it, the seller may rescind the contract notwithstanding any intermediate negotiation or litigation.

4.6   **Transfer**

4.6.1   The buyer does not prejudice his right to raise requisitions, or to require replies to any raised, by taking any steps in relation to the preparation or agreement of the transfer.

4.6.2   The seller is to transfer the property in the capacity specified in the agreement, or (if none is specified) as beneficial owner.

4.6.3 I f after completion the seller will remain bound by any obligation affecting the property, the buyer is to covenant in the transfer to indemnify him against liability for any breach of it and to perform it unless a covenant to that effect is implied by law.

4.6.4   The seller is to arrange at his expense that, in relation to every document of title which the buyer does not receive on completion, the buyer is to have the benefit of:

(a)   a written acknowledgement of his right to its production; and

(b)   a written undertaking for its safe custody (except while it is held by a mortgagee or by someone in a fiduciary capacity).

4.6.5   Where the title to the property is unregistered and the seller is retaining documents of title, he is at completion to endorse a memorandum of the sale to the buyer on the last document in each relevant title.

5   Pending Completion

5.1   **Responsibility for property**

5.1.1   The seller will transfer the property in the same physical state as it was at the date of the contract (except for fair wear and tear), which means that the seller retains the risk until completion.

5.1.2   If at any time before completion the physical state of the property makes it unusable for its purpose at the date of the contract:

(a)   the buyer may rescind the contract,

(b)   the seller may rescind the contract where the property has become unusable for that purpose as a result of damage against which the seller could not reasonably have insured, or which it is not legally possible for the seller to make good.

5.1.3   The seller is under no obligation to the buyer to insure the property.

5.1.4   Section 47 of the Law of Property Act 1925 does not apply.

5.2   **Occupation by buyer**

5.2.1   If the buyer is not already lawfully in the property, and the seller agrees to let him into occupation, the buyer occupies on the following terms.

5.2.2   The buyer is a licensee and not a tenant. The terms of the licence are that the buyer:

(a)   cannot transfer it

(b)   may permit members of his household to occupy the property

(c)   is to pay all outgoings including any premium the seller pays to insure the property

(d)   is to pay the seller a fee calculated at the contract rate on the purchase price (less any deposit paid) for the period of the licence

(e)   is entitled to any rents and profits from any part of the property which he does not occupy

(f)   is to keep the property in as good a state of repair as it was in when he went into occupation (except for fair wear and tear) and is not to alter it

(g)   is to quit the property when the licence ends.

5.2.3   The buyer's licence ends on the earliest of: completion date, rescission of the contract or when five working days' notice given by one party to the other takes effect.

5.2.4   The buyer's right to raise requisitions is unaffected.

6   Completion

6.1   Date

6.1.1   Completion date is twenty working days after the date of the contract but time is not of the essence of the contract unless a notice to complete has been served.

6.1.2   If the money due on completion is received after 2.00pm, completion is to be treated, for the purposes only of conditions 6.3 and 7.3, as taking place on the next working day.

6.1.3   Condition 6.1.2 does not apply where the sale is with vacant possession and the seller has not vacated the property by 2.00pm on the date of actual completion.

6.2   Place

Completion is to take place in England and Wales, either at the seller's solicitor's office or at some other place which the seller reasonably specifies.

6.3   Amount payable

6.3.1   Income and outgoings of the property are to be apportioned between the parties so far as the change of ownership on completion will affect entitlement to receive or liability to pay them.

6.3.2   If the whole property is sold with vacant possession or the seller exercises his option in condition 7.3.4, apportionment is to be made with effect from the date of actual completion; otherwise, it is to be made from completion date.

6.3.3   In apportioning any sum, it is to be assumed the seller owns the property until the end of the day from which apportionment is made and that the sum accrues from day to day at the rate at which it is payable on that day.

6.3.4   For the purpose of apportioning income and outgoings, it is to be assumed that they accrue at an equal daily rate throughout the year.

6.3.5   When any sums to be apportioned are not known or easily ascertainable a provisional apportionment is to be made according to the best estimate available. As soon after completion as the amount is known, a final apportionment is to be made and notified to the other party and any resulting balance paid, no more than ten working days later.

6.4   Rent receipts

The buyer is to assume that whoever gave any receipt for a payment of rent or service charge which the seller produces was the person or the agent of the person then entitled to that rent, or service charge.

6.5   Means of payment

The buyer is to pay the money due on completion in one or more of the following ways:

(a)   legal tender

(b)   a banker's draft drawn by and on a clearing bank

(c)   a direct credit to a bank account nominated by the seller's solicitor

(d)   an unconditional release of a deposit held by a stakeholder.

6.6   Notice to complete

6.6.1   A "notice to complete" means a notice requiring completion of the contract in accordance with this condition.

6.6.2 At any time on or after completion date, a party who is ready able and willing to complete may give the other a notice to complete.

6.6.3 A party is ready able and willing:

(a) if he could be, but for the default of the other party, and

(b) in the case of the seller, even though a mortgage remains secured on the property, if the amount to be paid on completion enables the property to be transferred of all mortgages (except those to which the sale is expressly subject).

6.6.4 The parties are to complete the contract within ten working days of giving a notice to complete, excluding the day on which the notice is given. For this purpose, time is of the essence of the contract.

6.6.5 If the buyer paid a deposit of less than 10 per cent of the purchase price, on receipt of a notice to complete he is forthwith to pay a further deposit equal to the balance of that 10 per cent.

7 Remedies

7.1 Errors and omissions

7.1.1 If any plan or statement in the contract, or in the negotiations leading to it, is or was misleading or inaccurate due to an error or omission, the remedies available are as follows.

7.1.2 When, as a consequence, there is a material difference between the description or value of the property as represented and as it is, the injured party is entitled to compensation.

7.1.3 The only circumstances which entitle the injured party to rescind the contract as a result of an error or omission are:

(a) where the error or omission results from fraud or recklessness, or

(b) where he would otherwise be obliged, to his prejudice, to transfer or accept property differing substantially (in quantity, quality, tenure or otherwise) from what the error or omission had led him to expect.

7.2 Rescission

If either party rescinds the contract:

(a) unless the rescission is a result of the buyer's breach of contract the seller is to repay any deposit paid by the buyer with accrued interest

(b) the buyer is to return any documents he received from the seller and is to cancel any registration of the contract.

7.3 Late completion

7.3.1 If there is default by either or both of the parties in performing their obligations under the contract and completion is delayed, the party whose total period of default is the greater is to pay compensation to the other party.

7.3.2 Compensation is calculated at the contract rate on the purchase price, or (where the buyer is the paying party) the purchase price, less any deposit paid, for the period by which the paying party's default exceeds that of the receiving party, or, if shorter, the period between completion date and actual completion.

7.3.3 Any claim for loss resulting from delayed completion is to be reduced by any compensation paid under this condition.

7.3.4 Where the buyer is in occupation of the property and completion is delayed, the seller may give notice to the buyer, before the date of actual completion, that he intends to take the net income from the property until actual completion.

7.3.5   The seller is only entitled to both compensation and income from the property in respect of the same period, if he exercises his option in condition 7.3.4.

7.4   After completion

7.4.1   Completion does not cancel liability for any apportioned sum payable under condition 6.3.5 or any compensation payable under condition 7.3.1.

7.4.2   The seller is to have no lien on any documents of title after completion.

7.5   Buyer's failure to comply with notice to complete

7.5.1   If the buyer fails to complete in accordance with a notice to complete, the following terms apply.

7.5.2   The seller may:

(a)   forfeit and keep any deposit and accrued interest

(b)   resell the property

(c)   claim damages.

7.5.3   The buyer is to return any documents he received from the seller and is to cancel any registration of the contract.

7.6   Seller's failure to comply with notice to complete

7.6.1   If the seller fails to complete, then the following terms apply.

7.6.2   The seller is to repay to the buyer the deposit with accrued interest.

7.6.3   The buyer is to return any documents he received from the seller and is, at the seller's expense, to cancel any registration of the contract.

7.6.4   The buyer retains his other rights and remedies.

8   Leasehold Property

8.1   Existing leases

8.1.1   The following provisions apply to a sale of leasehold land.

8.1.2   Before the contract is made, the seller is to provide the buyer with full details of the lease. The buyer is treated as entering into the contract knowing and fully accepting the lease terms.

8.1.3   The seller is to deduce a title which will enable the buyer to register the lease at H.M Land Registry with an absolute title or would enable him to do so if the title to the lease was registrable.

8.1.4   The seller is to comply with any lease obligations requiring the tenant to insure the property.

8.1.5   The transfer is to record that no covenant implied by statute makes the seller liable to the buyer for any breach of the lease terms about the condition of the property. This applies even if the seller is to transfer as beneficial owner.

8.2   New leases

8.2.1   The following provisions apply to a grant of a new lease.

8.2.2   The conditions apply so that:

"seller" means the proposed landlord

"buyer" means the proposed tenant

"purchaser price" means the premium to be paid on the grant of the lease.

8.2.3   The lease is to be in the form of the draft attached to the contract.

8.2.4   The seller is to deduce a title which will enable the buyer to register the lease at H.M Land Registry with an absolute title or would enable him to do so if the title to the lease was registrable.

8.2.5   The buyer is not entitled to transfer the benefit of the contract.

8.2.6 The seller is to engross the lease and a counterpart of it and is to send the counterpart to the buyer at least five working days before completion date.

8.2.7 The buyer is to execute the counterpart and deliver it to the seller on completion.

8.3. Landlord's consent

8.3.1 The following provisions apply if a consent to assign or sublet is required.

8.3.2 (a) The seller is to apply for the consent at his expense, and to use his best efforts to obtain it.

    (b) The buyer is to provide all information and references reasonably required.

8.3.3 Unless he is in breach of his obligation under 8.3.2, either party may rescind the contract by notice to the other party if three working days before completion date:

    (a) the consent has not been given; or

    (b) the consent has been given subject to a condition to which the buyer reasonably objects.

9 Chattels

9.1 The following provisions apply to any chattels which are to be sold.

9.2 Whether or not a separate price is to be paid for the chattels, the contract takes effect as a contract for sale of goods.

9.3 Ownership of the chattels passes to the buyer on actual completion.

Appendix C

Property Information Form

PROPERTY INFORMATION FORM

Property: _____

Seller: _____

Buyer: _____

1 Boundaries

Questions	Replies

1.1 Who owns all the boundary walls, fences, hedges, ditches or other boundary features?

1.2 Who accepts responsibility for repairing the above?

1.3 If there is no definite indication, please state which boundary features have been maintained or repaired by the seller or those which the seller considers to be his responsibility.

1.4 Has the position of any boundary feature been altered during the last 20 years?

2 Disputes

2.1 Please give full details of any past or current disputes which in any way relate to the property, its use or any adjoining or neighbouring property or their use.

2.2 Have there been any disputes relating to any covenants or any boundaries affecting the property?

3 Notices

3.1 Please give full details of all notices given or received that relate to the property, to its use or to its covenants or boundaries.

3.2 Please give details of any notices given or received relating to any adjoining or neighbouring properties or its covenants or boundaries.

3.3 Is the seller aware of any correspondence or negotiations with any local or other authority which might affect the property?

4 Guarantees

If the property has the benefit of any guarantees:

4.1 Please supply copies together with details or specifications of work done.

4.2 Please indicate what claims (if any) have already been made under the guarantee and with what result.

4.3 If appropriate, have notices of assignment of the guarantee been given in the past?

5 Services

5.1 Please give details of any services or conducting media other than mains which pass under or over any adjoining or neighbouring property.

5.2   Please give details of any services
       or conducting media other than
       mains which pass under or over
       the property and serve any
       adjoining or neighbouring property.

5.3   Please give full details of all legal
       rights enjoyed to ensure the benefit
       of uninterrupted services.
       e.g. easements, wayleaves,
       licences etc.

6   Facilities

6.1   With regard to the use of any joint
       facilities (such as accessway or
       drainage), please supply full details
       of all contributions made or
       requested towards the repair,
       renewal, maintenance or use of
       such facilities or any obligations for
       making such contributions.

6.2   Who is responsible for the
       collection of the contributions and
       for the renewal, repair or
       maintenance of such facilities?

6.3   Please give details of sums paid or
       owing.

6.4   Please indicate whether the
       payments are of a regular nature.

6.5   In order to repair or maintain this
       property or any of its boundary
       features, has the seller found it
       necessary to enter onto any
       adjoining or neighbouring property?
       If so, how has permission been
       obtained?

7   Adverse Rights

7.1   Please give full details of all
       overriding interests affecting the
       property as defined by the Land
       Registration Act 1925 Section 70(1).

7.2   Is the seller aware of any rights or
        other arrangements of either a
        formal or informal nature which
        affect the property other than
        those already disclosed in the draft
        contract? If so, full details should
        be supplied.

8   Occupiers

8.1   Please provide the full names, and
        ages if under 18, of all persons who
        are in occupation of the property.

8.2   (a) Do any of the people mentioned
        in 8.1 have any legal or equitable
        interest in the property or any
        rights of occupation?

        (b) If so, please supply full details
        and indicate if such person will sign
        the contract to confirm that vacant
        possession will be given on the
        contractual completion date.

9   Restrictions

9.1   If the property is subject to any
        restrictive covenant or other
        restriction which requires consent
        to be given for certain acts or plans,
        please provide written evidence of
        any such consent or approval.

9.2   Is the seller aware that any necessary
        consent was not in fact obtained?

9.3   Does the seller know who has the
        benefit of such restrictive covenants?
        If so, please provide the name and
        address of the person or company
        having such benefit or the name and
        address of his or its solicitors.

10   Planning

10.1   Has the seller (or to his knowledge any
        previous owner) carried out any
        alterations or additions to the property
        during the last 4 years?

10.2   If so, did such alterations or additions
        requireplanning consent, building
        regulations or bye-law approval or
        listed building consent?

11   Mechanics of Sale

11.1   (a) Is this sale dependent on the
        seller buying another property?

        (b) If so, what stage have the
        negotiations reached?

11.2   (a) Does the seller require a
        mortgage?
        (b) If so, has an offer been
        received or a mortgage certificate
        obtained?

11.3   How soon after exchange of
        contracts does the seller anticipate
        being able to give vacant
        possession of the whole of the
        property?

12   Outgoings

12.1   Has the seller paid any annual or
        periodic charges other than water
        and general rates or community
        charge which affect the property?

SELLER'S SOLICITORS

DATE

Reminder

1.   Copies of all relevant planning decisions, NHBC documents, guarantees and
        building regulation approvals should be supplied in addition to the information
        above together with the Fixtures, Fittings and Contents Form.

2.   If the property is leasehold, also complete Additional Property Information
        Form.

Appendix D

Fixtures, Fittings and Contents Form

FIXTURES FITTINGS AND CONTENTS

Address of the Property:

Place a tick in one of these two columns against every item.

	INCLUDED IN SALE	EXCLUDED FROM SALE (OR NONE AT THE PROPERTY)
TV Aerial		
Radio Aerial		
Immersion Heater		
Hot Water		
Cylinder Jacket		
Roof Insulation		
Wall Heaters		
Night Storage		
Heater		
Gas/Electric		
Fires		
Light Fittings: Ceiling Lights Wall Lights Lamp Shades N.B If these are to be removed, it is assumed that they will be replaced by ceiling rose and socket, flex, bulb holder and bulb.		
Switches		
Electric Points		
Dimmer Switches		
Fluorescent Lighting		
Outside Lights		

	INCLUDED IN THE SALE	EXCLUDED FROM SALE (OR NONE AT THE PROPERTY)
Telephone Receivers: British Telecom Own		
Burglar Alarm System		
Complete Central Heating System		
Extractor Fans		
Doorbell/Chimes		
Door Knocker		
Door Furniture: Internal External		
Double Glazing		
Window Fitments		
Shutters/Grills		
Curtain Rails		
Curtain Poles		
Pelmets		
Venetian Blinds		
Roller Blinds		
Curtains (Including Net Curtains): Lounge Dining Room Kitchen Bathroom Bedroom 1 Bedroom 2		

	INCLUDED IN THE SALE	EXCLUDED FROM SALE (OR NONE AT THE PROPERTY)
Bedroom 3		
Bedroom 4		
Other Rooms (state which)		
1		
2		
3		
Carpets and other Floor Covering:		
Lounge		
Dining Room		
Kitchen		
Hall, Stairs and Landing		
Bathroom		
Bedroom 1		
Bedroom 2		
Bedroom 3		
Bedroom 4		
Other Rooms (state which)		
1		
2		
3		
Storage Units in Kitchen		
Kitchen Fitments:		
Fitted Cupboards and Shelves		
Refrigerator/ Fridge-Freezer		
Oven		

	INCLUDED IN THE SALE	EXCLUDED FROM SALE (OR NONE AT THE PROPERTY)
Hob Cutlery Rack Spice Rack Other (state which) 1 2 3		

Kitchen Furniture:
    Washing Machine
    Dishwasher
    Tumble-Drier
    Cooker
    Other
    (state which)
1
2
3		

Bathroom Fitments:
    Cabinet
    Towel Rails
    Soap and
    Toothbrush Holders
    Toilet Roll Holders
    Fitted Shelves/
    Cupboards
    Other Sanitary Fittings		

Shower		
Shower Fittings		

Specimen Solutions to Workshop Problems

Chapter 3

Problem 1

1. Re-read section 2.17. The conveyance must be stamped with *ad valorem* stamps and a PD stamp. The stamping must be done within 30 days of completion.

     Re-read section 3.2. You must apply for first registration of your client's title within 2 months of completion.

     Now consider what entries will appear on the proprietorship and charges registers of your clients' title.

     The proprietorship register will presumably say that the title is absolute. Under the names of Bill and Ben as registered proprietors will appear a restriction. If you do not yet know why, you will do so when you have ploughed through Chapter 11.

     A notice of the restrictive covenant will be entered on the charges register and the mortgage will be registered there as a registered charge.
2. It will send a charge certificate to you, as you are acting for the lender, and you will forward this to the Building Society.

Chapter 5

Problem

(i)   D(ii). You must first find out what these restrictive covenants are. You do not seem to have a copy of the deed which created them. A copy of the application for registration of the land charge can be obtained from the registry, and the name and address of the person with the benefit of the covenants discovered. They might have been given by Ada to her neighbour when she sold him part of the garden in 1980. Once it is known what the covenants are, they must be listed in the contract as burdens on the land.

(ii) C(i). This is probably a second mortgage. Again, the name of the lender can be discovered, and you can find from him the sum that will be necessary to redeem the mortgage. You must be satisfied that there will be enough money available at completion to discharge both mortgages, before you commit your client to the contract.

(iii) The contract will promise vacant possession yet Ada's husband has protected his rights of occupation under the Matrimonial Homes Act 1983. The husband must be approached before contract, and asked if he will join in the contract to release his rights of occupation, and if he will cancel the registration of the Class F. He should be warned to obtain independent advice before agreeing to do this. If he will not cooperate, Ada must not enter into the contract, as she will not be able to fulfil her promise, and might be liable to pay heavy damages.

Now that you know that Ada is married, you should also consider the possibility that her husband has an equitable interest in the house. If he says that he does not, he can be joined in the contract to repeat that statement. If he says he does, he should be joined in the contract as a second trustee. Again, it should be suggested that he obtain independent advice unless it is clear that there is no conflict between himself and Ada, and that he is prepared to instruct you to act for him in the sale as well.

Chapter 6

Problem 1

It is usually the seller's responsibility to pay off all financial charges before completion, as they are removable defects. However, do not forget the general conditions. Look at standard conditions 3.1.1 and 3.1.2. The sale is subject to all public requirements. Your client has agreed to buy subject to the road charges. Also read 3.2.2. Your client is to bear the cost of complying with any outstanding public requirement. But now read 3.1.3.

The seller must have known about and received communications about the adoption of the road and the road charges. Presumably, this failure by the seller to reveal the charge outweighs the other terms, so that the seller must compensate the purchaser, i.e. reduce the purchase price.

Problem 2

(a) With regard to the side road, re-read section 6.2(c). Will Mr Jones have the right to walk and drive cars along the side road, or will he have to depend on a permission? If this is not made clear by the documents supplied, an additional enquiry must be made of the seller. Is there any possibility of the road being adopted, with consequent expense to your client? What do the local land-charge search and additional enquiries of the local authority reveal? What is the answer to question 3.3 on the property information form? With regard to the use of the garage, you need to check the title to see if the land is subject to any restrictive covenant prohibiting business use. Such a covenant may have been imposed when the developer sold the houses sixteen years ago. The developer might have created a development scheme, so that the covenants are enforceable not by the developer but by the owners of the other houses in the estate.

(b) Re-read section 6.5(d). Four years have passed since the garage was built, so no enforcement notice can be served requiring the garage to be demolished.

(c) There has been a change of use in the land from residential to business. There is no time-limit for the service of an enforcement notice, and the authority can stop the business use.

Problem 3

1. It does not matter that Joan did not make the searches and enquiries herself. Remember that compensation can be claimed under the Local Land Charges Act 1975 by anyone who knew of the contents of the search certificate before entering into the contract. Equally, if the replies to the additional enquiries are wrong because of negligence on the part of the district authority, damages will be

recoverable in tort by anyone who could have been expected to rely on the answers. However, the search and enquiries were made four months ago. Joan would be sensible to repeat them. No compensation is payable in respect of matters coming into existence after the date of the search. Alternatively, she could ask the seller's solicitor if he is willing to repeat the searches at his client's expense, or to arrange insurance under the Search Validation Scheme. If he refuses, she will have to repeat the search or arrange insurance.

2. The extension will certainly be development, so permission will be needed. What she must check is whether or not the development comes within the General Development Order. If it does, she will not need express planning permission. This is providing that the effect of the Order has not been negatived by an article 4 direction.

3. She should apply for it before exchange of contracts, so that if her application is rejected, she is not committed to the purchase of the house. Alternatively, she could enter into a contract that was conditional on her application for permission being successful (see section 5.10).

Chapter 7

Problem

The Finance Company is selling free from incumbrances. Both charges must, therefore, be cleared from the title. As it is the proprietor of the second registered charge, it cannot overreach the first mortgage, which will have to be redeemed by it from the proceeds of the sale. In respect of the first mortgage, therefore, there will be handed over the first charge certificate, and either form 53 or undertakings given by the solicitor to the Y Building Society in respect of it.

The second and any later registered charges will be overreached by the sale. All the Finance Company needs to hand over therefore is its own (i.e. the second) charge certificate, and a transfer executed by it.

Within 30 days of completion (i.e. the priority period given by the search) and having had the transfer stamped with a PD stamp and *ad valorem* stamps, you must apply for registration to the District Land Registry. The application will be for the discharge of the two registered charges, registration of the transfer to the Thompsons, and of the charge in favour of the Best Building Society. There will, therefore, after some months, issue forth from the Registry a charge certificate, containing in it a copy of the mortgage to the Best Building Society.

As it is an endowment mortgage, there must be sent to the society with the charge certificate a copy of the life policy, a deed executed by the Thompsons assigning it to the building society, and a notice of assignment receipted by the assurance company. (Re-read 2.12 and note that the instructions of the Best Building Society may have made it clear that it did not consider an assignment of the policy to be necessary, the Thompsons as a condition of the mortgage promising to execute an assignment if called upon to do so by the Society).

Chapter 8

Problem 1

(a) You could specify either the 1970 or the 1973 conveyance as the root, since both are at least fifteen years old. If you specify the 1970 conveyance, you will have to abstract the 1970 mortgage, and the receipt endorsed on it. If you specify the 1973 conveyance, these documents can be omitted. The 1973 conveyance, therefore, seems the better choice.

(b) Assuming that the 1973 conveyance is used as the root, you will have to abstract:

  (i) the 1950 deed creating the covenants. (See the exceptions to s.45 of the Law of Property Act.)

  (ii) the 1970 lease. Although this was created pre-root, it did not end until 1975, and so is part of the post-root title.

  (iii) the 1973 conveyance.

  (iv) the 1975 surrender. Remember that it is only leases that expire by effluxion of time that do not have to be abstracted. The purchaser is entitled to check on the validity of the surrender.

  (v) the 1973 mortgage.

If you are not following the protocol, you do not have to abstract the 1973 land charge search certificate, as it is not a document of title, but it would be courteous to do so. It will save the purchaser having to repeat the search against B, but not, you realise, against O'Connor.

Chapter 9

Problem 1

Yes. There is no discrepancy in the name of William Faulkner as it appears on the certificate and in the conveyance. But look at the dates. The priority period given by the search had lapsed before the conveyance was completed. Therefore, the search gives no protection against registrations against William's name that were made after the date of the search, and before the completion of the sale by him, i.e. between 1 June and 1 July. We therefore need to repeat the search to see if there is any such entry.

The search certificate against the names of Anthea Grumble is completely useless. It does not cover any part of her period of ownership, as it was made against her when she was buying. The search would have been made on behalf of the person making the mortgage loan to her, and would have been solely to find whether or not there was a bankruptcy entry against her name.

If Anthea is following the protocol, she should supply you with a recent land-charge search certificate against her name. This is of use, because it might give an early warning of trouble ahead, e.g. a class F land charge. However, another search will have to be made against her name just before completion, to cover her full period of ownership. If this reveals a new entry, she will be in breach of her contract.

Problem 2

Alan needs to check his client's title to that part of the land. There are three possibilities:

1. That the 1940 conveyance did not include the site of the water-garden, but that this extra land was bought by Vesta or her predecessor at some other time. Vesta must be asked if this is so, and asked where the title deeds are. If they are found, the transaction will proceed normally, except that two separate titles will be abstracted.
2. That the 1940 conveyance did include the site of the water-garden. Remember that the 1940 plan was said to be 'for identification only' and it might be completely unreliable. Evidence may be obtained from Vesta, neighbours, or large-scale maps of the area, as to what was occupied as 'Rosedene' in 1940. A special condition can be put in the contract that, for example, a statutory declaration will be supplied by Vesta that she has occupied Rosedene, including the water-garden, for the past fifty years under the authority of the conveyance. This may satisfy Paula.
3. That the 1940 conveyance did not include the site of the water-garden, nor was it ever conveyed to Vesta by some other deed. Over the years Vesta has simply encroached on her neighbour's land. In this case, it is most unlikely that Vesta can make good title to the piece of land, as she will not be able to deduce the true owner's title. A special condition should be put in the contract saying that the purchaser must be satisfied with a declaration by Vesta that she has occupied the land for however many years it is.

It is lucky for Vesta that this problem came to light before exchange of contracts. Otherwise, she would have promised good title to the water-garden, and then perhaps been unable to establish it.

Problem 3

The only difficulty is the question of revocation of the power. The Powers of Attorney Act 1971 does not entitle the purchaser to assume that Charles did not have any notice of revocation of the power. The conveyance took place more than 12 months from the date of the power, and there seems to be no statutory declaration made by Charles that he did not have notice of the revocation.

Charles can scarcely be asked to make one now. So the Act is useless. You cannot *presume* that Charles did not know of any revocation, and it is not something that can be *proved*, as no one knows what Charles knew, except Charles himself. What you now need is proof that the power was never in fact revoked, and the only person who can give evidence as to that is Bertha. If Bertha cannot be traced, there is a flaw in the paper title. You could take comfort from the fact that the conveyance took place several years ago, and no one has yet challenged its validity. If the conveyance of 1980 is void, because of the prior revocation of the power, Charles has been in adverse possession, and his successors will eventually acquire a title under the Limitation Act 1982.

These facts do show a loophole in the protection given by the Powers of Attorney Act 1971. The problem could have been avoided if Charles had made the statutory declaration as soon as he completed his purchase.

Problem 4

(a) Requisition 1   Is this condition valid? Re-read section 9.2(b).
    Requisition 2   The reply is quite correct. Re-read section 9.6(c).
    Requisition 3   The 1960 conveyance is pre-root.

However, it is arguable that the description in the 1974 deed is not complete without a copy of the 1960 plan. You cannot leave these problems until your colleague's return. See standard condition 4.1.1. You have three working days after receiving the replies to the requisitions in which to respond to them.

(b) An opportunity to revise Chapter 2. You will have to draft the conveyance, if you have not already done this, and send it to the seller for approval. When it is approved you must engross it, and send the engrossment to the seller for execution (see standard condition 4.1.2 for the time limits).

You must report on title to the XY Building Society, and ask them to provide the money in time for completion. You will draft the mortgage deed, and have it executed by your client. You must prepare a completion statement for your client, showing the balance of the purchase price that he must provide for completion.

Shortly before completion, you will do a search at the Central Land Charges Registry against the names of all the estate-owners revealed by the abstract of title and against which you do not already have a satisfactory search certificate. This will include the seller's name. You will also search against the name of James Brown, on behalf of the XY Building Society, to check that he is not bankrupt. You will complete within the priority period given by this search.

Chapter 10

Problem 1

(a) You should not consider it acceptable without further explanation from Eric. In 1973 the legal estate was owned by two personal representatives. We would, therefore, expect to find the next conveyance to be by both of them, bearing in mind that the authority of personal representatives to convey is only joint.

(b) The clue may be in the 1985 conveyance. A conveyance usually states the capacity in which the seller conveys. If the 1985 conveyance says that David conveys the estate 'as personal representative', there are two possibilities:

  (i) Charles was still alive on 1 April 1985. If this is so, the conveyance is void. The legal estate remain where it was, in Charles and David jointly. The legal estate can only be obtained by a conveyance from them both.

  (ii) Charles was dead on 1 April 1985. If so, the conveyance is valid. David, as the sole surviving personal representative, was competent to convey alone. Proof is needed of Charles's death. Strictly speaking, we cannot insist on seeing the death certificate itself, as it is a document of public record, but we can insist on being given the date of death, so that we can obtain a certificate for ourselves. In fact, if the seller has a copy of the certificate, he would be very churlish not to let us see it. We are not, of course, in the slightest bit interested in seeing the grant of representation to Charles's estate. We only want to check his death, not the identity of his personal representatives.

Suppose that the conveyance says that Charles conveys as 'beneficial owner'. How could his capacity have changed from being one of two personal representatives to being the sole beneficial owner?

The probable answer is that David was also the beneficiary, so that when Bertha's estate had been administered, the land was vested in David. If this is so, we must see the document of transfer. It is likely to be an assent, which under s.36(4) of the Administration of Estates Act 1925 must be in writing signed by Charles and David. So our requisition would be 'Provide an abstract of the assent made in favour of David'.

(If an assent is produced, we still have to worry about whether or not a memorandum of it was endorsed on the grant – see problem 3.)

If David and Charles had overlooked the necessity for a written assent – not having read chapter 10 carefully enough – the legal estate remained with them, and the 1975 conveyance by David alone is void. (An interesting point is that the equitable interest might have passed to David, and thence to Eric. Section 36(4) applies only to a legal estate. An assent in respect of an equitable interest can still be informal and inferred from circumstances (see Re *Edward's Will Trusts* [1982]). However, a purchaser requires the legal estate, not just the equitable interest.)

Suppose that having requisitioned for the missing assent, we receive instead an abstract of a conveyance whereby Charles and David convey the land on sale to David as purchaser? This would certainly explain why David was later able to convey as beneficial owner: it would be because he had bought the property. It does not, however, increase our confidence in the title. It is a conveyance on sale by two personal representatives to one of themselves. Do you remember the principle of trust law that a purchase of trust property by a trustee can be voided by the beneficiaries, no matter how fair the purchase price might be? Eric's title is voidable, and as we will be buying with notice, our title will be voidable too. It is possible that the only beneficiaries are David and Charles themselves, or that any other beneficiaries have, after independent advice, consented to the sale. If, however, no solution can be found, the title is bad, we could refuse it, and consider remedies for the seller's breach of contract in failing to make good title to the land.

Problem 2

The first thing that might occur to us is that we should have copies of the two grants, the one to Carol, and the one to Edward. Even with these, the title is unacceptable. Apparently Carol died still owning Blackacre in her capacity of Bill's personal representative. She was an administrator, so there can be no chain of executorship. When Edward

became Carol's personal representative, he did not thereby become Bill's. So he had no power to convey any of Bill's unadministered assets, including Blackacre. Blackacre can only be conveyed by the person who obtains a grant *de bonis non administratis* to Bill's estate. The person entitled to the grant might possibly be Edward; this would be due to his status as personal representative to the beneficiary entitled to Blackacre, Carol being entitled under the intestacy rules. The fact remains that Blackacre cannot be dealt with until the fresh grant to Bill's estate is obtained, and only the person who obtains that grant can convey Blackacre to Fred. (Had Carol been an executor, the chain of executorship would have existed. Edward could have conveyed Bill's assets because by becoming Carol's executor and proving her will, he would also have become Bill's executor.)

There is a final possibility. We have assumed that when Carol died, she owned Blackacre as personal representative. This is because the recitals make no mention of any assent. If, before she died, she signed an assent in her own favour, then she held Blackacre as beneficial owner, in which case Edward, as *her* personal representative, would be entitled to deal with it. The assent, however, would have had to be in writing.

Problem 3

What we should ask for is confirmation that a memorandum of the assent was endorsed on the grant in 1974. If it were, no subsequent conveyance by Cathy and Drew could have diverted the legal estate from Elaine in favour of a purchaser from themselves.

If it were not, there is, at least in theory, the possibility that Cathy and Drew, between 1974 and 1980, conveyed Blackacre to a purchaser for money or money's worth, who relied on a statement made under s.36(6) of the Administration of Estates Act 1925 that the personal representatives had not made any previous assent. If this were so, Elaine no longer had the legal estate in 1980. She could not convey it to Fred. (We do not have to worry about the possibility of the personal representatives having conveyed Blackacre after 1980 – remember that s.36(6) cannot remove the legal estate from a purchaser for money – i.e. Fred.)

So a requisition would have to be raised that Cathy and Drew confirm that no conveyance was made. They are, after all, the only people who can confirm it. Of course, they might now be dead or untraceable. In that case, the fact that Fred is living in Blackacre and has the title deeds is reassuring, and we might feel that we could advise our client-purchaser that the risk of the title being bad is very small.

Notice that the absence of a memorandum has been important because we were deriving title through the *beneficiary* who never protected her assent by a memorandum. Contrast the following abstract:

1972   Albert conveys to Bruce

1973   Bruce dies

1974   Grant of probate to Bruce's will to Carl

1975   Carl conveys on sale as personal representative to David

1976   David conveys to Elaine

Again we may query the absence from the grant of any memorandum of the conveyance. However, in this case the absence of a memorandum is not a defect in title. Even if Carl did convey to another purchaser after 1975, David would not lose the legal estate. So although it is important for a *beneficiary* to endorse a memorandum, it is not a matter of title if a *purchaser* from the personal representatives fails to do so. Nevertheless, as has been mentioned earlier, it would be sensible if he did.

NB

1. As you read about s.36(6), you may have been asking yourself, *why* do the personal representatives, having transferred the property to A, then seek to transfer it to B? Does the Act consider personal representatives peculiarly liable to lapses of memory? A double conveyance can occur in the case of badly drawn parcels clauses and maps, so that a border strip is conveyed twice. It can also happen that the deceased has two consecutive and separate personal representatives, e.g. on the making of a grant *de bonis non administratis*. It is possible that the administrator *de bonis non administratis* may not know of an assent made by his predecessor. However, if you feel that s.36(6) is a lot of fuss about nothing much, you have my sympathy. Still, if s.36(6) offers protection to a client who is buying from a personal representative, it is a conveyancer's job to procure it for him by putting the correct recital in the conveyance to him.

2. Another point worth mentioning here is that when reading an assent or a conveyance by a personal representative, check if it contains an acknowledgement for the production of the grant. Although the grant is a public document and copies can be obtained by anyone from the Probate Registry, a later purchaser will want to see the original because of the importance of checking for memoranda. Acknowledgements are discussed in Chapter 13, and you will see that the absence of an acknowledgement is not a defect in title.

3. Section 36(6) is sometimes said to have no relevance to registered title. Suppose you are buying from the personal representative of the dead registered proprietor, and you are considering the possibility of there having been a previous assent to a beneficiary. There are two possibilities:

(i) the beneficiary has registered himself as the new proprietor. If he does this, your pre-completion search of the register will disclose the new proprietor, and you will not complete the purchase from the personal representatives.

(ii) if he has not registered himself as the new proprietor, he has an unprotected minor interest, and your defence will be based on the Land Registration Act 1925 (a transferee for value taking free from an unprotected minor interest). However, if the beneficiary is living on the property, his interest is overriding, not minor. So you must realise that the Land Registration Act will not protect you against the earlier assent if the beneficiary is living in the house. So s.36(6) may be of use, and certainly no harm is done by putting the statement in the transfer that the personal representative has not made any previous assent.

Chapter 11

Problem 1

Do you remember the principle that *all* the trustees for sale must execute the conveyance? The fact that Robert retired from the partnership did not of itself divest him of the legal estate. You need to see a conveyance of the legal estate from Albert, Robert and Sidney to Albert and Sidney. This might take the form of a deed of retirement (see section 11.3(c)). Alternatively, you need evidence that Robert died before 1975, in which case the legal estate would have vested automatically in the surviving Bricks. If the legal estate was still vested in all three Bricks in 1975, the conveyance by two of them was void.

The search certificate is, at first sight, puzzling. The contract, or whatever it is that is protected by the C(iv) registration, would have had to be created by all three of them. The power of trustees (unlike personal representatives) to enter into a contract is joint only. Even if all of them entered into the contract, registration against only some of the estate-owners is not effective. Re-read section 4.5(c). Do you notice the discrepancy between the name on the deed, 'Sidney', and the name on the certificate, 'Sydney'? The certificate of search is useless, the search having been made against an incorrect version of the name. If we search again we probably shall find a C(iv) registered against Sydney.

If this is so, you must approach Miss Cooper's solicitor, and ask for an assurance that this land charge does not affect the land you are buying. There is a possibility that it does not, as it might be a contract in respect of other land owned by the Bricks. Another possibility is that it is protecting the contract by the Bricks to convey to Jennifer. If this is so, you can ask her solicitor to apply for cancellation of the registration. This should have been done by the solicitor as soon as the purchase by Miss Cooper was completed.

The solicitor may argue that the registration is protecting a void contract, an unenforceable contract, or one that was discharged by breach, and that he was satisfied as to this when he bought the land for his client. The answer should be that it is not your task to pass judgement on the validity of the contract; it is the seller's task to have the registration cancelled.

(This question is taken from part of the Law Society Summer 1988 paper.)

Problem 2

1. As both the Masons are registered as proprietors, you know that both owned the legal estate. They must have held it as joint tenants. There is no restriction on the

register, so you can assume that they owned the beneficial interest jointly, too. Therefore, when her husband died, Mrs Mason became sole owner of the legal estate and the beneficial interest *simply because her husband had died*. She does *not* trace her claim to ownership of even the equitable interest through the will. The will is completely irrelevant, therefore. To have the title registered in her own name, she need only produce her husband's death certificate.

2. The drawbacks of registration with a possessory title are set out in section 3.6(d). You can imagine that the building society will be reluctant to lend on the security of such a title. Notice, though, that the title was registered in 1974. Re-read section 3.7. Mrs Mason can apply to have the title upgraded to absolute.

3. The building society needs to know as much about the property as a purchaser would, so the searches made are the same as if the building society were actually buying the house. So you start by doing what in the context of a purchase would be called 'the pre-contract' searches and enquiries. Re-read Chapter 6, find the answers to the questions in the property information form, and make the local land-charge search and additional enquiries of the district authority. (For inspection of the property, you will be relying on the building society's surveyor.)

In this case there will be no contract for the grant of a mortgage, but these usual searches and enquiries may reveal things that would affect the value of the property. When the results of the searches are known, you will investigate the title and draft the mortgage deed. Before completion, you will make your pre-completion search at the district land registry, to enquire if there are any adverse entries on the register, either since the date of office copy entires obtained by you, or since the date when the land certificate was last officially compared with the register (re-read section 7.5).

You will complete the mortgage within the priority period given by the search. Completion will consist of your asking Mrs Mason to execute the mortgage and give you custody of the land certificate in return for the advance. It will have been part of the arrangement between herself and the society that you be able to deduct your fees and disbursements from the loan. You will then have to apply for registration of the mortgage as a registered charge, again before the priority period expires.

Note the searches you did *not* make:

(i) the coal board search, for obvious reasons;

(ii) the commons registration search – the house was built 30 years ago;

(iii) the public index map search – the title is registered;

(iv) the 'bankruptcy only' search at the Land Charges Registry. In this case the registered proprietor and the borrower are one and the same person. If Mrs Mason is insolvent, the register of her title will warn us. If the land registry search discloses no bankruptcy entry, you can safely lend money to her.

Suppose there had been a restriction on the register to the effect that no disposition by the sole survivor of the registered proprietors would be registered. You know that Mrs Mason has succeeded to her husband's share of the equitable interest under the terms of the will. Nevertheless, if she were *selling* the house, the simplest thing would be for her to appoint another trustee to act with her, so that the equitable interests are overreached. So again, for the purpose of making title to the house, the will would be irrelevant. It would only be of relevance when it had to be decided by the trustees how the proceeds of the sale were to be accounted for.

However, in this case Mrs Mason is keeping the house. It is probably better, therefore, to have the restriction removed, by proving to the Registrar the fact that she does now own the whole of the equitable interest. Probate of the will must be obtained, an assent in respect of the equitable interest made in her favour (but *not* in respect of the legal estate, as she owns this by virtue of the right of survivorship) and a statutory declaration made to the Registrar of these facts (see section 11.8(a)).

Chapter 12

Problem 1

You can see the problem. 21B has no direct access to the public road. The house can only be reached by crossing others' land. Pipes and wires must cross others' land to reach the public sewers and to obtain electricity, gas, telephone services, etc.

To deal with number 21, the question we have to ask here is 'What easements already exist over number 21 for the benefit of 21A and 21B?' In other words, what easements were reserved by Alice Brown when she conveyed to Catherine, because it is only the benefit of these easements that can be passed on to us. To stress a point that is obvious but can be forgotten in the heat of the moment, Alice can only pass to us the benefit of easements that already exist over number 21. She cannot create *new* easements over land she no longer owns.

If the title to number 21 is unregistered, you need a copy of the conveyance to Catherine. You will be looking in it for an express reservation over number 21 for the benefit of 21A and 21B of rights of way for pedestrians and vehicles, rights of drainage, and rights for all other necessary pipes and wires. You would also expect to see a right for the owners of 21A and 21B to enter number 21 for the purpose of inspecting and repairing the pipes, etc., and you would not be surprised to see a promise by the owners of 21A and 21B to contribute towards the cost of maintenance of the pipes, etc. If these rights were reserved, our client will succeed to the benefit of them. (If the conveyance to Catherine did contain a reservation, a copy of the conveyance – or even perhaps a duplicate – should have been kept with Catherine's deeds.)

If the conveyance does not contain an express reservation, there will have been a reservation implied into it, but, as we have seen, possibly only an essential means of access, so the pipes, wires, drains, and sewers would seem only to be there by virtue of Catherine's permission.

If the title to these properties had been registered at the time of the sale of number 21 to Catherine, any reservation of an easement in the transfer of part to Catherine would have been entered on the register of Catherine's title, and the benefit of it would have been entered on the register of Alice's title to 21A and 21B.

The absence of easements over number 21 would be a difficult problem to solve. The only person who can now grant an easement is Catherine, who may be unwilling to encumber her land. *She* may be willing to allow the pipes, etc., to remain where they are, but a purchaser from her may not be. The problem may be serious enough for our client to decide against buying number 21B.

If Alice finds that her failure expressly to reserve the necessary easements is making 21A and 21B unsellable, she should consider the contract that preceded her conveyance of number 21. As has been seen, the conditions in that contract might well have allowed her to put an express reservation of easements in the conveyance or transfer. She might now be able to apply to the court for rectification of the conveyance as it is not carrying out the terms of the contract but this right of rectification, if it exists, will not bind any purchaser of number 21 from Catherine, unless that purchaser has notice of it.

Number 21A presents a quite different problem. This is owned by the seller, so any easements your client needs over 21A can be granted by Alice. It is really a question of settling special conditions in the draft contract. Alice should promise your client in the contract that the conveyance will contain all the rights needed for access and services. These rights should be specified. She may wish to reserve easements, although from the plan, it is difficult to see why she would require any. The contract should also agree shared obligations as to maintenance and rights of entry as previously mentioned.

The special conditions should replace the standard condition. If the standard condition is not expressly excluded, it might 'top up' what the parties have expressly agreed to grant and reserve, contrary to their real intentions.

Problem 2

The enforcement of the covenant against Hebe has two aspects. One possibility is that the covenant could be enforced against her by A, or whoever has succeeded to the benefited land together with the benefit of the covenant. For the burden of the covenant to have passed with the land, it would have been essential for the covenant to have been registered as a D(ii) land charge against the name of the original covenantor, B. You need to make a land charges search against B's name. If a land charge is registered, the person with the benefit of the covenant may take action against Hebe. If no land charge is registered, the covenant is not an incumbrance on the land. The covenant cannot be enforced directly by A against Hebe.

However, the fact remains that A *can* sue B, as B promised that the covenant would *always* be observed. B can sue C, and C can sue Hebe. So despite lack of registration, Hebe should not have ignored the covenant.

The Contract   Clearly, if the covenant is registered, the covenant must be disclosed and the contract must list the covenant as a burden on the property. What must also be disclosed is the *breach* of the covenant. (Even if it is not expressly disclosed in the contract, the seller must give an honest answer to the enquiry on the property information form which asks if the seller has observed all the restrictions affecting the property.)

Usually, Hebe, having promised an indemnity to C, would like an indemnity from her purchaser. However, the purchaser will not be prepared to promise a general indemnity for he knows that the covenant has already been broken. The contract must make it clear, by substituting a special condition for the standard condition, that the purchaser promises an indemnity only in respect of breaches committed after the date of the conveyance.

The purchaser, apart from the indemnity point, may be concerned about the consequences of the breach. He does not want to find himself paying damages or having to dismantle the garage.

If a covenant has been broken, there are various ways to make the title acceptable to the purchaser. The seller might offer to indemnify the purchaser and his successors against the consequence of any breach (i.e. the seller will be promising to indemnify the purchaser against past breaches, and the purchaser will be promising to indemnify the seller against future breaches). This is not really satisfactory for either party if the consequences are likely to be serious, for example, if it had been the house itself, rather than a garage, that had been built in breach of covenant. The value of the indemnity depends on the seller's continued solvency (and traceability). The seller lives under a threat of one day having to find an unknown, but possibly large, sum of money.

Another possibility is taking out insurance against the risk of enforcement. The size of the premium will, of course, depend on the size of the risk.

(The purchaser will also be considering the planning position. Remember that express planning permission would have been needed, unless the garage came within the General Development Order. If the garage was built without planning permission, no enforcement notice can be served after four years has elapsed - see chapter 6.5.)

Problem 3

1. *The Restriction on the Proprietorship Register* Jacob must appoint another trustee, so that the transfer can be by two trustees. If the second trustee is appointed now, both will be named in the contract as sellers, and the contract will say that they will convey as trustees.

2. *The Property Register* The particulars in the contract may say '9 Havelock Street, Spa on Wells, as the same is registered with absolute title under title no KT1111111 at Tunbridge Wells District Land Registry'. An office copy of the entries on the register will accompany the contract, and naturally, the purchaser will want to know exactly what easements were granted and reserved by the 1965 conveyance. You must, therefore, obtain a copy of it. You could do this by asking the Equine Bank to photocopy the charge certificate. Alternatively, you could obtain an office copy of the deed from the Land Registry. The reservation of the easement certainly must be disclosed.

3. *Entry no.1 on Charges Register* If it was known what the 1922 covenants were, the contract could simply have said that the property was sold subject to entries 1 and 2 on the charges register of the title. (Not, notice 'subject to the entries on the charges register' as the sale is *not* subject to entries 3 and 4.) However, as no one knows what the 1922 covenants are, it is best for the contract to say not only that the sale is subject to the 1922 covenants, but also that there is no information about what the covenants are, and that no requisitions about them can be made by the purchaser.

   It is unfortunate that while it is quite clear that the covenants will bind the purchaser, as they are entered in the register, nobody knows what they are. This situation is not uncommon. The applicant for first registration produced the recent conveyances, all of which said the property was conveyed subject to the covenants, but the 1922 deed itself had been lost.

4. *Entry no.2* The contract will say that the sale is subject to the 1965 covenants. Again, the purchaser will see a copy of these before exchange of contracts.

5. *Entries 3 and 4* The sale is not subject to the mortgage, but there is no need to say this expressly in the contract because of the effect of standard condition 3 (see section 5.5).

6. *Fixtures and Fittings* Do not bother to rack your brain as to whether or not the shed is a fixture. Ask your client to fill in the fixtures fittings and contents form (in which all these items are included) and attach it to the contract.

7. *The Will?* Did you fall into the trap of thinking that the will was in some way relevant to the title to the home? It was not.

   After Naomi's death, Jacob was sole owner of the legal estate, by virtue of the right of survivorship. He owned it as sole trustee for sale. He could not however transfer it alone, because of the restriction on the register. The sale by two trustees would overreach the equitable interests.

   Naomi's will did affect the ownership of the equitable interests (but not the legal estate) but a purchaser does not have to investigate the interests of the beneficiaries. The will is of interest to the two trustees, as it determines how they should deal with the purchase price. It cannot all be given to Jacob. Some share of it must go to Ruth.

Note: You need to check, when looking at the office copies, whether the Greens were the applicants for first registration. If they were, you will have to ask the bank to let you see the pre-registration deeds to discover if the Greens gave an indemnity covenant in respect of the covenants when they bought. If they did, Jacob will need an indemnity from the purchaser. You will not need a special condition to provide for the indemnity, unless you consider the standard condition to be inadequate.

If the Greens were not the applicants for first registration, but were later transferees of the title, they apparently gave no indemnity covenant, as one does not appear on the proprietorship register. If they did not give an indemnity covenant, Jacob will not need one when he resells.

Chapter 13

Problem 1

1. the commencement – that is, 'This conveyance ...'
2. Date.
3. Parties. The two sellers will be one party; the two purchasers the other party.
4. Recital of sellers' ownership (in fee simple, subject as mentioned later in the conveyance, but otherwise free from incumbrances), and of the contract for sale.
5. Consideration – £30 000. (£500 is not being paid for the *land*, so exclude it.)
6. Receipt clause.
7. The fact that the sellers convey as beneficial owner. The capacity in which they hold the legal estate is that of trustees for sale, and the contract should have stated that they would convey in that capacity. The contract, however, seems to be silent on this point, so the effect of standard condition 4.6.2 is that they must convey as beneficial owners.
8. Parcels. A plan was probably used in drafting the particulars of the contract. If not, one should be used in the conveyance, unless the boundary between the northern and southern boundaries is well-established.
9. A reservation in the parcels clause of the right of way.
10. Habendum – to hold unto the purchasers in fee simple in equal shares subject to the 1960 restrictive covenants.
11. New restrictive covenant.
12. Indemnity and performance covenant *if* the sellers gave an indemnity covenant when they bought (standard condition 4.6.3).
13. Acknowledgement for production of retained deeds (this is a sale of part) and an undertaking for safe custody. (Query, could the sellers refuse the undertaking under standard condition 4.6.4 on the ground that they are fiduciary sellers? Perhaps not, as although they own the legal estate as trustees for sale, they hold on trust only for themselves.)
14. Certificate of value – consideration not exceeding £30 000.
15. Testimonium.
16. Any schedules referred to, for example, of retained deeds.
17. Execution of the document as a deed by sellers *and* purchasers, and attestation of their signatures.

Chapter 15

Problem 1

(a) *Consents*
1. *Assignment*   The need for the landlord's consent for assignment is obvious. This will probably be obtained before contract, but could be sought after contract (see section 15.3).

2. *User*

   (a) The landlord's consent is needed.
   (b) We do not know whether this is a headlease (i.e. granted out of the freehold) or an underlease. If it is an underlease, we need to consider the user covenants in the superior leases. A superior landlord generally has no direct right of action against an undertenant if he breaks a provision of the headlease. There is no privity of contract or estate between them. An exception to this rule is a restrictive covenant. A superior landlord can obtain an injunction against a subtenant who breaks a restrictive covenant in a superior lease if the subtenant had notice of the covenant when he obtained his sublease. This is because of the rule in *Tulk* v. *Moxhay* (1848) which has the effect of making a restrictive covenant an encumbrance on the land enforceable against anyone who takes with notice. However, as Pamela, by virtue of s.44 of the Law of Property Act 1925 is not entitled to see the headlease, she cannot be taken to have had constructive notice of its contents. This point can be pursued in any land law textbook, but it is not the major point which is as follows.

   If the subtenant's activities on the premises cause the tenant to be in breach of the covenants of the superior lease, the superior lease may be forfeited for breach of covenant. Therefore, for practical reasons a subtenant has to observe the user restrictions not only in his own lease, but all superior leases, as the forfeiture of a superior lease causes the end of all inferior leases derived from it. It is for this reason that user-covenants in a superior lease are often reproduced in the sublease. The tenant, knowing he can be controlled by his landlord, needs the same sort of control over his subtenant.

   So, to return to Pamela, she should ask if the lease she is buying is the headlease, or an underlease. If Vera's landlord is not the freeholder, he can be asked if any consent to change of use is needed under the terms of his own lease, and if it is, it should be obtained. It is as much in the interest of the landlord that consent is obtained as it is in Pamela's.

   Of course, it is also possible that there is a covenant on the freehold preventing use as a shop. If this covenant is registered either under the Land Charges Act 1972 or under the Land Registration Act 1925, it will bind Pamela as she will be treated as having actual notice of it. The risk of an unknown covenant is diminished if the contract between Vera and Pamela provides for deduction of the superior titles (diminished, not removed, because of the spectre – if the freehold title is unregistered – of the pre-root land charge).

   (c) The proposed change of use will need planning permission. It is a change from one class of use to another within the Use Classes Order (see section 6.5).

3. *Alterations*   Pamela will probably want to alter the inside of the premises. The lease should be checked to see if the landlord's consent is needed to alterations.

(b) The Option

An option to renew a lease is one that 'touches and concerns the land'. When a lease is assigned the new owner of it succeeds automatically to the benefit of such covenants. Therefore, the mere fact that Pamela becomes the new owner of the lease ensures that she has the benefit of this option. If Len is still the landlord, the option will be enforceable against him, and he will have to renew the lease. However, it is possible that Len has assigned the reversion to the lease. Let us assume that we have checked on this point and we find that he sold the reversion to Mary last year. Can Pamela enforce the option against Mary? It is true that a purchaser of a landlord's reversion takes subject to the burden of the landlord's obligations that touch and concern the land (s.142 of the Law of Property Act 1925), but the option is affected by other rules as well. We need to know if the title to the reversion is registered under the Land Registration Act 1925. If the title is registered, Mary will have taken free of the option unless it was a minor interest that was protected by an entry on the register, or was an overriding interest. The option is probably overriding. It is probably overriding under s.70(1)(g) as an interest belonging to a person in actual occupation of the land. So s.70(1)(g) ensures that Mary is bound by the lease and by the option. It is also possibly overriding under s.70(1)(k) (see section 3.15(e)).

If the title is unregistered, the option comes within the definition of an 'estate contract' and is registrable as a C(iv) land charge. If Vera did not register the land charge before Mary bought the reversion, Mary is not bound by the option and cannot be forced to renew the lease. The only remedy would be to sue Len for breach of contract. He promised to renew the lease if asked, but now cannot do so.

Notice that if Len had sold to Mary under a contract incorporating the standard conditions, Len could claim an indemnity against Mary if he were sued in such circumstances. Condition 3.3.6 provides that a purchaser of property subject to a lease shall indemnify the seller against all claims arising under the tenancy 'even if void against a purchaser for want of registration'. Mary might prefer to renew the lease, rather than face the cost of indemnifying Len.

Note   Suppose the option had not been to renew the lease, but instead to buy the landlord's reversion. Would this have made any difference? This option is one of the few covenants generally found in a lease that is not considered to touch and concern the land, but is treated as a personal agreement between the original landlord and the original tenant. For this reason, Pamela cannot claim she owns the benefit of the option merely because she owns the lease. However, unless the option is so drafted that it is exercisable *only* by Vera, there is nothing to stop Vera expressly assigning the benefit of the option at the same time as she assigns the lease. It has been held that if the option is drafted so that it is expressed to be exercisable by the original tenant and by assignees from her, then the assignment of the lease will also impliedly assign the benefit of the option (see *Griffith* v. *Pelton* [1958]).

The option creates an equitable interest in land which is capable of binding Mary but again it must either have been registered as a C(iv) land charge, or, in the case of a registered title, be protected by notice or caution, or be an overriding interest. The option could be overriding under s.70(1)(g) but probably not under 70(1)(k), as it is a provision in the lease that does not touch and concern the land and stands outside the relationship of landlord and tenant.

Problem 2

She is entitled to see the assignment to Enid. She must always see the assignment to the seller. This assignment is not yet fifteen years old. So Pamela is also entitled to see the assignment by Carol to Deirdre. This is over fifteen years old. Enid therefore satisfies her obligations under s.44 of the Law of Property Act 1925 by producing the 1940 lease and the 1973 and 1988 assignments. Pamela has no right to insist on investigating ownership of the lease between 1965 and 1973.

Note Pamela has no right to investigate the superior titles unless s.44 of the Law of Property Act 1925 has been altered by a term in the contract for sale.

Chapter 17

Problem 1, possible solutions

You need to work out how much the Archers will need to buy Greenbank, and the money they will have coming in.

Coming in

A. Sale proceeds

Contract price		£40 000
Less		
• redemption of first mortgage	£10 000	
• redemption of second mortgage	(unknown)	
Solicitor's fees and disbursements in connection with sale, purchase and mortgages say	£ 400	
Estate agent's fees say	£ 600	
at least	£11 000	£11 000
Less than		£29 000

Urgent step – to confirm redemption figure on first mortgage and to obtain redemption figure on second mortgage.

B. Net Mortgage offer

Amount of loan		£32 000
Less retention moneys	£ 2000	£ 2 000
		£30 000

So less (perhaps, *considerably* less) than £60 000 coming in

Going out

Purchase price		£60 000
Add stamp duty @ 1%		£ 600
Miscellaneous expenses, say		£ 200
Total - something over		£60 800

There is a shortfall. There are possible solutions.

1. Your clients must reconcile themselves to remaining in 5 King Street.
2. The Grasping Bank might be willing to transfer its mortgage from 5 King Street to Greenbanks. It will not then be necessary to find money to redeem it. The fees of the Bank's solicitors will have to be paid. You must check whether the Building Society's mortgage contains a covenant not to create a second mortgage without the Society's consent.
3. Increase the size of the loan from the Building Society. Your clients, before seeking to increase their borrowing, must consider their ability to repay.

If the transaction can continue, you must think about the deposit of £6000 to be paid on the exchange of contracts for the purchase of Greenbanks. Your clients will want to use the £4000 coming in from the sale of 5 King Street so make sure that the 5 King Street contract incorporates standard condition 2.2.2 unaltered. This leaves £2000 to find. Your clients do not appear to have any savings. Possibly the seller can be persuaded to accept a smaller deposit. Otherwise, your clients will have to arrange temporary finance, or use the deposit guarantee scheme. Both involve expense.

The two sets of contracts must now be exchanged as simultaneously as possible. This can be done by arranging exchange over the telephone. A simple method would be this:

Suppose Q is selling Greenbanks to the Archers, and the Archers are selling 5 King Street to S. S's solicitors will send S's part of the contract concerning 5 King Street to the Archers' solicitors, together with the payment of the deposit. (If the standard conditions apply, this will have to be by way of banker's draft, or a cheque on the solicitors' clients' account.) The accompanying letter will make it clear that the contract is not sent by way of exchange, but that the Archers' solicitors are for the present to hold it to the order of S. The Archers' solicitors then send their clients' part of the contract concerning Greenbanks to Q's solicitor, and the deposit, again making it clear that it is not sent by way of exchange. This is necessary because otherwise Q could force a contract on the Archers by returning his part of the contract. When they are ready to exchange, the Archers' solicitors will phone Q's solicitors, to say that they are about to exchange contracts on 5 King Street, and asking if they will be able to exchange the contracts on Greenbanks immediately afterwards. If the answer is 'yes', the Archers' solicitors phone S's solicitors, and the exchange of the contracts on 5 King Street is agreed, and the Law Society undertakings given, in this case, according to formula A. The Archers' solicitors immediately phone Q's solicitors, and contracts are exchanged for the purchase of Greenbanks.

This method does not remove all risk. It is possible that at the last minute while the Archers' solicitors are exchanging contracts on 5 King Street, Q may telephone his solicitors and withdraw his instructions to exchange. The Archers' solicitors will then find that when they telephone back to Q's solicitors, exchange does not take place. The risk of this happening in the small amount of time involved is small, and probably acceptable.

Notice the order of events. The contracts for sale are exchanged before the contracts for purchase, so there is no risk of the Archers being bound by a contract to buy, while not having disposed of their own house.

Problem 2: Possible Solution

The point about finances here is that Mrs Fawkes presumably owns part of the beneficial interest in The Plot, so *her* money will be partly financing the purchase of The Tower. If this is so, then The Tower should be conveyed into both their names, and the conveyance should declare how they hold the equitable interest.

Provided that there is no conflict of interest between Mr and Mrs Fawkes, you can act for them both, but you must receive Mrs Fawkes's instructions from her, not from her husband, and the point about the conveyance being to them both must be explained. If they cannot agree as to the ownership of the equitable interest there is a conflict between them, and you cannot act for them both.

Another reason why the conveyance should be to them both is that the mortgage to the Building Society should be by both of them. If the conveyance were to Mr Fawkes alone the Building Society would have to be warned that Mrs Fawkes contributed to the purchase price, and so has an equitable interest in The Tower. The Building Society would then be reluctant to accept a mortgage from Mr Fawkes alone, lest it be subject to the wife's interest.

An undertaking such as you have been asked for is common in chain transactions where a bridging loan has been obtained from a bank. If you are a solicitor or licensed conveyancer you are under an absolute duty to honour your professional undertaking, and any failure to do this would be looked upon as serious misconduct. For this reason you must only undertake to do what is within your own control. So the following precautions must be taken:

1. You must obtain your client's irrevocable instructions to give the undertaking.
2. You must only undertake to the bank to pay the net proceeds of the sale to it if and when they come into your hands. This covers the possibility that you may never receive the proceeds, e.g. because your client decides to transfer the transaction to another solicitor.
3. The undertaking is only in respect of the net proceeds after, e.g. deduction of your own costs, and redemption of mortgages, etc. Tell the Bank what deductions you will be making.
4. Undertake only to pay the proceeds into the account. Do not undertake to discharge the bridging loan from the proceeds. Otherwise, if the proceeds are insufficient, you may have to discharge the bridging loan from your own money. If the bank does not accept an undertaking in these guarded terms, you refuse to give an undertaking to the bank.

Problem 3

(a) Usually there is no conflict of interest between co-purchasers, and so it is possible to act for them all. However, if there is a conflict of interest the purchasers will have to be separately represented. So your answer depends on whether you can see the probability of a conflict of interest between the Savages and the Cowards. We will return to this point when we answer part (c).

(b) To begin with, check the overall position to see if there will be sufficient money to buy 'The Knoll'.

Coming in

A.	Net proceeds of sale of 22 Mount Road (This is an estimate made by the Savages, and should be checked.)	£ 7 000
B.	Contribution by the Cowards	£40 000
C.	The mortgage loan	£25 000
		£72 000

Going out

Purchase price of The Knoll	£72 000

(The expenses connected with the purchase, e.g. stamp duty of £720 and solicitors' fees and disbursements seen to have been taken into account in estimating the net proceeds of the sale, but this must be checked.)

The figures here seem to balance, but there is no surplus to meet any expenses that have been overlooked. The figure given for the net proceeds of the sale of Mount Road must be carefully checked to see if the Savages have foreseen all the expenses connected with both transactions.

Second, what about the position of the Savages? They have life savings of £50 000. They are going to contribute £40 000 towards the purchase and pay for the costs of conversion which are approximately £5000. This leaves them with only £5000. They need to obtain firm estimates for the costs of conversion. They must also be sure that they will have sufficient income to live on after most of their capital has been tied up in the house. Apparently they will have little more than their old age pension. The problem could become even more acute when one of them dies, and the other is living on the reduced pension. It will be difficult to realise their capital investment if they need to do so, unless the Savages cooperate.

(c) A decision must be reached as to how the equitable interest in The Knoll is to be shared. There must be a division of it into two shares, one for the Cowards and one for the Savages. Each couple will then be a tenant in common with the other couple. The Cowards' share can then be held by them jointly. This ensures that when one dies, the entire share will be automatically owned by the survivor. When the survivor dies, the share will pass over the terms of his or her will, i.e. to Sara. This will carry out the Cowards' wishes that only Sara will benefit from their deaths. The Savages' share will also probably be owned by them jointly, as again the right of survivorship, which is inherent in a joint tenancy, seems appropriate to the matrimonial home. (Notice that even if the couples' contributions had been equal, it would have been wrong for the conveyance to them to declare that they held the whole as beneficial joint tenants. This would not have carried out the Cowards' wishes, as it would mean that after their deaths their interests would be owned by their son-in-law and daughter jointly, rather than entirely by their daughter.) The problem lies in deciding the size of the two shares. The Cowards are contributing £40 000 of the total purchase price of £72 000, so possibly should have a share in proportion to their contribution, i.e. a five-ninths share. They are also paying for the costs of the conversion, but it is debatable if this adds anything to the capital value of the house. On the other hand, the Savages are bearing the expenses of the purchase.

The mortgage is another difficulty. The understanding between the Savages and the Cowards is that the Savages are to be solely responsible for the repayment of the loan. However, as they are giving the legal estate as security, not just the Savages' equitable interest, they will all sign the mortgage and covenant to repay. In other words, as far as the Building Society is concerned, all four of them are responsible, and the Cowards could be sued for debt. What would certainly happen if the Savages failed to make the monthly repayments is that the Society would sell the house, and the Cowards would lose their home.

It is possible to draw up the conveyance so that the legal estate is conveyed to the Savages alone on trust for sale for themselves and the Cowards. The mortgage of the legal estate would then also be solely by the Savages, and only the Savages would covenant to repay. This would mean that the Cowards could not be sued by the Building Society for debt, but it otherwise offers no solution, and indeed, creates other problems. The Cowards remain at risk if the Savages should fail to repay, as the Building Society would sell the property. The Cowards' equitable interests would not have bound the Building Society, as they would have been overreached by the mortgage (see *City of London Building Society* v. *Flegg* [1988]). It would be possible for the Savages to create a second mortgage without the concurrence of the Cowards. A safeguard against this in the case of registered title would be a restriction on the register, saying that no disposition by the registered proprietors would be registered unless the consent of the Cowards was obtained.

We can now see that the proposed arrangement is not completely satisfactory from the Cowards' point of view and as a result it is probably impossible for us to act for them as well as for the Savages without a conflict of interest. The Cowards should be separately advised.

Chapter 18

Problem

(a) Does the power authorise White to execute the conveyance? Yes. Re-read section 9.4(b).

White should hand over a facsimile certified copy of the power. Re-read section 9.4(e).

(b) This is not a security power, so death revokes it. More importantly, Green *knows* of the revocation, and for this reason any conveyance by White to him would be void. The person who will have the power to convey is Black's personal representative. He will be bound by the contract, as the contract for the sale of land is not discharged by the death either of the seller or of the purchaser. Can the personal representative convey *now* however? No. He must first obtain the grant, either of probate or letters of administration (see section 10.2). So there will be delay before the sale to Mr Green is completed.

(c) (i) The fact that his purchase may be delayed is no excuse for Mr Green to delay his sale. So he may decide to convey his present house on the agreed date, and find temporary accommodation. Mr Green may be tempted to stay where he is, and postpone completion of his sale until he completes his purchase. He may be thwarted by the purchaser, who can issue a writ for specific performance as soon as the agreed completion date has passed, or serve a completion notice and threaten to end the contract. If Green's purchaser is prepared to accept a delayed completion, when it takes place he may have a claim for interest under standard condition 7.3, or for damages.

(ii) It would be pointless for Mr Green to try to speed completion on by applying for a decree of specific performance. The personal representative cannot give a good title until he has obtained the grant, so the delay is inevitable.

If Mr Green does wish to discharge the contract, he could serve a completion notice. However, there are difficulties. It is not possible, whatever means are used, to serve notice on a dead man. Nor can the notice be served on his solicitors. A corpse has no solicitors, and death ends the retainer. Service would have to be on the personal representative. If Mr Black died without having appointed an executor he has no personal representative until letters of administration are granted. However, the rule is that pending the grant, an intestate's property is vested in the President of the Family Division. Could notice be served on him? If Mr Black died having appointed an executor, notice could be served on him. The trouble is that Mr Green cannot be sure who is the executor until he has seen a grant of probate. If the delay looks as if it is going to be substantial Mr Green would probably be forced to court for a declaration that the delay is unreasonable, being unable to serve a completion notice to establish that fact.

If Mr Green waits for the personal representative to obtain a grant, when completion takes place, he will be able to claim either interest or damages, and the claim will include any compensation he has had to pay to the purchaser from him.

Chapter 19

Problem

Presumably the contract does not repeat the statement as to the existence of the permission. So there is no possibility for action for breach of contract. Pauline will have to establish that the statement was a misrepresentation. If it is, the next question to decide is whether the representation was fraudulent or not, as this affects Pauline's remedies. To be fraudulent, the statement must have been made with the knowledge that it was false, or without belief in its truth, or reckless of whether it was false or true. A fraudulent misrepresentation could give Pauline the right to rescind the contract and to claim damages for the fraud. It seems difficult here for Pauline to prove fraud. Her remedies for non-fraudulent misrepresentation come from the Misrepresentation Act 1967. She has a right of rescission, (subject to the court's power under s.2(2) of the Act to award damages instead). She has a right to damages unless the representation was made without negligence.

The contract incorporates the standard conditions, and condition 7.1 restricts remedies for misrepresentation. (The condition has already been considered in this chapter in the context of misdescription, but it applies to misrepresentations as well.) When considering its effect, remember that a condition removing or restricting remedies for misrepresentation is void unless the condition is a fair and reasonable one to have been included in the contract having regard to all the circumstances known to the parties when the contract was made (s.3 of the Misrepresentation Act 1967). It is up to Roger to establish the validity of the condition. If he cannot do so, *or* if Pauline can establish that the misrepresentation makes a *substantial* difference, she will be able to rescind the contract. The right to rescission survives completion (s.1(b) of the Misrepresentation Act 1967) so it is possible that even if the house had actually been conveyed to Pauline, she could still ask for her money to be returned. This may make things very awkward for the seller, who may have used it to buy his new home, or otherwise put it beyond easy reach, and that sort of difficulty could be a reason for the court to exercise its discretion to award damages in place of rescission.

The remedy of rescission is an equitable one, and there are so-called 'bars' to obtaining an order for it. One is delay. Another is that rescission will not be awarded if it would prejudice innocent third parties who have acquired an interest in the property for value. If Pauline bought with the aid of a mortgage loan, rescission would destroy the mortgagee's security for repayment of the loan. This difficulty should be solvable by an arrangement being made for redemption of the mortgage when Pauline reconveys the land to Roger, in return for the purchase price.

If the exclusion clause is valid, and the misdescription makes a material difference, but not a substantial one, Pauline could not rescind, but could only claim damages.

Index